THE TURNING

OF

THE TIDES

By

Paul W. Shafer

and

John Howland Snow

The LONG HOUSE, Inc.

PUBLISHERS

1962

THE TURNING OF THE TIDES

The text of this volume has been divided into four parts. The first three describe a movement—how it started, what became its objectives, and to what extent those objectives were reached.

These three parts are entitled: *Currents, Tides,* and—*The Flood*.

The fourth part tells of the rising waters of a more recent stream, whose mounting effect gives the title to the book.

Parts I, III and IV are by John Howland Snow.

Part II is by the Hon. Paul W. Shafer of Michigan, Member of Congress from 1937 until his death in 1954. The original text was delivered in the House of Representatives on March 21, 1952.

Approximately two years were required for the preparation and publication.

CONTENTS

On the 12th of September 1905 a group of young men met together in lower Manhattan, New York. Conditions in America were not ideal. These young men had an ideal. Consciously or not, it had been borrowed from the social structures of the Old World.

The meeting took place in a loft above Peck's Restaurant, at 140 Fulton Street. Among the group were some who in later years were to become widely known for views which at that time were the catalyst bringing them together.

On that day nearly sixty years ago was organized the Intercollegiate Socialist Society.

The Society

Its godfather was Upton Sinclair. Others officiating at its birth included Jack London, Thomas Wentworth Higginson, J. G. Phelps Stokes and Clarence Darrow. Sinclair was twenty-seven. London, twenty-nine, was elected the first president. On the Executive Board were Morris Hillquit and Harry W. Laidler. Owen R. Lovejoy was the treasurer.

The purpose of the Society was "to promote an intelligent interest in Socialism among college men and women * * *"

About this time, and also in lower Manhattan, there was organized the Rand School of Social Science. Here, the I.S.S. established permanent headquarters in 1908.

[1]

Conditions, to repeat, were not ideal—anywhere—and to change those conditions these young intellectuals had plans. The plans, as we shall see, were put in operation.

The first step was to organize chapters of the I.S.S. in colleges and universities.

Walter Lippmann was president of the Harvard club in 1909 and Heywood Broun was a charter member. David J. Saposs, a student from Russia, was president at Wisconsin in 1910; Freda Kirchwey was president at Barnard. Walter Reuther was president, later, at Wayne.

Other names figured prominently in the early movement and among them were Bruce Bliven at Stanford, professors Vladimir Karapetoff at Cornell and Vida D. Scudder at Wellesley, Alexander Trachtenberg at Trinity, John Spargo at Amherst Agricultural College, Mary R. Sanford at Vassar and Eugene V. Debs at Columbia.

The Society progressed. Associated with its activities, and among its lecturers, writers and organizers, were Mrs. Ella Reeves Bloor, Algernon Lee, Jay Lovestone, Frances E. Perkins, Lincoln Steffens, Rose Pastor Stokes, Victor L. Berger of Wisconsin ("the first Socialist in Congress"), Bouck White, W. E. B. DuBois, Scott Nearing and the Reverend John Haynes Holmes.

The first annual convention was held in January, 1910.

By 1912 the I.S.S. had chapters in 44 colleges and universities and in five alumni associations. By 1917 chapters had been organized in 61 schools of higher learning and in a dozen graduate bodies.

From the very start the Society actively observed the socialist movement in German universities from its first impetus under Bismarck. The I.S.S. was in close intellectual contact with the Fabian Societies which were flourishing in the rarefied air of Britain's cloistered halls.

The League

In 1921 the Intercollegiate Socialist Society was ready for its next organizational step, and this was signalized by a change of name. The 16-year old I.S.S. in that year became the League for Industrial Democracy.

The L.I.D. was a membership society organized for the specific purpose of "education for a new social order based on production for use and not for profit."

Under its new name, the original Intercollegiate Socialist Society continued under the joint direction of Harry W. Laidler and Norman Thomas.

The League's first president was Robert Morss Lovett, a professor of English literature at the University of Chicago and an editor of *The New Republic*. Charles P. Steinmetz was a vice-president, and Stuart Chase was treasurer. One of its lecturers was Paul R. Porter, later with E.C.A. in Greece. The field secretary was Paul Blanshard. In 1926 one of the directors was Louis Budenz.

[2]

The chapters of the I.S.S. were now absorbed into a Student L.I.D., and by the mid-1930s there were some 125 such units. John Dewey was then a vice-president of the League together with John Haynes Holmes.

In 1941 Dewey became president and Reinhold Niebuhr treasurer. For better or worse, the L.I.D. was a fixture in the life of the Nation.*

The International

The scene must now shift, for a moment, to Britain. There, in 1883, had been organized the first Fabian Society. Its goal was socialism. Its method of patient, steady procedure was much later to become known as "gradualism". Its name derived from the Roman general, Quintus Fabius Maximus, who so successfully employed a similar strategy—of "delay, attack, delay"—against his arch enemy, the Carthaginian Hannibal. Its organizers were Beatrice and Sidney Webb, George Bernard Shaw, H. G. Wells and other intellectuals.

The hard core of the British Fabian Society, like that of the L.I.D., was never numerous. By 1932 the Society had only 1,867 members. But it was an operational success. Its *Forty-ninth Annual Report* gives the clue to much that has transpired, much that we shall find as we read. For it said:

"* * * we continue active association * * * with the League for Industrial Democracy of New York which carries on active propaganda in the United States on very similar lines to our own work here * * *"

The *Fifty-eighth Annual Report,* 1940, could boast that 15 member Fabians were in the House of Lords, 69 sitting in Commons. One of these, Clement Attlee, became Prime Minister in 1945. Another, a former member of the Executive Committee of the Society, was elevated to the Cabinet— as Minister of Education.†

In 1946, the Fabian Society's *Sixty-third Annual Report* announced the establishment of an International Bureau

"To prepare the ground for an international socialist policy in international affairs."

How successful the plan became we shall see.

The fashion

In America, meanwhile, John Dewey had organized the Progressive Education Association and in 1915 the American Association of University Professors. A new concept of education was becoming the vogue. Its development shows three distinct phases since 1905, and these may be defined as follows:

---

* Further details, and documentation for this Chapter, will be found in the Appendix, pages 160-1, and pages 174-5.

† *Cf.* footnote, page 102, and text, page 160.

[3]

1) The first student-organization; the period of its young ideals;

2) The period of social and educational development as these students were graduated into active life. They entered the drawing rooms of the newly-fashionable liberals, and they began the organized teaching of their views from the rostra of the classroom and of the pulpit;

3) The period of social, economic and political *bouleversement,* during which the disciples of the Fabianized movement took increasing possession of the guidance of labor, school and state.

Young theoreticians entered the pulpit; they entered the classroom; they entered the fields of textbook writing and revision; they entered the labor movement and the ranks of both of our major political parties. In 1933 the advent of the New Deal found them prepared. The Nation was absorbed in the drama of those first One Hundred Days.

At that time the L.I.D. membership totalled 5,652. And from that membership came many of the men and women whose names were shortly to become synonymous with "social change."

From an obscure loft in lower Manhattan had been graduated the first advocates of indoctrinated social revolution.

Its alumni were now in positions of vital power, and they used it. They influenced—for better or for worse—the course of the Nation and the conduct of its tens of thousands of schools.

Socially speaking, the loft was forgotten; the *milieu* was the now-fashionable liberal drawing room, the faculty club and the political caucus.

An open choice

It was this movement, open and at the same time subtle; known and yet generally ignored, which after forty years began to be discussed—not for its purposes but for its effects. Gradually, a counter-current could be discerned. Here, in ever-increasing numbers, were citizens who had determined that, whatever its blessings, there were signs that the movement's entirety was not in the permanent best interests of the Nation.

The entirety was known as "progressive education". As a movement, it was self-defined.

This is its early history, highly condensed. The beginning of its forceful development, of its program to mold the minds of America's youth and of her adult population, may be dated from 1932.

In that year the leadership of the movement announced plans which embraced a philosophy new to America as a whole, yet in essence as ancient as was the first Total State.

The movement has grown until now its program covers the civilized world. It has achieved power; it has given direction to that power; and it has found sources of boundless finance. In this last, we are going to observe a curious thing: Often that finance comes from channels which

[4]

would seem to be the last to subscribe to the doctrines announced by the movement itself.

What is the program?

Who are its advocates?

Whence comes its amazing finance?

What does it all mean to us—to our families, our homes, our daughters and our sons?

It is to these matters that the present book is addressed. At times your patience is going to be tried, for here is found not so much effect, as cause. The question it raises is a human one:

What is *best* for our schools—what is *best* for the 40,000,000 young citizens who are attending them and who, so soon, will be governing this great Country of ours?

There are two ways in which this question can be answered, and only two. These are:

1) By "Government"—as The State; or

2) By yourselves and neighbors—as citizens of the community in which you live.

In this decision regarding the public schools there is clear parallel to the mighty question which is so peculiar to our times. It is this:

Is the Nation, as well, to be run from Washington—or, is *local* government to recapture those functions which the Constitution reserves to you and to your neighbors; is it to be brought back home, where we know each other and know, therefore, what is going on?

So similar are these two questions that it may well be that to resolve the one is itself to resolve the other.

"Let us believe no man infallible or impeccable in government, any more than in religion; take no man's word against evidence, nor implicitly adopt the sentiments of others who may be deceived themselves, or may be interested in deceiving us."

John Adams, writing in the Boston *Gazette*, 1763.

PART II   The Movement
TIDES   In America's Schools

2. CHALLENGE

This document might be described as a product of freedom.

The whole thing started when, as guest speaker at a dinner in my home State, I mentioned having been invited by a superintendent of schools in my district to deliver a nonpolitical talk in the high school, but that the invitation subsequently was withdrawn by a somewhat embarrassed superintendent who explained that there had been objections from members of the school board. I further remarked that such experiences are far from unknown.

I was queried about these remarks by my home town newspaper, the Battle Creek *Enquirer and News*. I repeated them, and added the comment that there are "subversive activities and movements in some of the schools of the country and in some teachers' colleges."

The sequel was the appearance of an article quoting anonymous spokesmen of teachers in the area. These spokesmen denounced me for my comments and demanded that I either clarify and prove my charges, or retract them.

I replied through the press, and called attention to the anonymous character of this demand. While making clear that I had offered no blanket indictment, I stated the obvious truth that "an increasing number of Americans at the grass roots are disturbed over trends in educational philosophies and methods which run counter to the traditional American philosophy and principles of government."

The spokesmen then made their identity known, and the executive body of the Calhoun County branch of the Michigan Education Association adopted a resolution demanding that I either prove the charges or retract them.

[6]

Thereupon I invited representatives of the schools to meet with me to discuss the matter. Some sixty individuals, including superintendents, teachers and school board members, attended. Also present was a representative of the Michigan Education Association, apparently on the invitation of the teachers' group.

I said that I saw no valid reason for precipitating a community controversy over the cancellation of an invitation to speak. I again disclaimed "any intention of making a blanket criticism of the loyalty, conscientiousness or good faith of members of the teaching profession." I added, however, that I was fully aware—as they also must be—that "there are movements afoot in educational circles which are dedicated to the promotion of a system of planned and controlled economy, and a system of world government to which national sovereignty in matters of national defense is to be subordinated."

I stated that there could be no question of the right to discuss publicly the broad issues posed by this movement, but urged that I not be required to extend the discussion. The demand was repeated that I document the statements and I reluctantly agreed to do so.

Curiously, following the meeting, the two principal spokesmen for the teachers' group expressed the opinion that the matter might well be dropped. I reminded them of my promise, in the presence of some sixty persons, to provide the documentation. I added that I could not lightly break that promise.

Some weeks thereafter I received a letter from the two spokesmen. They again reversed their position, and repeated their insistent request for proof.

So far as I am concerned, there is no question that the issue upon which that insistence was focused was my reference to an educational movement which I labeled as "subversive".

Accordingly, I am not going to quibble over side issues.

I make no blanket indictment of the schools or of the teaching profession. I am going to document a movement which is closely identified with a program of certain "social planners"—a program which I believe bodes no good either for the schools or for the Nation.

Opinion

I certainly recognize that America is not perfect. I believe, however, that an educational movement, or philosophy, which "accentuates the negative" and which minimizes, ignores or denies the strength, accomplishments and potentialities of our Government and our own political, economic and social structure, is subversive.

I believe that an educational movement or philosophy which minimizes or denies the possibility of our people and institutions for self-improvement —save through the expanding agency of government—is subversive.

[7]

I believe that an educational movement and philosophy which pits class against class, which attributes only evil and viciousness to one group of citizens and only virtue to another group, and which proposes that the schools teach and promote such belief, is subversive.

I believe that an educational movement and philosophy which brands the capitalist or property owner as a foe of human rights, incapable of social conscience or responsibility, and hostile to the betterment of his fellow men, is subversive.

I believe that an educational movement and philosophy which insists, and teaches, that the only solution—and the desirable solution—of the problems of government, of economics and of social wellbeing, lies in bigger and bigger government, in power increasingly concentrated in a central government, is subversive.

I believe that an educational movement and philosophy which aims to convert our schools into agencies for promoting socialism, collectivism, government regimentation or the welfare state, is subversive.

I believe that a movement which arrogates to the educational profession—or to any other profession or segment of our national life—the awful responsibility of "social reconstruction", is subversive.

I believe that a movement which urges teachers, or any other group of people, to "deliberately reach for power and then make the most of their conquest", and which claims freedom from public examination and accounting, is subversive.

I believe that a movement which, in the name of "progressive education" and of "academic freedom", exhibits a cynical distrust of human motives and impulses, and which belittles old, inherited loyalties, and the truths and values established by ages of human experience, is subversive.

I believe that a movement and philosophy which aims to convert the public schools into agencies for the promotion of supernational authority or world government, and which urges the systematic eradication—beginning in the kindergarten—of nationalism, decreeing that nationalism and the loyalties which it involves must go, is subversive.

In all of this I am expressing my own opinion and judgment.

But in the material which follows I am not presenting personal opinion. I am documenting a movement—from the testimony of its own leaders and adherents.

If this documentation, therefore, results in misgivings with respect to certain schools and segments of the teaching profession, responsibility must rest upon the movement documented. Indeed, as I see it, one of the potential values of this documentation is that it defines—or at least undertakes, in good faith, to define—the entire movement with sufficient accuracy and objectivity that every citizen in the Country will be able to identify its advocates, and those who are not.

[8]

"One of the troubles in education—the same as in government in recent years—business men have allowed the theory boys and girls to run the show. They haven't taken the trouble to find out how the tax dollars going into education are being spent.* * *

"A serious look-see at the school system and what is being taught should be taken by business men in particular and the public in general."
Leslie Gould column. New York *Journal-American;* June 17, 1952.

3. STATEMENT

This documentation will show that a significant and influential segment of public school leadership in the United States proclaims—and has been proclaiming for years—the right and duty of teachers, school administrators and educational leaders actually to undertake to remake America.

Advocacy, expression and implementation of the movement is found in policy pronouncements of educational organizations; in professional books and journals; in the counsel and instruction of teachers of teachers and in textbook content and classroom techniques in elementary and secondary public schools, and in the colleges and universities.

The main features of the movement are these:

First. It proclaims that capitalism in the United States is doomed and that some form of collectivism, planned economy, government control, or outright socialization is both inevitable and desirable.

Second. The movement and its sponsors hold that the schools should actively participate in remolding our society along collectivist lines; that this should be done by means of indoctrination and guided study called "uncoerced persuasion"; and that the content and methods of instruction should prepare the child for participation in that collectivist order and "condition" him therefor.

Third. The movement calls for such revision of the educational system—its philosophy, procedures and subject matter—as is necessary to accomplish the purpose.

Fourth. The extremists hold that the transition to collectivism will in all probability involve class conflict; that, accordingly, the schools should adopt a class approach, align themselves with the "worker class", and utilize class conflict as a "potential resource".

[9]

Fifth. Advocates of the program recognize the inevitability of opposition and they propose certain "steps to power" designed to enable them to deal, defensively and offensively, with that opposition.

Sixth. The movement includes the doctrine that teachers are "engineers of social change"—through the agency of the public schools.

Seventh. The movement includes proposals for altering the form, philosophy and procedure of government in the United States.

Eighth. The program embraces the goal of world government, a supernational authority over and above the Government of these United States.

Ninth. It is a distinctly minority movement. It numbers, in my opinion, but a fractional percentage of the educational profession within its orbit. Because of this small percentage it is clear that teachers, in close collaboration with community groups, can bring the movement to a stop if they so desire.

I make no claim that the ensuing documentation is complete. I do claim, however, that the documentation is typical, and represents the basic premises and objectives of the movement—so stated by its own proponents.

I have attempted to identify my sources with painstaking care.

4. ATTACK

No responsible person wishes to place the school system, or teachers generally, under suspicion. Yet there are those who take advantage of that very fact in order to forestall legitimate citizen-investigation, and constant citizen-supervision, of the very institutions which—second only to the home and church—are responsible for the upbringing of our youth.

"Enemies of the schools"

In some quarters hypersensitivity to criticism verges upon a persecution complex. There are those who instantly cry "Smear!" It is no exaggeration to say that a segment of educational officialdom has declared open warfare upon critics of the schools.

Typical of the pronouncements is a resolution of the Michigan Education Association, adopted on August 25, 1951. This resolution condemns

the irresponsible attacks which are now being made on our schools, their personnel and procedures, attacks which often are designed to discredit the public schools, reduce their financial support, curtail their program, and destroy free public education for all children.

The MEA pledged its resources to "expose and combat" such "vicious attacks."

The National Education Association, at its 1951 convention, resolved that

The NEA believes that one of the year's most challenging problems is presented by attacks of front organizations and pressure groups on the public schools, on their teachers and administrators, and on the quality of instruction. The Association believes in and welcomes honest and constructive criticism but condemns general and irresponsible attacks on schools. Often the real purpose of such attacks is found to be the reduction of school costs and the curtailment of the public school system.[1]

---

[1] *NEA Journal,* September 1951; p. 383.

The *Thirtieth Yearbook* of the American Association of School Administrators, NEA, quotes an article in *McCall's* of September 1951:

Public education in America is under the heaviest attack in its history. This attack is not aimed at the improvement of free public education. It is aimed at its destruction.

The *Yearbook* was not alone in its appraisal of this article. On October 2, 1951, the *Daily Worker* stated:

It should be "must" reading for every P.T.A. group and every parent in this country.

This is no isolated instance of communist approval of the overall movement.

The AASA *Yearbook* continues:

In some cases this pressure may be sparked by organizations or individuals who are authoritarian in intent, seeking to destroy the American way of life by undermining public confidence in the schools. They are persistent, devious, and clever in the way they twist statements and acts of educational leaders and by innuendo and association create doubt of the motives and methods of the entire public-school system. (*P. 258*)

It is claimed that the "attacks" are the result of a "central command", that they emanate from persons "who have no competence to judge educational matters."[2]

As proof of the "central command" the fact is noted that flare-ups occur in widely separate communities. My own home city of Battle Creek is listed as the scene of one, although between 1948 and 1950 its citizens voted and levied a million and a quarter dollars in extra taxes for school rehabilitation—and despite the fact that Battle Creek is named in the May 1948 *School Board Journal* (pp. 31-2) as a model of public support of schools.

One report, on the Pasadena controversy, was made to the National Education Association's 88th Delegate Assembly, held on July 3, 1950 at St. Louis, Mo. In this report,[3] Harold Benjamin, chairman of the NEA's National Commission for the Defense of Democracy Through Education, branded the opposition to the Pasadena superintendent as "The Enemy"—and proceeded to describe him.[*]

David Hulburd charges in his book *This Happened in Pasadena:*

It is a fact that certain forces, vicious, well organized, and coldly calculating, would like to change the face of education in the United States. (*P. ix*)

---

* *Editor's Note:* The designation had been used six years earlier by Dr. Howard A. Dawson, long a high official of the National Education Association. Addressing the Representative Assembly of the NEA, Dawson said: "When I make the statement that there are powerful enemies to the cause of education sitting in the Halls of the United States Congress, it becomes an easy matter to cite the evidence. ° ° ° For years the House Committee on Education has been deliberately filled by a minority known to be enemies of public education."
Congressional Record. Vol. 90, Part 10; p. A3937. September 8, 1944.

[2] *Fact Sheet,* Community Relations Service of New York City, March 1, 1951.
[3] *Defense Bulletin No. 35.* National Commission for the Defense of Democracy Through Education, NEA. 1950.

This statement is going to reveal itself as an amazingly accurate description of the movement to be documented.

Academic freedom's double standard

The consequences are serious. Anyone who ventures adverse comment on the schools finds he has spoken at his peril and that he has incurred the wrath of powerful, organized groups. Even elected school officials—school board members—discover they are not immune.

Is comment to be restricted to what certain educators declare permissible? Is a double standard to be applied?

Certainly for three decades the most intense pressure on the schools has come not only from within the profession but from lay supporters of this movement. No denunciation, no labeling of these zealots as "The Enemy", no accusation of a plot "under central command", has been heard from educational officialdom. Quite the contrary.

Advocates of this movement insist that the schools need "thorough reconstruction". They charge that "educational leadership has too much interest in the matter of pleasing boards of education." They accuse the schools of furthering social chaos. They allege that "after 150 years, American education has left us as vicious socially and as dishonest as we were before that education began". They denounce "the commonplaces of American education" as "faint voices from a distant and mythical land" when compared to progress within the Soviet.

Teachers are told to emancipate themselves from the domination of business interests and to "cease cultivating the manners and associations of bankers."

Teachers are told to "abandon smug middle-class traditions". They are warned "to restate their philosophy of education, reorganize the procedures of the schools, and even redefine their own position in society."

These are typical statements which have emanated—and still emanate —from the advocates of the movement. For years its spokesmen have been applauded to the echo for their attacks. And adherents of the movement are not bashful in claiming credit for the results.

One director of the Progressive Education Association, Vinal H. Tibbets, declared in 1945 that "the impact [of the Association] upon educational thinking and practice is immeasureable". He asserted that, though the Association's largest annual membership was under 11,000, "probably no group so small, except the early Christians, has ever made such progress in so short a time in changing the direction of a social movement".[4]

Yet criticism of the movement becomes the mark of "The Enemy"!

The ultimate effect of cowering before such outcries would be to estop all objective examination of our schools, however proper or just.

---

[4] *Progressive Education,* March 1945; p. 3.

[13]

"It is clear from this brief survey that a collectivist economy is better equipped to raise the aggregate demand to the required level than to reduce a surplus demand. It is possibly better equipped than a capitalist state to combat inflation as well as deflation. Its chief asset in this respect is that it is able to rationalize institutions, introduce a fiscal system more nearly fraud-proof than is possible in a capitalist régime and, consequently, to exercise control over incomes dependent on personal position and market conditions, leaving individuals only such sums as are considered necessary in order to encourage them to work and to use their initiative and organizing ability."

Pierre Mendès-France and Gabriel Ardant, in *Economics and Action* (p. 143). Published by Unesco, Paris; Columbia University Press, New York. 1955.

PART II   The Movement
TIDES   In America's Schools

5. THE MOVEMENT

Sensitivity to objective examination is particularly acute with respect to any suggestion that collectivism is being fostered in the schools. The reaction is an air of injured or indignant innocence.

As an example, take the monthly bulletin issued by superintendent C. C. Trillingham of the Los Angeles County, Cal., public schools:

Anyone who knows about the general educational program of the schools today knows that the charges that the schools are leading the country toward socialism, that the fundamental skills are being ignored, and that there is no attempt to discipline youngsters, are untrue. That these are the results of a premeditated program of so-called "progressive education" is sheer nonsense.[1]

In *The Pasadena Story,* issued by the National Commission for the Defense of Democracy Through Education of the NEA, sensitivity to the charge of socialism is marked. Of those who so charge, it says:

They apparently claim that this country has already moved into, or is rapidly moving toward, some form of socialism, collectivism, or statism. They contend that subversive elements have sifted into public education and that many teachers are seeking to change the American way of life. They charge that John Dewey's progressive education is an instrument designed to break down American standards and weaken the fabric of American society. They oppose Federal aid to education on the ground that it is a collectivist measure. They oppose certain educators who they assert are seeking to indoctrinate the youth of the country for a changed social and economic order. (*P.* 23)

The *Defense Bulletin* issued by Harold Benjamin, NEA Commission chairman, refers to such allegations in another way. "The Enemy", says Mr. Benjamin,

has whipped up pseudo-popular revolts there [in Pasadena] against teachers, administrators, and school programs on the grounds that they are indoctrinating the children

---

[1] This bulletin was published in the October 1950 *Education Digest;* p. 39.

[14]

in communism, socialism, or at least mentioning democracy, and they are helping to increase taxes.[2]

Dean Ernest O. Melby of the New York University School of Education says that "most of the attacks being made on public education are dishonest and unjustified", and that

Schools must deal with controversial issues. In doing so they are sometimes accused of leftist leanings by persons who fail to realize that teaching about communism is not the same thing as teaching communism. What the schools are trying to do is to equip boys and girls to deal with the present ideological conflict successfully.[3]

Dean J. B. Edmondson of the University of Michigan School of Education is more emphatic. Among "threats", he lists

the insidious efforts of some persons to create the false impression that teachers are committed to a "progressive philosophy of education" that is socialistic and communistic in its influence on children and youth.[3]

If I understand the English language, these statements constitute a categorical denial of the existence of any such movement. The denial is inexplicable. It means to me that educators who speak and write in this vein are less than frank with people.

Dr. William H. Kilpatrick, long a professor of education at Teachers College, Columbia University, New York, made the matter perfectly clear nearly twenty years ago. On February 27, 1935 he addressed the Department of Superintendence of the National Education Association—now the American Association of School Administrators, NEA. With respect to members of the teaching profession, he stated:

There are many who think that our social-economic system should be radically reconstructed. To this proposal, opinion responds over a wide range from an extreme yes to an extreme no, with all gradations in between. Some who are most anxious to bring about this social-economic reconstruction urge the school to take an active part in helping to build the new social order. To this proposal also, opinion responds over a wide range from an extreme yes through intermediate positions to an extreme no.[5]

The present documentation is concerned with the militant minority of the profession veering in the direction of what Dr. Kilpatrick called the "extreme yes".

More specifically, it reveals an organized, vocal and aggressive element which is dedicated to the support of a movement for social-reconstruction-through-the-schools.

---

[2] *Eighth Report* (*L-1267*), Senate Investigating Committee on Education, California Legislature, 1951; p. 93.
[3] *NEA Journal,* October 1951; pp. 441-2.
[4] *NEA Journal,* September 1951; pp. 381-2.
[5] *NEA Proceedings,* 1935; p. 567.

"Obsessed by a vision of what they believed to be a rational, peaceful, cooperative society in which everyone would have an abundance of food, clothing, recreation and medical care, a highly influential group of educators seriously modified the vision of education as a process whereby children would learn to 'think for themselves', to include indoctrination with a set of ideas which, whatever their merits, were widely at variance with earlier beliefs. That a definite element of idealism motivated the group should be readily granted; but it should also be recognized that when they used idealistic phrases such as 'cooperation', 'social planning', 'democracy', and 'production for use, not for profit', their eyes were on the stars. The brightest star of all was what they then called 'the socialist experiment in Russia.' "

A. H. Hobbs: *The Vision and the Constant Star.* THE LONG HOUSE, INC. 1956. *(P. 37)*

PART II   The Movement

TIDES   In America's Schools

6. THE PHILOSOPHY OF "SOCIAL CHANGE"

Some four or five years after his appointment as a professor of education at Teachers College, Columbia University, Dr. George S. Counts read a paper before a conference of the Progressive Education Association in Baltimore, Md. This was in February, 1932.

The paper, *Dare Progressive Education Be Progressive?,* is the necessary starting point in the documentation which I am undertaking.

Because of the major—even dominant—rôle which Dr. Counts has played in the history of the movement, it is important to become somewhat acquainted with him and with his views.

Dr. Counts' rôle is attested not only by the Baltimore address. It is attested by his authorship, in 1932, of the monograph, *Dare the School Build a New Social Order?;* by his chairmanship of the Progressive Education Association Committee on Social and Economic Problems which one year later issued *A Call to the Teachers of the Nation;* his service as research director of the American Historical Association's Commission on Social Studies; and his editorship, for several years, of *The Social Frontier,* official journal of the movement.

Collectivist philosophy

In 1932 Counts was an enthusiastic commentator on the "great collectivist experiment" in Soviet Russia. He was one of a number of American educators who, in keeping with a custom encouraged by the Communist organization in the United States, made pilgrimages to the Soviet to view—under proper chaperonage—the workings of that experiment.

His estimate of collectivism is clearly expressed:

The world today is full of social experimentation. There is one experiment, however, that dwarfs all others—so bold indeed in its ideals and its program that few can contemplate it without emotion. * * * Soviet Russia is endeavoring with all the

[16]

resources at her command to bring the economic order under a measure of rational control. * * * She issues to the Western nations and particularly to the United States a challenge—perhaps one of the greatest challenges of history. But she issues it not through the Communist International, nor through the Red Army, nor through the Gay-Pay-OO (political police), as most of our citizens naïvely and timorously believe, but through her State Planning Commission and her system of public education.[1]

Dr. Counts left no doubt as to where his sympathies lay:

In the societies of the West in general and in the United States of America in particular the evolution of institutions proceeds for the most part without plan or design, as a sort of byproduct of the selfish competition of individuals, groups and enterprises for private gain. In Russia, on the other hand, since the days of 1917, the Soviet government has sought to promote the rational and orderly development of the entire social economy. * * * a whole civilization is harnessing its energies and is on the march toward consciously determined goals. (*P. 7*)

Further:

If the revolution is successful the social order which is emerging today in Soviet Russia will first of all be collectivistic. In its essence this means that the institution of private property, at least insofar as it applies to land and the tools of production, will be abolished. It also means that no individual will be able to acquire great wealth, that the motive of personal gain will cease to drive the wheels of the economic order *. * *, and that land, railroads, factories, mills, shops, houses, and natural resources will be owned collectively and administered in the interests of all. (*Pp. 24-5*)

In the Soviet, Counts stated,

new principles of right and wrong are being forged. Under such conditions the commonplaces of American education sound like faint voices from a distant and mythical land. (*P. 324*)

Soviet education is clearly superior to our own:

The idea of building a new society * * * is certainly no worse than the drive towards individual success which permeates not only the schools but every department of culture in the United States. If one were to compare the disciplined effort of the Soviet to industrialize the country, to socialize agriculture, to abolish poverty, to banish disease, to liquidate unemployment, to disseminate knowledge, and generally to raise the material and spiritual level of the masses, with the selfish scramble for wealth and privilege * * * in America, one would find small grounds for complacency. Whatever may be said on the other side concerning the regimentation of opinion and the restriction of individual freedom, there exists in Soviet Russia today an idealism and a driving passion for human betterment which contrasts strangely with the widespread cynicism of the United States. It is only natural that this idealism and this passion should sweep through the schools * * * (*Pp. 328-30*)

Dr. Counts closes his book:

This cultural revolution possesses a single mighty integrating principle—the building of a new society in which there will be neither rich nor poor * * * in which a condition of essential equality will unite all races and nations into one brotherhood. * * * A devotion to the common good and a deep interest in the oppressed of all lands penetrate and color every aspect of the cultural life of the country. That the pursuit of the goal may often be blind and unintelligent during the current period of stress and experimentation is only to be expected. (*Pp. 338-9*)

Counts' *Dare the School Build a New Social Order?* was reviewed in 1933 by J. I. Zilberfarb, identified as a member of the State Scientific Coun-

---

[1] Counts: *The Soviet Challenge to America*, 1931. Foreword; pp. ix-x.

[17]

cil, Commissariat of Education, U.S.S.R. Counts, said Zilberfarb, "continues to make great strides ahead", and, in a letter accompanying the review, expressed his pleasure at "the remarkable progress which you have made in challenging capitalism".[2]

Clearly, Zilberfarb saw in Dr. Counts the makings of a true "comrade".

Sixteen years later Counts and others found themselves denounced as "a vociferous group of Trotskyites and other anti-Communists".[3]

The occasion for this "denunciation" was Dr. Counts' uninvited appearance at the International Cultural and Scientific Conference in New York City late in March 1949.* He challenged delegates to account for the disappearance in the Soviet of several scholars who had incurred the displeasure of the Stalin régime and co-sponsored a rival mass meeting held at the same time as the Communist-sponsored conclave.

"* * * the molding of the minds of both young and old."

Sadder and wiser, in 1951 Counts was writing:

The Soviet leaders boast every hour of the day about their grandiose achievements * * * Yet they have to their credit one truly staggering achievement about which they say nothing—their all-embracing system of mind-control. * * *

The Soviet system of mind control is the product of perverted genius. It is the most comprehensive thing of its kind in history, surpassing immeasurably its predecessor under the tsar. * * * Employing with complete ruthlessness and singleness of purpose all the resources of science, of mechanical invention, of medicine and psychology, it is able to attain power and reach heights of efficiency which dwarf the efforts of earlier despotisms.

The system embraces all of the organized processes and agencies for the molding of the minds of both young and old.[4]

Yet for upwards of twenty years Dr. Counts held other views—and it was during those years that the collectivist philosophy crept so deeply into the life of America's schools. And the question raised is this: To what extent has our Nation been sheltering a movement designed "for the molding of the minds of both young and old"?

How many of our 40,000,000 young citizens are studying under teachers who absorbed the philosophy of others like Dr. Counts?

How many policies of our Government have been influenced by men and women who absorbed these philosophies in the schools?

---

* The sponsors of this Conference included Theodore Brameld, W. E. B. DuBois, Albert Einstein, Robert Morss Lovett and Gene Weltfish. Among the delegates were Scott Nearing and Alexander Trachtenberg.

[2] *Progressive Education*, February 1933; p. 71 *et seq.*
[3] *Daily Worker*, March 28, 1949.
[4] *NEA Journal*, January 1951; pp. 29-32. MIND CONTROL IN THE SOVIET UNION.

"But the teacher is entrusted with the custody of children and their high preparation for useful life. His habits, his speech, his good name, his cleanliness, the wisdom and propriety of his unofficial utterances, his associations, all are involved. His ability to inspire children and to govern them, his power as a teacher, and the character for which he stands are matters of major concern in a teacher's selection and retention."

> *A. L. Goldsmith v. The Board of Education of Sacramento City High School District et al.* Third Appellate District. March 12, 1924. 66 *Cal. App.*, p. 168.

PART II

TIDES

The Movement

In America's Schools

7. THE FIRST "CALL"

The basic premise of the movement is categorically stated, and with almost monotonous repetition. The premise is that capitalism is doomed, and that some form of collectivism, planned economy, government control or socialization, is desirable and inevitable in its stead.

Whatever euphemisms are encountered, the movement must be appraised in this light.

The premise was laid down by Dr. Counts at the Baltimore meeting in 1932:

We live in troublous times; we live in an age of profound change; we live in an age of revolution.

A new world is forming, he asserted, and

we hold within our hands the power to usher in an age of plenty, to make secure the lives of all, and to banish poverty forever from the land.

What did Counts propose?

The achievement of this goal * * * would seem to require fundamental changes in the economic system. Historic capitalism, with its deification of the principle of selfishness, its reliance upon the forces of competition, its placing of property above human rights, and its exaltation of the profit motive, will either have to be displaced altogether, or so radically changed in form and spirit that its identity will be completely lost.

Dr. Counts made it quite clear that this meant

a coordinated, planned, and socialized economy.

He stated:

That under such an economy the actions of individuals in certain directions would be limited is fairly obvious. No one would be permitted to build a new factory or railroad whenever and wherever he pleased; also, no one would be permitted to amass great riches by manipulating the economic institutions of the country.[1]

---

[1] *Progressive Education,* April 1932; pp. 261-2. Dare Progressive Education Be Progressive?

[19]

Pronouncement of doom

In *Dare the School Build a New Social Order?* Counts was explicit:

If the machine is to serve all, and serve all equally, it cannot be the property of the few. * * *

* * * If property rights are to be diffused in an industrial society, natural resources and all important forms of capital will have to be collectively owned. Obviously, every citizen cannot hold title to a mine, a factory, a railroad, a department store, or even a thoroughly mechanized farm. This clearly means that, if democracy is to survive in the United States, it must abandon its individualistic affiliations in the sphere of economics. * * * (*P. 45*)

* * * We must * * * insist on two things: First, that technology be released from the fetters and the domination of every type of special privilege; and, second, that the resulting system of production and distribution must be made to serve directly the masses of the people. Within these limits, as I see it, our democratic tradition must of necessity evolve and gradually assume an essentially collectivistic pattern. * * * (*P. 46*)

Continuing, Dr. Counts says:

* * * The growth of science and technology has carried us into a new age where ignorance must be replaced by knowledge, competition by cooperation, trust in Providence by careful planning, and private capitalism by some form of socialized economy. (*P. 48*)

As a sequel to Counts' Baltimore address, the Progressive Education Association Committee on Social and Economic Problems, of which Counts was chairman, was formed in 1933. It was this Committee that issued *A Call to the Teachers of the Nation.*

An introductory statement by Dr. Willard W. Beatty, president of the Progressive Education Association, carefully emphasized that the text "does not commit either the Board of Directors of the Association or the members of the Association, individually or as a whole, to any program or policy embodied in the report." Nevertheless, the Committee included Merle E. Curti, John S. Gambs, Sidney Hook, Jesse H. Newlon, Dr. Beatty, Charles L. S. Easton, Frederick L. Redefer and Goodwin Watson, in addition to Dr. Counts—all leaders in the progressive education movement.

The *Call* states its premise:

Clearly, if democracy is to survive * * * it must be dissociated from its individualistic connections and be rephrased in terms of the collectivist reality. In the highly integrated social order of the twentieth century individual men cannot own and operate the means of production as they did at the time of the founding of the nation. As a consequence, the fulfillment of the old ideal requires a reversal of loyalties at certain points. Today the individual can be guaranteed freedom for cultural and spiritual growth only by the abandonment of economic individualism. Liberty of persons is no longer to be attained through freeing business enterprise from restraints but rather through deliberate organization in the name of material security for all. Thus the democratic tradition has come to the end of an era. If its spirit is to live on, its forms must suffer radical change. (*P. 17*)

The 1933 premise is perfectly clear.

The "new" compulsion

The same premise underlies the 170 pages of *Conclusions and Recommendations* of the Commission on Social Studies, published by the American Historical Association in 1934. Its Committee on Direction included Isaiah Bowman, George S. Counts, Carlton J. H. Hayes and Jesse H. Newlon. Excerpts follow:

Under the molding influence of socialized processes of living * * * there is a notable waning of the once widespread popular faith in economic individualism; and leaders in public affairs, supported by a growing mass of the population, are demanding the introduction into economy of ever wider measures of planning and control.

Cumulative evidence supports the conclusion that, in the United States as in other countries, the age of individualism and *laissez-faire* in economy and government is closing and that a new age of collectivism is emerging.

As to the specific form this "collectivism" * * * is taking and will take in the future, the evidence at hand is by no means clear or unequivocal. * * * Most likely, it will issue from a process of experimentation and will represent a composite of historic doctrines and social conceptions yet to appear. (*P. 16*)

The Commission of the American Historical Association was emphatic that

Almost certainly it will involve a larger measure of compulsory as well as voluntary co-operation of citizens in the conduct of the complex national economy, a corresponding enlargement of the functions of government, and an increasing state intervention in fundamental branches of economy previously left to individual discretion and initiative—a state intervention that in some instances may be direct and mandatory and in others indirect and facilitative. In any event the Commission is convinced * * * that the actually integrating economy of the present day is the forerunner of a consciously integrated society in which individual property rights will be altered and abridged. (*Pp. 16-7*)

Collectivism, according to the Commission, is

the future already coming into reality * * * (*P. 36*)

Essentially the same premise is found in the report of the Committee on Education for the New America of the Department of Superintendence of the National Education Association—now the American Association of School Administrators, NEA. This report was presented at the Department's meeting in Cleveland on February 28, 1934 by Dr. Willard E. Givens. Givens was then superintendent of schools at Oakland, Cal., and for many years thereafter was executive secretary of the NEA. The text reads:

This report comes directly from the thinking together of more than one thousand members of the Department of Superintendence.

* * * We are convinced that we stand today at the verge of a great culture. We are now entering an epoch in which man can bring forth a civilization of abundance, of tolerance, and of beauty. * * *

But to achieve these things, many drastic changes must be made.

Now comes the first pertinent statement:

A dying laissez-faire must be completely destroyed and all of us, including the "owners," must be subjected to a large degree of social control.

[21]

The following is more definite:

A large section of our discussion group, accepting the conclusions of distinguished students, maintain that in our fragile, interdependent society the credit agencies, the basic industries and utilities cannot be centrally planned and operated under private ownership. Hence, they will join in creating a swift nationwide campaign of adult education which will support President Roosevelt in taking these over and operating them at full capacity as a unified national system in the interest of the people.'

Here was the outline—however vague—of the "new" compulsion.

Controls—"good" and "evil"

The decade between 1934 and 1944 saw two monthly publications, *The Social Frontier* and its successor, *Frontiers of Democracy*, launched to promote the movement. The former, edited by Dr. Counts with William H. Kilpatrick as board chairman, numbered among its directors more than sixty well-known American educators.

The lead editorial of the initial issue, October 1934, bore the title "Orientation". Here was stated the basic premise which the magazine was designed to promote:

For the American people the age of individualism in economy is closing and an age of collectivism is opening. Here is the central and dominating reality in the present epoch. * * *

* * * [THE SOCIAL FRONTIER] represents a point of view, it has a frame of reference, it stands on a particular interpretation of American history. It accepts the analysis of the current epoch presented above and outlined in greater detail in Conclusions and Recommendations, Report on the Social Studies of the Commission of the American Historical Association.

THE SOCIAL FRONTIER assumes that the age of individualism in economy is closing and that an age marked by a close integration of social life and by collective planning and control is opening. For weal or woe it accepts as irrevocable this deliverance of the historical process. (*Pp. 3-4*)

The second issue, November 1934, elaborated editorially the acceptance of collectivism, and its inevitability:

THE SOCIAL FRONTIER is not engaged in any battle for collectivism as such. That issue has been decided by the forces of history. As Prof. Walton Hamilton says in the last paragraph of a brilliant article in the Encyclopedia of the Social Sciences, the "commitment to collectivism is beyond recall."

* * * Accepting the rise of a collectivist order as irrevocable, it [THE SOCIAL FRONTIER] refuses to adopt a fatalistic attitude toward the question of the form which collectivism is to take in the United States. * * *

* * * THE SOCIAL FRONTIER will throw all the strength it possesses on the side of those forces which are striving to fashion a form of collectivism that will make paramount the interests of the overwhelming majority of the population. (*Pp. 3-4*)

In April 1935 the magazine editorialized:

Loudest in the chorus of praise for freedom and imprecation for collectivism are the grateful beneficiaries of our inherited economic institutions. To them freedom is God and collectivism is Satan.

' *NEA Proceedings,* 1934; p. 647.

* * * The mistaken notion that democracy and freedom are identical with the institutions of property and profit should not be allowed to go unchallenged. On the contrary, teachers and laymen should make clear by all means at their disposal that a collectivist social order is not only necessary in a world of large scale production, corporate control, and human interdependence, but also that under these circumstances only social ownership and democratic control of the means of production can secure a free and democratic life. (*P. 9*)

In the same issue—April 1935—a second editorial pronounced:

The end of free business enterprise as a principle of economic and social organization adequate to this country is at hand. (*P. 8*)

Nor did *The Social Frontier* blink at the prospect. Quite the contrary:

And finally, is economic regimentation really evil? Must it necessarily result in the dehumanization of man? No general answer to these questions is possible. It all depends on who does the regimenting and the purpose the process is intended to serve. If regimentation is imposed by the few people at present in power, for the purpose of maintaining that power, it is evil because dehumanizing. The end products then are material, cultural, and spiritual poverty for the vast masses of people. But if regimentation is the consequence of the human urges of the millions who seek a life of work, dignity, security, and material and cultural plenty, it is humanizing and consequently good. Such regimentation is no regimentation at all; it is rather humanization, liberalization, and socialization. (*June 1935; pp. 5-6*)

"** * * they want a new deck.*"

This theme was followed by many contributors to *Progressive Education* in the early 1930s, and to *The Social Frontier* and *Frontiers of Democracy* in the decade during which those journals were successively published. A few typical citations will suffice.

Writing under the title "Teachers Must Be Leaders", Jesse H. Newlon, director of the Lincoln School,* Teachers College, Columbia University, said:

To effect a more equitable distribution of the national income, a curb must be put upon the operation of the profit motive. The making of profit can no longer be regarded as the chief aim of production. Production must be primarily for use. Integration and planned control of the agencies of production and distribution are inescapable in production primarily for use. They can be achieved only through organs of economic planning that can exercise wise control over credit and over many basic industrial and agricultural operations. To accomplish these ends will necessitate fundamental modifications of our forms and processes of government, both national and local, in order to adapt them to contemporary needs.[1]

In an address before the Sixth World Fellowship of the New Education Fellowship—this being the international organization of the Progressive Education Movement—at Nice, France, in 1932, Dr. Harold Rugg, profes-

---

* The Lincoln Institute of School Experimentation was developed in 1927, based upon the curricular investigational work of the Lincoln School. Its activities included all the Teachers College Schools, and such special investigations as might be assigned to it. In 1928 the name was changed to Institute of School Experimentation. It was discontinued in 1934 but reactivated in 1943 as the Horace Mann-Lincoln Institute of School Experimentation. The same year, 1943, the Schools were consolidated and have since been known as the Horace Mann-Lincoln School.

[1] *Progressive Education*, October 1932; pp. 410-3.

[23]

sor of education at Teachers College, Columbia University, declared:

The world is on fire, and the youth of the world must be equipped to combat the conflagration. Nothing less than thoroughgoing social reconstruction is demanded, and there is no institution known to the mind of man that can compass that problem except education.[4]

Granville Hicks, at the time assistant professor of English at Rensselaer Polytechnic Institute, Troy, N. Y., and later a member of the editorial board of *New Masses*, stated the premise now being documented:

Today the majority of those authors who make any attempt to portray contemporary life frankly admit that the capitalist system is doomed.[5]

Norman Woelfel, subsequently managing editor of *The Social Frontier* and later professor of education at Ohio State University, defined his concept of "social change". This, he said,

* * * implies that there be no unnecessary delay in making completely public the ownership and control of the natural resources and the industrial structure of the nation.

He frankly advised that

* * * we must not blindly shrink from the fact that it may require some use of force against those at present privileged.[6]

Dr. Henry Pratt Fairchild* wrote:

The old economic structure is a house built upon the sands, and the President [Roosevelt] instead of doing anything to install a firm foundation or to move the house over to bedrock, contents himself with putting in a new beam here, shoring up a wall there, and spreading whitewash liberally wherever he can find an exposed surface.

This is the tragedy of the New Deal. * * *

There are many, even in capital-minded America, * * * who will not be satisfied with a New Deal—they want a new deck.[7]

Such are the movement's beliefs

Broadus Mitchell, associate professor of economics at Johns Hopkins University, criticized all talk of correcting the economic order "within the framework of the present system". He pointed to a small "but rapidly growing" group of economists

which finds the only practicable exit in the common ownership of the social means of production and in their operation for use rather than for profit.[8]

---

* *Who's Who in America*, Vol. 26, 1950-1, lists Professor Fairchild as a social scientist, a member of the Planned Parenthood Federation since 1939, and a Council member of the American Association of University Professors. Faculty of New York University.
[4] *Progressive Education*, December 1932-January 1933; pp. 11-18.
[5] *Progressive Education*, January-February 1934; pp. 49-54. THE SOCIAL INTERPRETATION OF LITERATURE.
[6] *Ibid.*, pp. 7-12. THE EDUCATOR, THE NEW DEAL, AND REVOLUTION.
[7] *The Social Frontier*, October 1934; pp. 15-18.
[8] *The Social Frontier*, April 1936; pp. 215-7.

Many of these educators use the phrase "social design". This is a polite term for government control or ownership. Thus, Dr. Theodore Brameld, professor of education at New York University, wrote:

We need today a design for tomorrow. We need an American design which encompasses and unifies the partial, contradictory, often destructive plans of our traditional economy. We need a design where nature's goods at last are consciously, collectively controlled by the majority of our people.[9]

A few months earlier, Dr. Harold Rugg had written:

A large-scale, sustained-yield economy can be operated here if a practicable social design and an efficient and socially acceptable scheme of control can be provided. Both seem to me to be called for; the design must be comprehensive enough to cross any boundaries, either of States or personally owned properties that interfere with the efficient and humane operation of the social system. The central control to administer it must be created by the people themselves.

And, adds Professor Rugg,

that, it seems to me, is what we must teach.[10]

These beliefs *are* being taught, and their exposition and advocacy are by no means confined to the journals which I have been quoting.

Stuart Chase, addressing the Department of Superintendence of the NEA at its Atlantic City meeting on February 25, 1935, said:

If we have even a trace of liberalism in our natures, we must be prepared to see an increasing amount of collectivism, government interference, centralization of economic control, social planning. Here again, the relevant question is not how to get rid of Government interference, but how to apply it for the greatest good of the greatest number.[11]

Writing in the *Thirteenth Yearbook* of the Department of Superintendence of the NEA, 1935, Dr. John L. Childs, professor of education at Teachers College, Columbia University, said:

* * * Under present industrial conditions democratic control can be made a reality only by the collective ownership of those industries whose coordinated administration is essential to the success of a planned economy. (*P. 133*)

* * * Enough data are now available * * * to show the general direction in which we must go. Industrialism points to national social planning. Our national ideal of social democracy requires that this planning be under collective control. Collective control cannot be made a reality in a regime of private ownership of the basic industries. * * * we need not prematurely assume that collective planning and dictatorial bureaucratic regimentation of social life are necessary correlatives. (*Pp.137-8*)

The citations could be endless. But few things could more graphically illustrate the collectivist premise than the final lines of a report on an educators' tour of the Soviet written by Dr. Goodwin Watson, professor of education at Teachers College, Columbia University, and a member of the board of directors of *The Social Frontier:*

---

[9] *Frontiers of Democracy,* January 15, 1940; pp. 111-2, 126-7.
[10] *Frontiers of Democracy,* October 15, 1939; pp. 9-11.
[11] *NEA Journal,* April 1935; pp. 107-10.

For each of us there were sights we approved and others we disapproved, but how about the balance of judgment on the new civilization as a whole? One became skeptical and remained rather unfavorable toward Soviet life. A half dozen who came prepared to find a bad situation had been transferred into warm admirers of the Communist scene. None who came with high expectations had been disappointed. The sum total would be more than 95 percent favorably influenced by this brief study. We had not always been comfortable, but we had been aware of a society directed toward the sustenance of major human values.

One question lingered in our minds. Anna Louise Strong had stated it for us. "I wish I knew," she said, "whether it will take longer for the Russians to develop efficiency or for America to develop socialism. Then I'd know where I wanted to live."*[12]

Such is the philosophy that has been permeating America's teaching for years. The documentation speaks for itself.

Is it any wonder that collectivism is a "trend"?

Is it any wonder that thousands of our young citizens have "strange" ideas?

---

*Editor's Note: Anna Louise Strong's preference may be gathered from the following testimony:

"* * * the Institute of Pacific Relations contributor Anna Louise Strong was for many years editor of the English language Soviet propaganda magazine *Soviet Russia Today*."[1]

She was "Identified as a member of the Communist Party by one or more duly sworn witnesses"; she "Collaborated with agents of the Soviet Intelligence apparatus as shown by sworn testimony"; she wrote for "official publications of the Communist Party or the Communist International or for a Communist government or for pro-Communist press services"; she was "Affiliated with *Amerasia*" and the "Committee for a Democratic Far Eastern Policy."[2]

(This Committee was cited as communist by Attorney General Tom Clark in a letter to the Loyalty Review Board, released April 27, 1949—and as a communist front by the California Committee on Un-American Activities, *Report*, 1948; p. 148.)

Anna Louise Strong was employed by the *Moscow Daily News* and is listed "among American IPR personnel as collaborating with agents of the Soviet intelligence apparatus * * *"[3]

[1] Senate Committee on the Judiciary. *Report No. 2050.* July 1951-June 1952. INSTITUTE OF PACIFIC RELATIONS, p. 96.
[2] *Ibid.*, p. 158.   [3] *Ibid.*, p. 171.
[12] *The Social Frontier*, February 1937; p. 143.

"Scholars have for the most part a diseased way of looking at the world. They mean by it a few cities and unfortunate assemblies of men and women, who might all be concealed in the grass of the prairies. They describe the world as old or new, healthy or diseased, according to the state of their libraries,—a little dust more or less on their shelves. When I go abroad from under this shingle or slate roof, I find several things which they have not considered. Their conclusions seem imperfect."
Henry David Thoreau: *Journal.* (*Circa* 1842)

PART II
TIDES

The Movement
In America's Schools

8. ACTION

This movement involves not only beliefs, but action—by teachers and school administrators, in and through the public schools.

Therein lies its ominous significance.

And therein lies the importance of patiently following its documentation.

There can be no question of a teacher's right to accept and, as a citizen, to promote outside the classroom a premise that capitalism will or should be replaced by collectivist socialism.

The right of personal belief and advocacy is one thing. It is something else, however, when teachers become agents and advocates of collectivism before the involuntary audience of their pupils. And it is something further that public education be the agency and medium for the accomplishment of the purpose.

Personal belief cannot—and must not—be pleaded when it cloaks the proposal that

the school take an active part in helping to build the new social order.*

To "deliberately reach for power"

Many terms are encountered to describe the techniques involved. The blunt word *propagandize* is rarely used; *indoctrination* is the word employed. And the question of just what constitutes *indoctrination* becomes a subject of hair-splitting controversy among the educators concerned.

Some hesitate to advocate outright indoctrination, accepting collectivism as the "frame of reference", as the "orientation" of our children's teaching. A "democratic vision" is presented to the pupil, and his loyalties

---
* *Cf.* page 15.

[27]

are then enlisted in its behalf. The entire procedure is defined as—"uncoerced persuasion".

By whatever name it is called, the premise remains—the schools are actively to participate in building "a new social order", and to prepare children for participation therein.

The school system, its procedures and its curricula are to be revised to whatever extent may be necessary to achieve the goal.

But let its advocates reveal this in their own words.

The whole point, the entire purpose, of Dr. Counts' original Baltimore address, of his subsequent monograph, and of the *Call to the Teachers of the Nation* which he inspired, was that the teachers and the schools were to do something about it. The *Call* was not simply a call to belief; it was a dynamic call to action.

In the Baltimore speech, Counts elaborated the achievements of the movement since 1921. He held that there still was something lacking. The corrective? Dr. Counts gave it:

> If progressive education is to be genuinely progressive, it must emancipate itself from the influence of [the "upper middle class"], face squarely and courageously every social issue, come to grips with life in all of its stark reality, establish a theory of social welfare, fashion a compelling and challenging vision of human destiny, and become somewhat less frightened than it is today at the bogeys of *imposition* and *indoctrination*.[1]

The "challenging vision of human destiny" is collectivism.

Changes in our economic system will, of course, require changes in our ideals, Counts declared. And the schools must actively promote the change in "ideals":

> To my mind [wrote Counts], a movement honestly styling itself progressive should engage in the positive task of creating a new tradition in American life, a tradition possessing power, appeal, and direction.
>
> But, you will say, is this not leading us out upon very dangerous ground? Is it not taking us rather far from the familiar landmarks bounding the fields that teachers are wont to cultivate? My answer is, of course, in the affirmative. * * *
>
> You will also say, no doubt, that I am flirting with the idea of indoctrination. And my answer is again in the affirmative, or, at least, I should say that the word does not frighten me. We may all rest assured that the younger generation in any society will be thoroughly imposed upon by its elders and by the culture into which it is born. For the school to work in a somewhat different direction with all the power at its disposal could do no great harm. At the most, unless the superiority of its outlook is unquestioned, it can but serve as a counterpoise to check and challenge the power of less enlightened or more selfish purposes. (*Pp. 262-3*)

In *Dare the School Build a New Social Order?* Counts wrote:

> Such a vision of what America might become in the industrial age, I would introduce into our schools as the supreme imposition, but one to which our children are entitled—a priceless legacy which it should be the first concern of our profession to fashion and bequeath. The objection will, of course, be raised that this is asking

---

[1] *Progressive Education*, April 1932; p. 259.

teachers to assume unprecedented social responsibilities. But we live in difficult and dangerous times—times when precedents lose their significance. (*P. 54*)

This was his counsel:

That the teachers should deliberately reach for power and then make the most of their conquest is my firm conviction. To the extent that they are permitted to fashion the curriculum and procedures of the school they will definitely and positively influence the social attitudes, ideals, and behavior of the coming generation. * * * It is my observation that the men and women who have affected the course of human events are those who have not hesitated to use the power that has come to them. (*Pp. 28-9*)

To instruct children "for their share in the new order"

The teachers' rôle is made crystal clear by an injunction which should do more to alert us to what is going on than all of "The Enemy" put together:

If the teachers are to play a positive and creative rôle in building a better social order, indeed if they are not to march in the ranks of economic, political, and cultural reaction, they will have to emancipate themselves completely from the domination of the business interests of the nation, cease cultivating the manners and associations of bankers and promotion agents, repudiate utterly the ideal of material success as the goal of education, abandon the smug middle-class tradition on which they have been nourished in the past, acquire a realistic understanding of the forces that actually rule the world, and formulate a fundamental program of thought and action that will deal honestly and intelligently with the problems of industrial civilization. They will have to restate their philosophy of education, reorganize the procedures of the school, and redefine their own position in society.[2]

Dr. Counts outlined the rôle of the schools:

In the collectivist society now emerging the school should be regarded * * * as an agency for the abolition of all artificial social distinctions and of organizing the energies of the nation for the promotion of the general welfare. This, of course, does not mean that the individual should not be encouraged to succeed. It means instead that he should be given a new measure of success.

Throughout the school program the development of the social order rather than the egotistic impulses should be stressed; and the motive of personal aggrandizement should be subordinated to social ends. In promotion practices, in school activities, in the relations of pupils and teachers and administrators, the ideal of a cooperative commonwealth should prevail. * * * All of this applies quite as strictly to the nursery, the kindergarten, and the elementary school as to the secondary school, the college, and the university. (*P. 21*)

Plainly, this blueprint shows the schools—from your nursery through the university—as agencies for promoting a collectivist order.

Further, said Willard W. Beatty, president of the Progressive Education Association, the educator

who would contribute materially to social planning [must] be prepared to undertake the instruction of children for their share in the new order.[3]

---

[2] *A Call to the Teachers of the Nation;* p. 20.
[3] *Progressive Education,* October 1933; p. 304.

No wonder why TFA doesn't reach any S.S. teachers

As Dr. Jesse H. Newlon would write, over seven years later,
the so-called child-centered school goes into the ashcan.[4]

To create "a socialist America"

A strategic wedge was driven in 1934 following the *Conclusions and Recommendations* of the American Historical Association's Commission on Social Studies.

Its point of entry was adroitly chosen. The Commission proposed to consolidate the traditional high school subjects of geography, economics, sociology, political science, civics and history, into a single category designated as the "social studies". Here was the most strategic of all teaching areas for the advancement of a particular philosophy.

Success in enlisting teachers in this field in the cause of a "new social order" would have an influence out of all proportion to the number of teachers involved.

The Commission's *Conclusions and Recommendations* were addressed particularly to this area of instruction. The purpose, then stated, is now clear:

The Commission * * * deems desirable * * * the incorporation into the material of social science instruction in the schools of the best plans and ideals of the future of society and of the individual. (*P. 27*)

Bearing in mind the Commission's dictum that collectivism "is the future already coming into reality", its recommendations clearly indicate how the schools are to "best" serve this "future":

Organized public education in the United States, much more than ever before, is now compelled, if it is to fulfill its social obligation, to adjust its objectives, its curriculum, its methods of instruction, and its administrative procedure to the requirements of the emerging integrated order. * * * It must recognize the new order and proceed to equip the rising generation to cooperate effectively in the increasingly interdependent society and to live rationally and well within its limitations and possibilities. (*Pp. 35-6*)

To "condition" the child for this "new" order,
emphasis will be placed on the development of the social and creative rather than the acquisitive impulses. (*P. 40*)

What this all meant was summed up by Professor Harold J. Laski, philosopher of British socialism. He stated:

At bottom, and stripped of its carefully neutral phrases, the report is an educational program for a socialist America.[5]

To "carry the pupils with them"

It is to be noted that Laski's analysis incurred neither wrath nor protests of injured innocence on the part of his ideological *confrères* within the American school systems. The public heard little, or nothing, about it.

---

[4] *Frontiers of Democracy*, April 15, 1941; pp. 208-11.
[5] *The New Republic*, July 29, 1936; p. 343.

[30]

Dr. Harold Rugg, in his address before the New Education Fellowship at Nice, France, in 1932, said:

Before the school can be used as an agent for social regeneration, it must undergo thorough reconstruction.* * *

How is the problem to be attacked? The first step is the building of a new program of work, a new content for the curriculum, directly out of the problems, issues and characteristics of our changing society.

Therefore,

Our new materials of instruction shall illustrate fearlessly and dramatically the inevitable consequence of the lack of planning and of central control over the production and distribution of physical things.

The task was specific:

Thus through the schools of the world, we shall disseminate a new conception of government—one that will embrace all of the collective activities of men; that will postulate the need for scientific control and operation of economic activities in the interests of all the people. Political government in a new connotation, then, including economic government and social government."

Dr. Norman Woelfel holds that with "our thin crust of culture breaking before our eyes", the educators' "ancient tactics of care and tact and impartiality are, of course, basically futile today":

If we wish to mutter longer the old rhetoric about democracy, as we pursue under capitalism our almost secret routine in the schools, that is a possible choice also, but there can be no assurance that it will long remain a possible alternative. If we will, as teachers, individually and then collectively, make this fundamental choice between clearly distinct social ideals, further procedures will be envisioned more clearly.`

And, as Woelfel said a few months later,

* * * in doing all this, they should endeavor to carry their pupils with them."

To "remake the curriculum"

Dr. John Dewey, while exceedingly dexterous at manipulating words, makes it equally clear that the program calls for classroom action. Because of his immense influence, I quote Dr. Dewey at some length:

I do not think * * * that the schools can in any literal sense be the builders of a new social order. But the schools will surely as a matter of fact and not of ideal *share* in the building of the social order of the future according as they ally themselves with this or that movement of existing social forces. This fact is inevitable. The schools of America have furthered the present social drift and chaos by their emphasis upon an economic form of success which is intrinsically pecuniary and egoistic. They will of necessity, and again not as a matter of theory, take an active part in determining the social order—or disorder—of the future, according as teachers and administrators align themselves with the older so-called "individualistic" ideals— which in fact are fatal to individuality for the many—or with the newer forces making for social control of economic forces. The plea that teachers must passively accommodate themselves to existing conditions is but one way—and a cowardly way—of making a choice in favor of the old and chaotic.

" *Progressive Education*, December 1932-January 1933; pp. 11-18.
` *Progressive Education*, February 1934; pp. 7-12.
` *The Social Frontier*, October 1934; p. 9.

If the teacher's choice is to throw himself in with the forces and conditions that are making for change in the direction of social control of capitalism—economic and political—there will hardly be a moment of the day when he will not have the opportunity to make his choice good in action. If the choice is conscious and intelligent, he will find that it affects the details of school administration and discipline, of methods of teaching, of selection and emphasis of subject-matter. * * * The task is to translate the desired ideal over into the conduct of the detail of the school in administration, instruction and subject matter. Here, it seems to me, is the great present need and responsibility of those who think the schools should consciously be partners in the construction of a changed society. The challenge to teachers must be issued and in clear tones. But the challenge is merely a beginning. What does it mean in the particulars of work in the school and on the playground? An answer to this question and not more general commitment to social theory and slogans is the pressing demand.

The view was expressed by Dr. Jesse H. Newlon during a panel discussion before the Department of Superintendence, NEA, on February 26, 1935. Dr. Newlon, professor of education and director of the Lincoln School,* Teachers College, Columbia University, insisted that

the school will be employed either to support the existing order or to build a better social order."

Why studies and textbooks must be made over is outlined by James M. Shields, former supervising principal of elementary schools at Winston-Salem, N. C.:

It fairly staggers one to consider the tremendous task ahead in revision of our existing instructional literature if it is to be of any use at all in a collectivist society. Hardly a public school textbook now in use but is saturated with the profit psychology. Arithmetics are permeated with profit and loss, gain, "making" money. One would hunt in vain through their pages for an incentive to economic cooperation. Even geographies are replete with production for gain. And as for histories! No wonder the Russians started from scratch in creating an entire new educational literature under the Soviet system. Almost we may have to discover America anew."

Professor Rugg fully concurred, saying:

* * * a necessary first step in educational reconstruction lies in the remaking of the curriculum."

The first move had been to consolidate the "social studies" in 1934.

To "change the very lives of the children in their care"

Is "indoctrination" permissible? This question is much debated. In many instances views expressed by the same educators are contradictory. Dr. Rugg, for example, wrote in 1936 that he did not advocate "the construction of any theoretical social order and its 'teaching' in the schools"." Three years later he insisted upon a "scheme of central control", adding,

---

* Cf. footnote, page 23.

" The Social Frontier, October 1934; pp. 11-2. Can Education Share in Social Reconstruction?
" NEA Proceedings, 1935; pp. 540-1.
" The Social Frontier, June 1936; pp. 281-4.
¹²,¹ The Social Frontier, October 1936; pp. 12-15.

"that is what we must teach".[14]

John Dewey had this to say:

If teachers who hold that there is an intrinsic relation between actualization of democracy and social planning of economic institutions and relations hope to bring others to the same conclusions by use of the method of investigation and free cooperative discussion, I see nothing undemocratic in the procedure. It looks to me like an education procedure, and, moreover, to be of the same sort that teachers who have been led to accept the conclusion might then use with their own students.[15]

And what about the students? As Dr. Rugg already had said—in so many words—

To change the outlook and procedure of teachers is to change the very lives of the children in their care.[16]

That is the question which faces every parent in America. And the essence of that question is:

Do the people of this Country want "the very lives of their children" to continue to be so changed?

There is another question: Given the choice, would the "children" themselves accept such guidance of their "very lives"?

[14] *Frontiers of Democracy,* October 15, 1939; pp. 9-11.
[15] *The Social Frontier,* December 1938; p. 72.
[16] *The Social Frontier,* October 1936; pp. 14-5.

"By and large, the textbooks commonly used by the 7,000,000 secondary school children of America are poorly written, show a lack of scholarly competence and are generally on a 'very low level' * * *

" '* * * You would be perfectly amazed at some of the stuff in them. There is a notable tendency * * * to play down what this country has accomplished and to place the emphasis on defects * * * on the one-third of the population who are underfed rather than the two-thirds who are well fed

" 'They emphasize the small number of large corporations, rather than the large number of small ones. The authors point to the few wealthy people of this country rather than to the fact that we have the greatest distribution of wealth in all the world.

" '* * * What you get is a critical attitude that is destructive in its influence.' "

Benjamin Fine, reporting an interview with Dr. Ralph W. Robey, assistant professor of banking, Columbia University, following an extensive survey of textbooks conducted by a committee of which Dr. Robey was the head. (*The New York Times*, February 22, 1941; pp. 1 and 6)

PART II   The Movement
TIDES   In America's Schools

9. CLASS-WARFARE

Should public schools become the battlegrounds of class warfare?

Should teachers engage—or even acquiesce—in such warfare?

What a shock that such questions can seriously be asked in these United States! Yet is it not even more shocking to find supposedly responsible educators answering in the affirmative?

Extremists, of course, believe that the transition to collectivism will lead to open conflict—political or worse—between what they call the owner and worker classes of society. They hold that the schools cannot escape this "conflict", and that teachers must cast their lot, in classroom and out, with the "worker" class.

Class warfare is a Marxist tenet. And whether or not they accept the label, such advocates of collectivism-through-the-classroom embrace this Marxist tenet.

Dr. Counts showed strong leanings toward it:

If democracy is to be achieved in the industrial age, powerful classes must be persuaded to surrender their privileges, and institutions deeply rooted in popular prejudice will have to be radically modified or abolished. And according to the historical record, this process has commonly been attended by bitter struggle and even bloodshed. Ruling classes never surrender their privileges voluntarily.

* * * There is little evidence from the pages of American history to support us in the hope that we may adjust our differences through the method of sweetness and light.[1]

The same theme is found in *A Call to the Teachers of the Nation:*

Even the taxpayers have no special claim on the schools; they are but the tax collectors of society; ultimately school revenue comes from all who labor by hand or brain. This the teachers should never forget. Their loyalty therefore goes to the great body of the laboring population—to the farmers, the industrial workers, and the

---

[1] Counts: *Dare the School Build a New Social Order?* Pp. 50-1.

other members of the producing classes of the nation. They owe nothing to the present economic system, except to improve it; they owe nothing to any privileged caste, except to strip it of its privileges. (*Pp. 19-20*)

This, mind you, is being taught—however covertly—in schools all over the United States.

Communism "contained" abroad—while taught at home

Dr. Norman Woelfel does not hesitate to suggest the use of force:

If we wish the intelligent utilization of the marvelous natural resources and the superb productive machinery which America possesses, for all of the people, with common privileges * * * that is possible, although we must not blindly shrink from the fact that it may require some use of force against those at present privileged.[2]

For years one of the most vigorous advocates of collectivism-through-the-schools has been Dr. Theodore Brameld, professor of education at New York University. Brameld has declared that "realistically minded teachers might profit by greater acquaintance with Marx". Though disclaiming advocacy of Marxism, Brameld pointed out that "several of his"—Marx'—"basic postulates are likewise those of a considerable group of progressive educators", especially Marx' belief that "the profit system is the root of our social troubles" and his insistence that "collectivism has to replace it".[3]

Scores of textbooks contain such attacks on profits, and on individual rights and enterprise. The attacks are both open and subtle, and they have been causing thousands of graduates to enter business life with scant faith in the most expansive force on earth—the hope of self-betterment, and the hope of legitimate gain.

In the background is always the thought of possible violence. Brameld, for instance, declared that violence, in Marx' view, was to be avoided if possible, "but it should not be characterized categorically as immoral under all circumstances". He called attention to Marx' statement in a letter to his friend Kugelmann that "the solution cannot proceed along pleasant lines." He emphasized the Marxist principle that

the opposition of the class in control of capitalist society is so tremendous that nothing short of counter-opposition frequently bordering upon, indeed crystallizing into, illegality will suffice to defeat it.[4]

And Brameld held that, from Marx' standpoint,

the teacher who wishes to conduct his activity—within the schools and without—in behalf of the collectivist ideal must free himself from the fallacy that the choice before him is naught or all. * * * Teachers, first, should recognize that unless they choose to follow the older educational philosophy of neutrality they must accept a point of view consonant with the requirements of the new America. They must then influence their students, subtly if necessary, frankly if possible, toward acceptance of the same position.[5]

[2] *Progressive Education,* January-February 1934; pp. 7-12. THE EDUCATOR, THE NEW DEAL, AND REVOLUTION.
[3] *The Social Frontier,* November 1935; pp. 53-6. KARL MARX AND THE AMERICAN TEACHER.
[4] *Science and Society—a Marxian Quarterly,* Fall 1936; pp. 1-17.
[5] *The Social Frontier,* November 1935; pp. 53-5.

Discussion flared in educational circles. The class approach found vigorous espousal in *The Social Frontier*. An editorial in the February 1936 issue asserted:

> To us the class approach to society appeals as * * * an extremely useful point of departure for a method of bringing about those changes which are necessary for an equitable distribution of the goods of life. (*Pp. 134-5*)

Then follows this argument:

> If we wanted a society dominated by either men or women, by Negroes or Nordics, by Jews, Catholics, Protestants, or atheists, we would approach society with a sex, race or religious orientation. But we want a society dominated by and managed in the interest of those who create national and cultural wealth. We want a society in which goods will be produced for use, and not for the profit of owners of means of production. We want a society in which the wealth-creating resources and instruments will be owned collectively, controlled democratically, and managed efficiently. We want a society in which the fruits of economic effort will be distributed in such a way as to liberate the masses of the people for creative and appreciative experiences in the realms of culture.
>
> In the process of creating such a society the needed classification—and we have indicated that classification of one kind or another is necessary for social engineering—is the classification of "worker" and "owner".

Another editorial from *The Social Frontier* states:

> There is no hope for the significant practice of education in a social order based on private property and profit. * * * That there is no hope for education worthy of that name under capitalism needs no arguing.

The editorial proceeds with increasing candor:

> The suggestion that teachers align themselves with labor, no doubt, implies advocacy of the class struggle. But the truth might as well be realized that radical redistribution of power and the fruits of power in society is brought about not by pointing out how reasonable and efficient that distribution might be, but by the organized, daring, and effective bid of a socio-economic class for mastery over social machinery and resources * * * undertaken by those to whom these steps are a matter of life and death.
>
> It will be said that class struggle spells violence, that it is inconsistent with the function of the teacher who is an agent of society as a whole. These arguments are not tenable. Class struggle need not necessarily lead to a violent seizure of power. * * * If there should be violence, the onus will fall on the shoulders of those few who cannot gracefully surrender their privileges in the face of a popular decision. Moreover, while the teacher is an agent of society whose function is to contribute to the common good, the common good can best be served now by promoting a class good— the good of that class whose security and dignity can be achieved only if our economic resources are collectivized and democratized. The interests of labor are now the interests of society. The teacher should consider that if he does not consciously identify himself with labor he unwittingly sanctions the continuation of the reign of the small group which now holds power over the life of the nation.[′]

Deliberate class-division

Returning for the moment to *The Social Frontier* editorial of February 1936, one finds teachers being urged to join a "class"—which "class" is at the same time to be made conscious of itself:

[′] *The Social Frontier*, October 1935; pp. 7-8. EDITORIAL.

In view of the absence of a class mentality among the workers, it would be reasonable to assume that it is the problem of education to induce such a mentality, rather than to take an existing mentality and base a course of action upon it.

This thesis is expressed by Dr. John L. Childs, professor of education at Teachers College, Columbia University:

The institutions and practices of our historic American economic individualism are in irreconcilable conflict with the patterns of life implicit in the present interdependent industrial economy. * * * The collective, scientific planning and utilization of resources, material and human * * * is incompatible with the continuance of the historic profit system. * * *

If affairs are studied in relation to vital national trends the "class" concept seems to many to be less doctrinaire than the "classless" doctrine. So also from an empirical point of view does the notion of a deepening conflict of interests between owners and workers correspond more closely to the actual situation than does the view that all will collaborate in the transformation of our economic system.

Childs is convinced that "we shall not make the transition to an effectual planning society by the collaboration of all groups" and that "educators can play an important rôle" in the transition only as they accept this premise. Therefore, he concludes:

Educators, aware of what is now involved, * * * should not find it difficult to decide where they belong in this deepening struggle of classes.[1]

Even among liberal educators this provoked dissent. Childs agreed that "the experimentalist educator will not encourage the preaching of violence and class hatred", because "his experience teaches him that when passions of this sort are aroused, it is generally chance operating as brute force, and not intelligence which decides the issue." Such tactics, he warned, "might also lead to a sweeping reaction which could easily result in some form of Fascist control."

But, Childs insisted, the teacher

will recognize that democracy involves the right of a majority to make its will prevail, even if the power of government and law must be utilized to coerce reluctant minorities entrenched in outmoded institutional arrangements. Political democracy is not to be opposed to engaging in group and class struggles.[2]

Dr. Boyd H. Bode, professor of education at Ohio State University, saw what this meant. He warned that clever phraseology

must not be permitted to obscure the fact that this proposed scheme of education is deliberately aimed at fostering a disposition which will make the pupil intolerant and 'sore' with respect to the contrast between employers and workers.[2]

Haven't you heard employers remark on just this attitude among their junior staff? Haven't you observed it yourself? If so, another question is clearly posed:

Is the alien doctrine of class-warfare to be permitted to remain in the teaching of our youth?

[1] The Social Frontier, April 1936; pp. 219-22. CAN TEACHERS STAY OUT OF THE CLASS STRUGGLE?
[2] The Social Frontier, June 1936; pp. 274-78.
[2] The Social Frontier, November 1938; pp. 38-40.

10. THE ANTICIPATED RESISTANCE

From the very outset of the movement its leaders have recognized the inevitability of opposition. The emphasis which they placed upon it, and their plans to devise a strategy to overcome it, indicate significantly the long-range planning of the movement.

Dr. Counts showed this in *Dare the School Build a New Social Order?:*

We know full well that, if the school should endeavor vigorously and consistently to win its pupils to the support of a given social program, unless it were supported by other agencies, it could act only as a mild counterpoise to restrain and challenge the might of less enlightened and more selfish purposes. (*P. 24*)

It was the realization of inevitable opposition which prompted Counts' injunction that teachers "deliberately reach for power and then make the most of their conquest". He warned that

The power that teachers exercise in the schools can be no greater than the power they wield in society.

Therefore, teachers

must be prepared to stand on their own feet and win for their ideas the support of the masses of the people. (*Pp. 30-1*)

The problem is stated in *A Call to the Teachers of the Nation:*

Thus we are brought face to face with the paradox: The school must participate in the task of social reconstruction, yet until society is already transformed the school can scarcely hope to function effectively. (*P. 23*)

Opposition, the *Call* stated, would be characterized by

the ignorance of the masses and the malevolence of the privileged. (*P. 26*)

The opposition defined

No one saw more clearly the grass-roots meaning of this movement than did Harold J. Laski. The program, he said,

is a direct criticism of the ideals that have shaped capitalist America; the ideals, also,

[38]

that American capitalists still stoutly hold. To them it says in effect: We want you to agree to the trial of educational practices built upon the assumption that you and all that you are stand in contradiction to the needs of America. Our spirit is a denial of your spirit. Where you deny, we affirm, where you affirm, we deny. What you think are the safeguards of America are the things we believe will work disaster for it. We ask you to allow the schools to be used for the destruction of those safeguards.

How would the schools be "used"? Laski continues:

We want to fill them with teachers who will analyze critically all the things for which you stand. We want to create in the schools a new generation which will realize that your ideals, your purposes, your methods, are both dangerous and obsolete. We believe that it is to the interest of America—even, on a long view, to your interest—to help us to realize our program. Cannot we rely, in this crisis of America's destiny, upon your willing support for this adventure?

And Laski, socialist subject of socialist Britain, concludes:

Virtually * * * the report [of the Commission of the American Historical Association*] asks the present owning class in America to cooperate in facilitating its own erosion. I know of no historical experience that makes that demand likely of fulfillment. * * * The report, I believe, underestimates the passion with which men cling to the religion of ownership; and its impact upon the votaries of that faith would, if they read it, lead less to conviction that conversion was desirable than to the angry perception that the liberal teacher is an even more dangerous heretic than they have hitherto been accustomed to affirm.[1]

Laski's amazing statements were not considered newsworthy by the "capitalist" press, and few advocates of our competitive system troubled themselves to discover if that system were being undermined in the schools. However, as "capitalists" eventually might find it out, the problem before the collectivists was clear enough.

I proceed to the various proposals they made for meeting it.

---

* Four members of the Commission refused to join in the 1934 report. They were: Frank W. Ballou, superintendent of schools at Washington, D. C.; Edmund E. Day, of the University of Michigan; Ernest Horn, of the University of Iowa; and Chas. E. Merriam, of the University of Chicago.

[1] *The New Republic,* July 29, 1936; pp. 342-5.

11. THE STRATEGY OF INFILTRATION

However verbose and vague the leaders may be in describing their "new" social order, no vagueness is apparent in the measures they regard as necessary to prepare the profession, and particularly its "progressive" element, for the struggle to attain it.

Their agenda includes professional tenure—job security, in other words —a war chest, and provision for legal aid. It includes "academic freedom", deference to their own "trained judgment" and a minimum of "interference" by the public. And it calls for "more liberal school boards"—as long as these institutions survive as unavoidable evils in their path.

The agenda includes professional "solidarity"; unionization of teachers; enlistment of the support of kindred "liberal forces", and utilization of the "class approach" as a "resource" in the campaign. In some instances the promoters do not scruple to justify resort to slyness and deceit.

Finally, an all-out effort for adult education is planned. This is to assure general acceptance of the collectivist idea.

The *Call to the Teachers of the Nation* flatly says that

any program of education designed for the coming generation, if it is to be successful, must march hand in hand and be closely coordinated with a program of adult and parent education.

The *Call* asserts that the profession

must fight for tenure, for adequate compensation, for a voice in the formulation of educational policies, they must uphold the ancient doctrine of academic freedom and maintain all of their rights as human beings and American citizens. (*P. 24*)

The *Call* continues:

Also they must insist on the public recognition of their professional competence in the field of education; they must oppose every effort on the part of publishing houses, business interests, privileged classes, and patriotic societies to prescribe the content of the curriculum. (*Pp. 24-5*)

[40]

* * * The progressive-minded teachers of the country must unite in a powerful organization * * * In the defense of its members against the ignorance of the masses and the malevolence of the privileged, such an organization would have to be equipped with the material resources, the legal talent, and the trained intelligence necessary to wage successful warfare in the press, the courts, and the legislative chambers of the nation. (*P. 26*)

It is hard to spot a detail which has been overlooked.

A minority corps d'élite

The *Conclusions and Recommendations* of the American Historical Association's Commission stressed that the public must take second place:

If the school is to discharge the highly conservative function of relieving tensions in American society and of bringing thought and reason to bear on social adjustment, then reliance must be placed on the trained judgment of those to whom the actual content of public education is entrusted. (*P. 125*)

If the teacher is * * * to free the school from the domination of special interests * * * there must be a redistribution of power in the conduct of education. * * * The boards of education will have to be made more representative. (*P. 128*)

Dr. Harold C. Hand, associate professor of education at Stanford University, illustrates this latter point:

Given the present class-composition of virtually all of our boards of education, and the. administrator-dominated type of teachers' organization to which the vast majority of the affiliated teachers now belong, what hope that such a splendid program of democratic education could be translated into actual practice in the classroom?[1]

John Lloyd Snell concluded:

Few of the many needed departures from the traditional secondary school curriculum may be expected to emanate from high school boards as they are set up at present in California.

Kenneth D. Benne, in his presidential address before the American Education Fellowship—formerly the Progressive Education Association—spoke emphatically in 1951:

One other lesson teachers must learn. This is the lesson of organized professional responsibility and solidarity to protect schools and teachers in the responsible, daring and open study, discussion and experimentation which the teaching task requires; to enlist the aid and support of other forces and groups who, like progressive teachers, are devoted to a democratic future for America and the world in protecting the transformation of the schools, to oppose forces and groups which would make of schools the passive and impotent hawkers of harmless, irrelevant, and outworn knowledge and values, the agents of social reaction.

Superintendent Virgil M. Rogers of Battle Creek, Mich., during a panel discussion at the annual meeting of the NEA at San Francisco, July 1951, stated:

[1] *Frontiers of Democracy*, October 1939; p. 24.
- *Frontiers of Democracy*, February 15, 1940; pp. 141-2. SOCIAL ATTITUDES OF CALIFORNIA SCHOOL BOARD MEMBERS. (Snell at the time was principal of the Leggett Valley High School, Cummings, Cal.)
Progressive Education, April 1951; p. 196.

Teachers must close ranks professionally, remove the schisms, and solidly unite professionally in every community and throughout the nation.[4]

A united combat group

The "solidarity" cannot be termed exclusive. Dr. Theodore Brameld, in discussing the possible contributions of Marxism to the profession, said:

Particularly would he [Marx] be pleased to see that at least a few teachers have already gone so far as to unionize themselves as a class, conscious of interests fundamentally separate from most school boards or from others sympathetic with the status quo.[5]

Again Brameld wrote:

Marxism would applaud * * * the statement of Professor Newlon in *The Social Frontier*: "Teachers, if they are really opposed to suppression that is fascism must prepare to join in an organized way with the liberal forces seeking to build a better society, with labor, farmers, professionals, and all others who do the actual productive work of the country, in the struggle of the people against special privilege."[6]

John Dewey makes the matter perfectly clear:

Organization among teachers is imperatively needed to stem the rising tide of brutal reaction and intimidation. * * * it is foolish to suppose that this organization will be adequate unless it is supported by wider and deeper organization with others who have a common interest in the reconstruction of the present regime of production for personal gain and personal power. * * *

What can be done? The direct answer is: Join locals of the American Federation of Teachers where they exist; help form them where they do not exist. * * * I would heartily second the motion of Heywood Broun* for an alliance of teachers with the Newspaper Guild. Actors and writers are organized or are beginning to organize. Ministers in the churches, while not yet widely organized for other than purely professional purposes, have spoken, through their various organizations, more and more openly about the injustices of the present order.

What is needed is an aggressive alliance of these various groups. Divided, we may fall. United, we shall stand, and in standing shall do our special work.[7]

Norman Woelfel has described such a combat group as

a united front of radically inclined educators.

These radically inclined educators, he said, must

form their defensive lines under the banner of basic convictions, ally themselves with all other social groups of similar orientation among the people, and fight heroically against whatever forces elect to lay down the gauge of battle.[3]

Dr. John L. Childs held that

the present conflict of classes presents not only a *problem*, it also presents a *resource*.

---

* *Editor's Note:* Heywood Broun was the organizer of the Newspaper Guild, which for years was known for its leftist views. He was a charter member of the I.S.S. club at Harvard in 1909.

[4] Mimeographed release of the NEA, issued at the time.
[5] *The Social Frontier*, November 1935; pp. 53-6.
[6] *Science and Society—a Marxian Quarterly*, Fall 1936; pp. 1-17.
[7] *The Social Frontier*, April 1935; pp. 11-12.
[3] *Progressive Education*, January-February 1934; p. 11, and March 1934; p. 161.

It was Childs' judgment that the educators'

struggle for academic freedom and adequate support for the public schools [is] related to the deepening conflict of class interests in American society.

This is because the educators'

experience indicates that not all classes in the economic life of the United States are so situated objectively that they will be inclined to favor this fundamental social reconstruction.

Indeed, Childs adds,

a small, but economically and politically powerful, class of owners is already taking active measures to forestall it.

Conversely,

honest appraisal of conditions convinces him that certain elements of the population are much more likely to respond to this program of socialization than are others. If, as this movement of workers—farm, factory, office, and professional—gathers momentum, he finds that class cleavages in American life grow sharper, he will not thereby be deterred from continuing his work of political and economic organization.

Far from being deterred, teachers should welcome allies in the conflict:

* * * In my opinion, the chance for a peaceful, orderly transformation of our economy will be increased, not lessened, by an open alliance of professional groups, including educators, with the working class."

Task forces of "social change"

Dr. Childs already had expressed the belief that

If the schools are to be kept free to perform their important intellectual function * * * they will need the support of those groups whose interests will be advanced by the change from capitalism.'"

One reference to the potential power of the teaching profession, and the strategic employment of that power, was an editorial in *The Social Frontier* of January 1935. The title—*1,105,921*—represented the number of teachers in schools and colleges in 1930 according to the fifteenth Federal Census. That one out of every forty-five persons gainfully employed was engaged in teaching was noted as

a fact of far-reaching social significance—a fact whose meaning has been fully grasped neither by society at large nor by the teaching profession.

Elaborating on this significance, the editorial states:

* * * The responsibility of educational workers for shaping the program of the school has become perpetual and inescapable. They could not be mere instruments if they tried. * * * In large part, therefore, the actual administration of the school must be left to those who are technically competent—the teachers of the country. The only alternative is chaos and cultural regression.

The next sentence is significant:

In the very nature of the case no clear mandate covering the details or even the major outlines of an educational program can be given by society to educational workers.

" *The Social Frontier,* June 1936; pp. 274-8.
'" *The Social Frontier,* April 1936; pp. 219-22.

In other words, "society" is to remain silent, while "educational workers" determine what they will.

The editorial continues:

* * * In the state now emerging organized education must take its place alongside the other great coordinate functions of industrial society and become an integral part of government.

This seems to me to add up to an amazing, totalitarian, free-from-accountability-to-anyone-but-themselves rôle for certain members of the teaching profession. Here is a "handsoff" notice to the "educationally incompetent" lay public, including, presumably, members of your local board of education.

Such a rôle would mean total power for those who guide the movement. It would mean total subservience of the people to that power—and the deliverance of every single child in America to its domination.

As for the use of power, the editorial states:

to those who say that the profession dare not show independence in the formulation of either educational or social policies, it should be pointed out that the potential power of teachers in terms of today and tomorrow has never been put to the test.

* * * With the enfranchisement of women the teachers of the country have become a potential political force to be reckoned with. They have the power to throw the fear of God and of unemployment into the hearts of many a machine politician. THE SOCIAL FRONTIER is of the opinion that the judicious and courageous use of this power in advancing the interests of education and protecting the civic and professional rights of teachers is a responsibility which they can no longer escape.*

An additional factor is cited:

The strength of the teachers * * * is by no means to be gauged by statistics. Their strength is strategic and functional as well as numerical. They spread over the country in a fine network which embraces every hamlet and rural community. And the function which they perform brings them into close and sympathetic relations with the rank and file of the people of the nation. No occupational group in society is equally favorably situated.

And the editorial concludes:

All they lack is organization, vision, and courage. Perhaps these things will come.

Thus have the task forces of "social change" infiltrated the Nation's schools—while spokesmen declare that no such movement exists.

---

* *Editor's Note:* Nine years later, the "potential political force" of organized teachers had become a reality. Dr. Howard A. Dawson, high official of the National Education Association, addressed the Representative Assembly of the NEA as follows:

"My friends, we have recently had some demonstrations of the power of the influence of teachers working in a righteous cause. * * *

"It was no political accident that Claude Pepper will again sit in the Halls of the United States Senate to lead the fight for the common people of Florida and of the Nation. The school teachers of that State made their contribution. In the primary election of that State, Federal aid was an issue; Federal aid won.

"Again, my friends, it was no political accident that the not-so-distinguished Republican Senator from Oregon [Rufus C. Holman] will not again grace the Halls of Congress." (In this case the man elected was Wayne Morse.)

Congressional Record. Vol. 90, Part 10; p. A3937. September 8, 1944.

"For the time will come when they will not endure sound doctrine; but after their own lusts shall they heap to themselves teachers, having itching ears;

"And they shall turn away *their* ears from the truth, and shall be turned unto fables."

II Timothy 4: 3, 4.

PART II
TIDES

The Movement
In America's Schools

12. THE STRATEGY OF INDOCTRINATION

One proposal for overcoming public opposition at least has the virtue of candor. Stated by Willard W. Beatty, president of the Progressive Education Association, the proposal is this:

schools cannot offer their children instruction in political or economic doctrines which differ materially from those understood and accepted by the adult community. * * * A double burden therefore rests upon the educator who would contribute materially to social planning. He must be prepared to undertake not only the instruction of children for their share in the new order, but also leadership and guidance of the adult community in its groping for individual and social security in this rapidly changing world.[1]

How is this to be done? Professor Rugg, for instance, urged "a dramatic nation-wide campaign for social reconstruction", insisting that "this step is a necessary preliminary to the rebuilding of the social-science program of the elementary and secondary schools".[2]

Eight years later, in 1942, Rugg's advocacy reached a climax unequalled openly before or since. To President Roosevelt, to U. S. Commissioner of Education John Studebaker, and to public school superintendents throughout the Nation, he addressed open letters which bore the resounding title, *The Battle for Consent: Gentlemen, This Is Our Moment —If.*

Here he proposed an all-out, Government-financed and directed campaign to wage a "war-at-home over a free, abundant, and creative world"; to promote world rehabilitation and "full employment at abundance level." The program included economic planning by Government; "interjection of social capital into the system" by Government "if private initiative does not act promptly to maintain full employment"; and the proposition that "with our giant resources we need not fear the national debt."

---

[1] *Progressive Education,* October 1933, p 304
[2] *Progressive Education,* January-February 1934, pp 3-5.

Dr. Rugg announced that educators who have reached

much the same conclusions and affirmations more than all else crave a chance to teach these great ideas to their high school youths and to the prospective teachers in the colleges of education. They want to write them into the new textbooks that will be made to herald the new day.

To do this, he said, "would be a thrilling experience"—

I know, for I tried to do it during the great depression in my *Man and His Changing Society*—a series of books which was studied by some 5,000,000 young Americans until the patrioteers and the native Fascist press well-nigh destroyed it between 1939 and 1941.

Teachers' colleges as "Pointers of the Way"

Professor Rugg called for an office of education for peace. It was to have "unlimited resources", and "a budget running into billions if necessary, to reach ten, twenty, thirty million Americans day after day, week after week, without let-up." He called for an "all-out campaign over every trunk line of communication in this country, a nation-wide barrage of ideas and attitudes that will reach every city, town and hamlet—a barrage day after day, month after month, not letting up for years to come."

This campaign requires a pamphlet-bulletin-article-book-writing program that would dwarf anything that has ever been dreamed of in this or any other country. The nation's finest novelists, poets, essayists, columnists, and other publicists, drafted to write. Drafted, I say. The nation's scholars in the social sciences—economics, politics, government, history and sociology, social psychology and public opinion—drafted to organize topics, to outline material, to collaborate with the professional writers in preparing books, pamphlets, bulletins, articles printed by Government printing presses and syndicated at cost throughout the country.[1]

One month later Rugg warned:

There may not be time enough * * * to silence the isolationist, exploitive back-to-normalcy, die-hard right and their vicious press.[4]

The fantastic proposal was snubbed. Reluctantly, then, he wrote:

I am unhappy to report that the hoped-for attack from Washington has not been forthcoming. * * * I very much fear that as in the past we shall be driven back upon private initiative to take the lead.

Rugg lost no time in developing this "private initiative", and issued the following summons to teachers' colleges:

Let them become powerful national centers for the graduate study of ideas and they will thereby become forces of creative imagination standing at the very vortex of the ideational revolution. Let us make our teacher education institutions into great direction-finders for our new society. . . . Pointers of the Way . . . dynamic trail blazers of new frontiers.[5]

Here, in the teachers' colleges, is the tactical center of the movement.

---

[1] *Frontiers of Democracy*, December 15, 1942; pp. 75-81.
[4] *Frontiers of Democracy*, January 15, 1943; pp. 101-8.
[5] *Frontiers of Democracy*, May 15, 1943; pp. 247-54.

[46]

Deception "in a truly Bolshevik manner"

There remains one further device for circumventing opposition. I refer to slyness and outright deception.

This is what Dr. Theodore Brameld was talking about in 1935 when he said that teachers favorable to the collectivist philosophy and program must

influence their students, subtly if necessary, frankly if possible, toward acceptance of the same position.[*]

It is the method referred to in the May 1937 issue of *The Communist*:

* * * Only when teachers have really mastered Marxism-Leninism will they be able skillfully to inject it into their teaching at the least risk of exposure, and at the same time to conduct struggles around the schools in a truly Bolshevik manner. (*P. 440*)

In February 1951 an article in *Progressive Education* discussed circumstances where outright deceit might be employed—apparently without editorial repudiation of the possibility. The article is signed by A. Max Carmichael, professor of education at Ball State Teachers College, Muncie, Ind.:

* * * Our teacher will have to choose whether * * * to try to live up to the principles which he morally can accept, and risk being discharged; or whether * * * to temporize with the situation, abiding actually or ostensibly by the decision of those in control, but here and there, perhaps, secretively failing to abide by the injunction, and not stating his position too openly in the wrong places. Some teachers can find moral justification for this latter procedure under these circumstances. It seems to me that the individual teacher will have to make up his mind in terms of the alternatives before him; to wit, how well he can make an adjustment if discharged, how likely he is to get caught, etc. It seems a shame to have to talk in these terms, but one must meet opposition that is without moral principle in ways that implement one's long-time goals rather than the more immediate ones. Ultimately, force may often best be met with force and with its accompanying deceit. Let me here add that so long as no threat of discharge exists, I see no reason for any other behavior than that of candid discussion. Even in the case of threat, there is little need for innuendoes, name-calling, sarcasm, even though there may be occasion for deceit. (*P. 110*)

Thus parents and children are subjected to a technique which enables the more militant advocates of this movement to

conduct struggles around the schools in a truly Bolshevik manner.

And for over twenty years such philosophy has been present within our schools—for the "education" of our youth.

---

[*] *The Social Frontier*, November 1935; pp. 53-5. KARL MARX AND THE AMERICAN TEACHER.

"Therefore, let us not sleep, as others do; but let us watch, and be sober. "❋ ❋ ❋

"But prove all things; hold fast that which is good."

1 Thessalonians 5: 6, 21.

PART II
TIDES

The Movement
In America's Schools

13. THE SUBTLE USE OF THOUGHT

Leaders of the movement are naturally interested in the personal views of members of the teaching profession. How, otherwise, can teachers be trained as "engineers of social change"?

This is illustrated by a survey conducted in 1936 by the John Dewey Society for the Study of Education and Culture. The survey, together with its findings, is described in the Society's *First Yearbook,* issued in 1937. The description is written by Dr. George W. Hartmann, associate professor of education at Teachers College, Columbia University. It is entitled, "The Social Attitudes and Information of American Teachers".

In opening discussion, Dr. Hartmann offers this thesis:

Any system of public education that seeks to equip the nation's youth for effective participation in the life of a complex society cannot be indifferent to the social, political, economic, and general philosophic attitudes of its teachers. ❋ ❋ ❋ We cannot doubt that the teacher's personal acceptance or rejection of significant institutional practices and proposals has at least some influence upon the actions and opinions of his pupils and consequently upon the thoughts and behavior of future citizens of the country. ❋ ❋ ❋ In a period of rapid social change the particular attitudes of the teacher lose whatever irrelevancy they may have appeared to possess in a stabler era and become instead crucial matters for urgent consideration. (*P. 174 ff*)

Questionnaire to teachers

Now, the first to condemn inquiries into a teacher's political or economic views—let alone his "philosophic attitudes"—are these very educators, when inquiries come from "busybodies, patrioteers, American Fascists", and others similarly described. Yet one phase of this 1936 survey was the circulation, among 9,300 junior and senior high school teachers, of a "testing instrument" listing 106 propositions to which the teacher was asked to express agreement or dissent. According to Dr. Hartmann, 3,700 usable replies were obtained.

[48]

The 106 questions were rated according to prevailing "liberal" or "conservative" views. In this summary 30 are listed, not to show the canvass was "loaded" but to indicate the "liberal" preference and the percentage of high school teachers who in 1936 were in accord with it. Replies are shown in italics:

Capitalism is immoral because it exploits the worker by failing to give him the full value of his productive labor. *Yes; 40%.*

The regular calling of conventions for the revision of State and national constitutions at 10-year intervals would eliminate some of the evils of social lag. *Yes; 68%.*

A policy of maximum international cooperation is morally superior to national isolation from world affairs. *Yes; 90%.*

The United States Supreme Court should be deprived of its power to declare acts of Congress unconstitutional. *Yes; 19%.*

Our national health would suffer if physicians were made civil servants like the public-school teachers and placed on the Government payroll. *No; 69%.*

Persons who wish to bring about a "New Social Order" make poorer teachers than those who adhere strictly to their own specialty. *No; 65%.*

Indoctrination by conservatives plays a smaller part in American schools today than radical propaganda. *No; 69%.*

A satisfying life for the masses of people can be secured without introducing important economic changes. *No; 75%.*

Most of the 10,000,000 or more unemployed will never again find steady work at good wages in a capitalist society. *Yes; 49%.*

Production for use and present-day capitalism are incompatible systems. *Yes; 53%.*

Cheaper electric light and power could be had if the industry were owned and operated by governmental units. *Yes; 75%.*

Transport service would deteriorate if all railroads were owned and managed by the Federal Government or one of its agencies. *No; 65%.*

We need a Government marketing corporation empowered to buy and process farm products and to sell them here and abroad. *Yes; 47%.*

The coal mines of the nation should be taken over by a public agency and run for the benefit of all the people. *Yes; 50%.*

All foreign trade should be a monopoly of the Federal Government. *Yes; 22%.*

No government has a right to experiment with different social policies. *No; 83%.*

The best way to secure decent homes for most of the people will be for the Government to build them for its citizens on a large scale basis. *Yes; 41%.*

All farm mortgages should be assumed by the Federal Treasury at an interest rate not in excess of 1 percent. *Yes; 28%.*

The practice of birth control should be discouraged. *No; 88%.*

Genuine individual liberty will flourish under socialism as it never did before. *Yes; 18%.*

For most people the opportunity to exercise beneficial personal initiative would be increased by life in a socialist state. *Yes; 21%.*

The formation of a comprehensive anticapitalist Farmer-Labor political party in the United States would contribute greatly to our social progress. *Yes; 42%.*

[49]

An improved American nation will result from step-by-step advances in the socialization of the means of production and distribution. *Yes; 74%.*

Capitalism can be abolished only through a violent seizure of power by anticapitalists. *No; 81%.*

If we put capable men into office, most of our social problems would be solved. *No; 21%.*

The best form of society is one in which an intelligent and forceful elite rules over the stabilized masses. *No; 64%.*

Although some persons take advantage of it for unworthy ends, at bottom our industry is organized on a fundamentally ethical basis . *No; 28%.*

It is as difficult for a man of property to support basic social change as for a camel to go through the eye of a needle. *Yes; 40%.*

The behavior of the capitalists is doing more to discredit and undermine capitalism than all of the activities of anticapitalistic groups. *Yes; 71%.*

Teachers should affiliate with some genuine labor organization of their own choosing. *Yes; 37%.*

Questionnaire to students*

A similar project is described by its director, Dr. Theodore Brameld, as

An educational exploration of the future of democracy for senior high schools and junior colleges.[1]

This particular "exploration of the future of democracy" questioned pupils of the Floodwood, Minn., high school under the auspices of the University of Minnesota. Like the previous example, it involved a series of propositions to be affirmed or denied. Returns were rated on the basis of the "liberal" answers.

Here are some of the propositions, with the "liberal" rating in italics:

There should be Government ownership and control of radio stations. (*Affirm*)

Liberal interpretation of the Constitution has permitted too great expansion of the powers of the Federal Government. (*Deny*)

If European countries want to establish left-wing governments after the war, we should support them. (*Affirm*)

A program to legalize and educate for birth control should be instituted in the nation. (*Affirm*)

The power of unions should be curtailed. (*Deny*)

America has never been interested in imperialistic gains. (*Deny*)

Should any plan of socialized medicine be established, the caliber and the ability of the medical profession would fall. (*Deny*)

Family life is in need of no change in its traditional form. (*Deny*)

What this country needs is more TVA's. (*Affirm*)

If the creed of the postwar world be the betterment of the common man, then it follows that public medicine should become a main part of that program. (*Affirm*)

---

* A third questionnaire, somewhat different, is presented without comment in the *Appendix*, pp. 163-4, where a 1956 Jugoslav questionnaire is also reviewed.
[1] Brameld: *Design for America*, 1945; title page.

[50]

If medical care is to be made available to all families at costs they can afford, these costs must be shared by all. (*Affirm*)

The Federal Government should finance Government projects for the advancement of the arts. (*Affirm*)

The Constitution needs some radical modifications. (*Affirm*)

There is need of a change in our constitutional pattern which would eliminate State boundaries and set up a system of representation based primarily on economic and geographical regions. (*Affirm*)

There is too much bureaucracy in Government already. (*Deny*)

Our economic base must be shifted from rugged individualism to economic planning. (*Affirm*)

The chain of middlemen that connects the producer with the consumer is unnecessary. (*Affirm*)

The more State authority and the less Federal authority, the better. (*Deny*)

Unless business makes a profit, the worker will be unemployed. (*Deny*)

Economic planning and control of production by Government could never eliminate depressions and unemployment. (*Deny*)

Without individual competition for profits, our economy would slow up and soften. (*Deny*)

Income taxes on the rich should be greatly increased. (*Affirm*)

Wealth should be much more equally distributed. (*Affirm*)

The Government should take over much larger areas of northern Minnesota iron mines now entirely in private hands. (*Affirm*)

The indoctrination is subtle. During the student year it is a detail of the work. It is an item to be done. No talk is raised; no sound is heard. Yet here, fitting significantly into the pattern of the whole, its warning rings out like a trumpet call.

Thus the very philosophy of the Republic is being undermined within our schools.

"I am more & more convinced that Man is a dangerous creature. & that power whether vested in many or a few is ever grasping &, like the grave cries give, give, The great fish Swallow up the Small, and he who is most strenuous for the Rights of the people, when vested with power, is as eager after the prerogatives of Government."
Abigail Adams, writing to her husband, the future President of the United States. 1776.

PART II   The Movement
TIDES   In America's Schools

14. THE SECOND "CALL"

To a large extent the second World War diverted educators from the program of social-reconstruction-through-the-schools. This was true even of the most outspoken advocates of the movement.

Then came a postwar statement of policy by the Progressive Education Association, issued under its new name, the American Education Fellowship. The statement was adopted at Chicago on November 29, 1947. It reviewed the movement of the thirties, cited its eclipse during the war period, and proceeded to issue a new "call" to the teachers of the Nation.[1]

The statement set forth a broad basis of agreement within which the larger group, not part of the militant leadership, could work. It provided a common ground for those who openly advocate socialism and others who either do not advocate socialism, or who do not want to so appear to their colleagues or the public.

The original *Call to the Teachers of the Nation,* while drafted and approved by a responsible committee of the Progressive Education Association, was never formally adopted—a fact which the Association's president, Dr. Willard W. Beatty, emphasized at the time.

The 1947 statement, however, was first adopted by the board of directors of the American Education Fellowship, then by the delegates at the Chicago convention, and subsequently was submitted to a vote of the AEF membership by ballot printed in the magazine *Progressive Education.* The statement was approved by a majority of the ballots returned.

Thus the postwar statement has an official status lacking in the earlier pronouncement. It also reflects a new strategy, one of euphemism, camouflage and ambiguous double-talk.[2]

---

[1] *Progressive Education,* November 1947; pp. 258-62 and 269, and February 1948; pp. 33, 40-1, 46 and 52.
[2] *Progressive Education,* January 1948; pp. 6-9 and 29. Archibald W. Anderson: REPORT ON THE NATIONAL CONFERENCE.

The policy committee, of which Dean Ernest O. Melby of the New York University school of education was chairman, designated one of the most radical leaders of the movement to prepare the draft. The man was Theodore Brameld.

Archibald W. Anderson, assistant professor of education at the University of Illinois, states that Brameld's draft was discussed at length by the AEF board, and by delegates at the Chicago meeting. The directors, Anderson says,

appointed a committee to attempt certain modifications which seemed desirable. It was this modified form which was finally presented to the conference as a whole.¹

The new strategic terminology

Comparison of the two drafts discloses how the more forthright Brameld proposals were modified:

Brameld draft: America is out of step with the world.

Final statement: Since the end of the war, America has shown a singular reluctance either to take cognizance of the democratic nature of these movements or to deal with the serious social problems which have called them forth.

Brameld draft: The two great constructive purposes which should now govern the AEF * * * are:

1. To channel the energies of education toward the reconstruction of the economic system—a system which should be geared with the increasing socializations and public controls now developing in England, Sweden, New Zealand, and other countries; a system in which national and international planning of production and distribution replaces the chaotic planlessness of traditional "free enterprise"; a system in which the interests, wants and needs of the consumer dominate those of the producer; a system in which natural resources such as coal and iron ore, are owned and controlled by the people; a system in which public corporations replace monopolistic enterprises and privately owned public utilities; a system in which Federal authority is synchronized with decentralized regional and community administrations; a system in which social security and a guaranteed annual wage sufficient to meet scientific standards of nourishment, shelter, clothing, health, recreation, and education are universalized; a system in which the majority of the people is the sovereign determinant of every basic economic policy.

Final statement: * * * two great constructive purposes have first claim for active support.

1. The reconstruction of the economic system in the direction of far greater justice and stability; a system to be secured by whatever democratic planning and social controls experience shows to be necessary; a system in which social security and a guaranteed annual wage sufficient to meet scientific standards of nourishment, shelter, clothing, health and recreation are universalized; a system in which the will of the majority with due regard for the interests of all the people is the sovereign determinant of every basic economic policy.

Brameld draft:

II. To channel the energies of education toward the establishment of genuine international authority in all crucial issues affecting peace and security; an order therefore in which all weapons of war (including atomic energy, first of all) and police forces are finally under that authority; an order in which international eco-

---
¹ *Ibid.,* p. 9.

[53]

nomic planning of trade, resources, labor distribution and standards is practiced parallel with the best standards of individual nations; an order in which all nationalities, races and religions receive equal rights in its democratic control; an order in which "world citizenship" thus assumes at least equal status with national citizenship.

Final statement:

2. The establishment of a genuine world order, an order in which national sovereignty is subordinate to world authority in all crucial interests affecting peace and security; an order therefore in which all weapons of war and police forces are finally under that authority; an order in which international economic coordination of trade, resources, labor and standards parallels the best practices of individual nations; an order geared with the increasing socializations and public controls now developing in England, Sweden, New Zealand and certain other countries; an order in which all nationals, races and religions receive equal rights; an order in which "world citizenship" thus assumes at least equal status with national citizenship.

That the economic system should be "geared with the increasing socializations and public controls now developing in" certain countries is stated in both drafts, simply under different headings. Note, too, that the Brameld draft, particularly Point I, is an explicit, detailed advocacy of teaching socialism. The revised statement is less clear.

Nonetheless, beneath its verbal outer garments the socialist slip is plainly seen.

The seven missing words

Both drafts deal with "classroom indoctrination":

Brameld original: In "taking sides" against the unworkable economic system and unworkable nationalism, and with a workable system and workable internationalism ✿ ✿ * The school should become a center of experimentation in attaining communities of uncoerced persuasion.

Final statement: In implementing the above outlook there should be no attempt to indoctrinate for any political party or for any given economic system. It is vital to maintain democratic, intelligent discussion and decision but also to make sure that the process will lead to conclusions. This can only be done by informed teachers who have convictions of their own—convictions which they do not foist upon their students but which at appropriate age levels they share with students. The task is to experiment with techniques of learning which look toward intelligent social consensus, not to superimpose prejudgments or dogmatic doctrines. Only thus can majority rule eventually become rule by an informed majority who understand what they want and how, democratically, to get what they want. The school should become a center of experimentation in attaining communities of uncoerced persuasion.

Both drafts contain this identical wording:

[The schools today] may study and endorse the United Nations, to be sure; and that is helpful. But they seldom face the contradiction between high-minded objectives for all nations and the still dominant power of sovereignty for each nation. Students are taught that internationalism is desirable; they are also taught that the United States is supreme in its own right. They are taught that all countries must cooperate; they are also taught that we should keep the secret of atomic energy. They are taught that we should support the efforts of common peoples in other parts of the world to rise in power; they are also taught to be uncritical of a foreign policy when it* serves to thwart those efforts.

---

* In the Brameld draft, *when it* read *which.*

[54]

At this point there had been seven additional words in the Brameld draft, to wit:

in countries like Greece, China and Spain.

That was 1947, when the "efforts of common peoples" in those three countries were following the communist line. The seven words were deleted in the final text.

The missing paragraph

Brameld's concluding paragraph read:

To prove that education is not a mere mirror of dominant ideologies, not a device for bolstering outmoded economic systems and diseased nationalisms, but rather that education is a penetrating critic, dynamic leader, and imaginative recreator which anticipates dangers before they crystallize into calamities, which helps simultaneously to reshape the culture of America and the world in accordance with the imperatives of our revolutionary age—this is the supreme obligation of the American Education Fellowship in our time. This is its new policy.

Here is the frank statement that the movement is to help "reshape the culture of America and the world."

The paragraph was not present in the final statement.

New goals and old

Among the specific tasks to which the AEF should devote itself is this:

5. There should be extensive educational practice in building detailed social designs which come to grips with problems arising in, for example, social planning. Intensive study is needed of experiments and institutions already under way such as the Tennessee Valley Authority, the postal system, the consumer cooperative movement, the social-security programs of America and Europe. Psychological problems such as motivations and incentives; political problems such as bureaucracy and reorganization of State and Federal Governments; social problems such as neighborhood life and the role of women; economic problems such as the place of private property in an evolving democracy,* problems of civil rights such as those raised by the President's Committee on Civil Rights—these are equally pressing.

The final draft stressed that

Vital education of the adult population at the "grass roots" should occupy a place of importance comparable to education of youth, and should include all the issues exemplified above.

Ideological confrères

Regardless of its double-talk, the AEF statement constitutes a new "call" to teacher activity, in and out of the classroom, in support of increasing controls and of the subordination of these United States to world government.

---

* In the Brameld original, the phrase *evolving democracy* read *increasingly socialized order.*

[55]

It urges the AEF to

push for recognition by the United Nations of the need to lift UNESCO above its present purely advisory status.

The statement continues:

Cooperation with the United States Office of Education is also important, looking toward crystallization of its own objectives and toward the provision of more authority to assist in improving the public schools. The National Education Association, American Federation of Teachers, Association for Childhood Education, and American Association for Adult Education should learn of the new AEF program, and should consider its reformulated ends and means just as they have done during the earlier period of AEF history.

The statement calls on the AEF to

support the democratic potentialities of the labor movement, the consumer cooperative movement, and quasi-political groups of sufficiently similar intent.

Brameld had said,

such as the Political Action Committee and Union for Democratic Action.

This phrase was not present in the final statement.*

The AEF statement urges that the editorial policy of *Progressive Education* be

explicitly geared to these purposes.

Meaning of the second "call"

The statement emphasizes that even the traditional objectives of the movement must be subordinated to the task of "world government." It concludes as follows:

In making these important recommendations, the AEF will continue to support the kind of experimentation for which it is most famous.* * *

In terms of organizational imperatives, however, such objectives are now subordinate, even while indispensable, to the larger, more audacious and magnetic objectives impelled by a world in crisis. Faced by the alternatives of economic chaos and atomic war, on the one hand, of world-wide plenty and enforceable international order, on the other hand, the AEF should become the clearest, most purposeful educational spokesman for the second of these alternatives. Thus, and only thus, can it become even more the great vanguard influence which it has been for nearly three decades— an influence which, as before, is certain to extend far beyond its own membership and even its own country.

Such is the official program of the movement—despite claims that it does not exist.

---

*Editor's Note: The Union for Democratic Action is discussed extensively by the House Committee to Investigate Un-American Activities. The Committee lists the affiliations of fifty leaders of the UDA with agencies and fronts of the Communist Party. *Report No. 2277, June 25, 1942.* SPECIAL REPORT ON SUBVERSIVE ACTIVITIES AIMED AT DESTROYING OUR REPRESENTATIVE FORM OF GOVERNMENT.

The PAC hardly requires comment.

"In cooperation with Jack London, Upton Sinclair, and a score of others prominent in the activities of the League for Industrial Democracy, I have preached the gospel of collectivism to the youth of America.

"Our watchword now, as thirty-five years ago, should be: 'Education for a new social order based on production for use, and not for profit.' "

> Leonard D. Abbott, an editor of *Current Literature* in 1905 and one of the nine persons who signed the original call for an Intercollegiate Socialist Society in that year. From *Thirty-five Years of Educational Pioneering*. League for Industrial Democracy. 1940. (*P.* 24)

PART II
TIDES

The Movement
In America's Schools

15. CONTINUITY OF THE MOVEMENT

The strategy of carefully phrased euphemism is well calculated to cloud the actual purposes of the movement. And the strategy is widespread. For example, the *Twenty-fifth Yearbook* of the American Association of School Administrators, NEA, asserts:

> The supreme problem of our society in our day, then, is the retention of the essence of our liberties—freedom of education, opportunity, choice of career, suffrage, speech, press, and assembly—while creating and establishing the controls of a democratic social order in which individual lives merge in a supreme entity of purpose and being that in itself is the ultimate goal. That means, inevitably, a vast stepping-up of the functions of government on all levels; it means a vastly increased emphasis in our schools upon education for civic and economic understanding and competence; it means a fundamental shift in emphasis throughout our whole educational program, from helping to educate the individual in his own right to become a valuable member of society to the preparation of the individual for the realization of his best self in the higher loyalty of serving the basic ideals and aims of our society.[1]

Dr. Counts and others had said all that twenty years ago—and they said it clearly, with no equivocation.

Denial . . . and reply

The basic doctrines are widely camouflaged and as vehemently denied. For example, when William H. Kilpatrick and other disciples of the movement are accused of radical views, a typical statement runs like this:

> It might be remembered, however, that these radical theories had been advanced in the thirties, when it was not uncommon for genuine liberals to espouse points of view which they no longer hold.[2]

---

[1] *Twenty-fifth Yearbook,* American Association of School Administrators, NEA. February 1947; pp. 43-44. Schools for a New World.
[2] Hulburd: *This Happened in Pasadena*, 1951; p. 53.

Yet the very year that statement was published, Kenneth D. Benne was urging a new "call" to the teachers of the Nation (April, 1951). And in his presidential address at the national conference of the American Education Fellowship, Benne said this new "call"

must have many elements in common with its forerunner of 1933.

He stated that

the way of thinking which the [original] *Call* represented was never absent after 1933 from the thinking and activities of organized progressive education.

He credited this "way of thinking" with influencing the National Education Association "to somewhat similar though more cautious conclusions."

Two short years previous to that statement, the same Kenneth D. Benne, professor of education at the University of Illinois, was interpreting the rôle of the public school educator in these words:

The central counsel of this number of *Progressive Education* to teachers and school administrators is that they come to see themselves as social engineers. ⁰ ⁰ ⁰ The must equip themselves as "change agents."[1]

Such clarity lends little dignity to dismissals of the "radical theories" of the movement's leaders in the 1930s as "points of view which they no longer hold."

The program consistently follows Dr. Counts' advice that teachers "deliberately reach for power"—all such bland disclaimers notwithstanding.

" * * and then to act concertedly."*

The collectivist view is stated by Dr. John L. Childs:

The fundamental interests of teachers as teachers are not restricted to the effort to get an adequate material and spiritual support for the public school. Teachers are also concerned with the effort to organize and maintain a society that can make a productive use of the human product of the schools. * * *

⁰ ⁰ ⁰ We must develop a more sensitive regard for the cultural aspects of human existence, and be prepared to support a vastly extended program of community services. This, in turn, means frank commitment to the "welfare state", and to the planned organization of the productive enterprises of our country. The real issue is no longer one of social and economic planning versus an individualistic system of *laissez-faire;* it is rather one of what forces are to do the planning, by what means are controls to be exercised, and for what purposes. * * *[1]

This statement alone refutes the claim that there is no movement among the teachers of our children—for the "reorganization of our economy".

American educators fall into three categories, says Childs: Those in the *first* category "fortunately are very few". They believe in the communist

[1] *Progressive Education,* May 1949; p. 201.
[1] *Progressive Education,* February 1950; p. 118.

solution. The *second* group, "numerically large", feels that the "resolution of social, economic and political problems" is not properly the responsibility of educators as educators, but believes educators are justified in employing pressure tactics to secure greater support for the schools.

The *third* group, says Childs, includes the progressive educators:

This third group * * * believes that in the long run both the material and the spiritual interests of public education depend upon the achievement of a reorganization of our economy. They therefore do not have faith in a policy that insists on teachers working separately as a mere educational pressure group * * * to develop * * * a more socialized economy. This group of educators also believes that there is an intimate connection between the domestic effort to achieve a more socialized economy and the world effort to develop a democratic system of collective security.[5]

Theodore Brameld calls this "Reconstructionism". He states:

The kind of education here being discussed encourages students, teachers, and all members of the community not merely to study knowledge and problems considered crucial to our period of culture, but to make up their minds about promising solutions, and then to act concertedly.[6]

Analysis thus discloses that the strategic terminology neither abandons the basic premises of the movement nor does it alter them.

It serves, on the contrary, to emphasize them.

---

[5] *Ibid.*, p. 120.
[6] Brameld: *Ends and Means in Education*, 1950; p. 86.

"I know not how it is, but mankind seems to have an aversion to the science of government. Is it because the subject is too dry? To me, no romance is more entertaining."
John Adams, writing to George Wythe, January 1776.

PART II
TIDES

The Movement
In America's Schools

16. THE STRATEGY OF "EDUCATING AWAY" THE REPUBLIC

The threat to our Bill of Rights is shown—with no possibility of successful refutation—in a series of articles by Dr. Norman Woelfel. This is his conclusion:

It may be necessary, paradoxically enough, for us to control our press as the Russian press is controlled and as the Nazi press was controlled. However, even if this were truly the only way out it is not "control" that we should fear, for we already have a very vicious type of control. We need only to look carefully at the objective in whose name control is exercised. Democratic objectives are open, intelligent, creative; they are pointed at the welfare of every individual and at the realization of a great common culture. Surely we could have nothing to fear from a press controlled to reflect, realize, and glorify such objectives.

The press, radio and cinema can no longer be left to the

owners and their hireling practitioners if we wish social salvation.[1]

The above was published in 1946. So the total control of press, radio and cinema is not some former aim, "no longer held." It is a present—and pressing—threat.

Changes in government structure proposed

Proposals are made to change the entire structure of our government. Such proposals have been put forward since the beginning of the movement, and they have been numerous. They embrace a total alteration of the successful philosophy and procedure of our Federal, three-branch system.

In 1932 the premise was laid down that

Democracy of course should not be identified with political forms and functions—

---

[1] *Progressive Education,* May 1946; p. 266 ff. COMMUNICATIONS. A series of articles by Dr. Woelfel in the October 1945, and the January, February and May 1946 issues.

with the federal constitution, the popular election of officials, or the practice of universal suffrage.[2]

By the end of the year this vague outline became more definite:

To accomplish these ends will necessitate fundamental modifications of our forms and processes of government, both national and local, in order to adapt them to contemporary needs.[3]

This was followed by the views of Dr. Rugg in 1933:

Must we not build systematically the attitude among the young people of the world that the trend toward representative democracy has produced nothing more than important *experiments* in government?

An "attitude" must be "systematically built" that

every form of government on earth today must be regarded frankly as an experiment, tentative, and to be changed as new social and economic conditions develop.[4]

One year passed, and the premise took a further development:

[Teachers] should proceed to a consideration of the changes in its [the Constitution's] provisions which the rise of industrial civilization is making desirable or necessary. And in doing all this, they should endeavor to carry their pupils with them.[5]

If I am not mistaken, the American Constitution provides for orderly change—but it does not provide for change deliberately indoctrinated by organized minority groups, professional or otherwise.

The same year, 1934, Stuart Chase declared that an abundance economy requires

the scrapping of outworn political boundaries and of constitutional checks and balances where the issues involved are technical.[6]

Three years went by, and in 1937 the *First Yearbook* of the John Dewey Society published the questionnaires to teachers and students previously cited. Here were proposals that regular ten-year conventions be held for revision of State and Federal constitutions; that the power of the Supreme Court to declare as unconstitutional acts of the Congress or of the President, be removed; and the flat suggestion of

a change in our constitutional pattern which would eliminate State boundaries and set up a system of representation based primarily on economic and geographic regions.[7]

[2] Counts: *Dare the School Build a New Social Order?*, 1932; p. 40.
[3] *Progressive Education*, October 1932; pp. 410-3.
[4] Rugg: *The Great Technology*, 1933; p. 270.
[5] *The Social Frontier*, October 1934; p. 9.
[6] *NEA Journal*, May 1934, p. 147. *Who's Who in America*, Vol. 27, 1952-3, lists Stuart Chase as affiliated with Unesco in 1949. He was for some years treasurer of the League for Industrial Democracy.
[7] *First Yearbook*, John Dewey Society, 1937; p. 174 ff. THE TEACHER AND SOCIETY.

Advocates of this movement, ever quick to hurl the "Fascist!" epithet at critics, are here advancing a proposal that has striking similarity to the Fascist corporate state!

Another proposal is that the Supreme Court have a "substantial miority" lay membership, and that Henry Wallace be one of the "minority" Justices.[8]

This steady development of the original premise is posed against the claim that "no such plan exists", that "charges" are "general and not specific".

Preparation for a world collectivist state

The encouragement of a flippant, casual attitude toward our Government yields ominous byproducts. One is the calm acceptance of big government; another is an ever lessening appreciation of the fundamental principles of the Republic.

For example, "fear of a centralized governmental administration and control" is dismissed as a "bogeyman"—not because a trend in that direction does not exist but because the trend is deemed inevitable, even desirable. Arnold E. Joyal, professor of educational administration at the University of Maryland, argues that there is nothing to fear in this "inevitable trend" if people only

realize that the federal government is as much our government as is the state, or the city, or the school district. It is *our* creature. It is capable of functioning only with *our* sanction.[9]

Nothing is said of the historic impossibility of controlling a centralized government; there is no hint that government, to be successfully controlled and watched, must be "kept near home".

On the contrary, those to whom we entrust our children's schooling are teaching theories which, if not squelched, will bring an end to all idea of local self-government, and of our American governmental form.

In 1943, Dr. William H. Kilpatrick denounced

the threefold governmental arrangement of the President, Senate and House,

claiming it was

a misconceived system

because it

embodies inherent conflict where there should be inherent cooperation.[10]

A system of self-government by which millions of people achieved the greatest individual freedom in the history of the world, is "misconceived"!

---

[8] *The Social Frontier*, April 1937; pp. 197-8. TELEGRAM TO PRESIDENT ROOSEVELT from the directors of *The Social Frontier* and the Fellows of the John Dewey Society.
[9] *Frontiers of Democracy*, February 15, 1941; pp. 142-6.
[10] *Frontiers of Democracy*, March 15, 1943; pp. 164-5.

A "new" theory charges that system with conflict between its parts—because there has been balance among those parts!

And in 1949 comes attack upon the very essence of personal liberty upon which the Republic stands. Kenneth D. Benne provides an illustration. Teachers and school administrators, he says, are "change agents", "social engineers". To what end?

> The engineering of change must be anti-individualistic, yet provide for the establishment of appropriate areas of privacy and for the development of persons as creative units of influence in our society.

The concept of man's natural rights is "unscientific". Accordingly,

> That a wise social policy will establish areas of privacy for persons and voluntary associations within the society is undoubtedly true. In such areas private judgment may rule. But the determination of the proper boundaries of these areas must, in an interdependent society, be based on a collective judgment.[11]

Thus is prepared a creeping acceptance of the "trend" toward a collectivist state. By constantly indoctrinating people along such lines, the Republic can be "educated away", for the philosophy at its base will be gone. It then is but a step to the world superstate.

That this is no mere opinion of mine, that this is no phantasy divorced from world events, will be seen from documentation which ensues.*

It will be seen as a terrible, actual reality. It has been taught with ever increasing tempo throughout the schools of the Nation. Yet I believe the thing can be stopped, for I am convinced that the great majority of our fathers, mothers, teachers *and students* can and will organize to stop it —once they see what it is.

It would be my suggestion that this be done at community level—where schools can be citizen-controlled, and watched.

---

* The concept that "a wise social policy will establish" the "areas" of a man's privacy is a concept which acknowledges the supremacy of The State—as it was before the historic American Revolution set men free. It certainly is a concept which Americans in every walk of life should actively challenge when a Prime Minister of France—writing for UNESCO in 1955—flatly asserts that

"* * * a collectivist economy * * * is able * * * to exercise control over incomes dependent on personal position and market conditions, leaving individuals only such sums as are considered necessary in order to encourage them to work and to use their initiative and organizing ability." (*Cf.* p. 14)

[11] *Progressive Education,* May 1949; pp. 206-7.

"To us our venerable progenitors bequeathed the dearbought inheritance of liberty, to our care and protection they consigned it, and the most sacred obligations are upon us to transmit the glorious purchase, unfettered by power, unclogged with shackles, to our innocent and beloved offspring."
From the Preamble to the *Suffolk Resolves*. Massachusetts, September 1774.

PART II
TIDES

The Movement
In America's Schools

17. THE TEACHING OF WORLD COLLECTIVISM

America's teachers are to be the handmaidens of a welfare state in their own Country and of a global WPA to embrace the world—with themselves and other citizens picking up the check.

Global income tax proposed

Notwithstanding denials and smear, the global WPA has already been proposed. Methods have been put forth to finance it. One method is outlined by Dr. Lewis Mumford, who for some years was on the Committee on Teacher Education of the American Council on Education. Addressing a Conference on World Order in Rochester, N. Y., November 13, 1951, Mumford proposed

a World Equalization Tax upon nations, graded to accord with their wealth and productivity. * * * This would permit the creation of a World Equalization Fund, operated under the United Nations, to provide grants-in-aid for health, education, social services, technical assistance and even outright gifts of food when temporary conditions, such as exist now in India and Israel, demand it.

This should be a "universal policy", said Mumford. It

would be hard [for other nations] to resist, all the more because we ourselves, as the wealthiest nation in the world, would by the very principles we uphold, have to pay the largest tax and receive the smallest amount of tangible benefits.

Now, just how America can be the "wealthiest" nation in the world, when America is in debt to the most astronomical figure in all history, never has been made clear to me.

Nevertheless, that is what these people assert—and they are teaching it in our schools.

The proposal means a world collectivist state, America-financed.

[64]

Global textbook supervision

The philosophy which advocates changing the basic structure of the Republic is a philosophy which leads logically to a collectivist organization of the world. This will now be further seen.

Isaac Leon Kandel, of Teachers College, Columbia University, states:

> Nations that become members of UNESCO accordingly assume an obligation to revise textbooks used in their schools. * * *

> For the present there is no provision for the scrutiny of textbooks in the UNESCO Constitution on the assumption that they are matters within the domestic jurisdiction of the member nations in which the Organization is prohibited from intervening. Under these conditions, each member nation, if it is to carry out the obligations of its membership, has a duty to see to it that nothing in its curriculum, courses of study, and textbooks, is contrary to UNESCO's aims. * * *

> * * * unilateral efforts to revise the materials of instruction are futile. The poison of aggressive nationalism injected into children's minds is as dangerous for world stability as the manufacture of armaments. In one, as in the other, supervision of some kind by an international agency is urgent.[1]

"Conditioning" by Unesco and the U.S. Department of State

Here is an internationalism far deeper than generally suspected. And a glimpse of what that internationalism means is shown with disconcerting frankness in the *Report* of President Truman's Commission on Higher Education:

> The role which education will play officially must be conditioned essentially by policies established by the State Department in this country, and by ministries of foreign affairs in other countries. Higher education must play a very important part in carrying out in this country the program developed by the UNESCO and in influencing that program by studies and reports bearing upon international relations.* * * The United States Office of Education must be prepared to work effectively with the State Department and with UNESCO. *who wants to censor our textbooks*

This is placed before the strict judgment of the reader. As previously noted, in 1947 the policy statement of the American Education Fellowship disclosed a major addition to the traditional program of the movement, namely,

> the establishment of a genuine world order, an order in which national sovereignty is subordinated to world authority in all crucial interests affecting peace and security * * *[3]

Theodore Brameld, in his *Ends and Means in Education,* particularly welcomed the idea of supergovernment:

> * * * The world of the future should be a world which the common man rules not merely in theory, but in fact. It should be a world in which the technological potentialities already clearly discernible are released for the creation of health, abundance,

---

[1] *NEA Journal,* April 1946; p. 175.
[2] *Report* of the President's Commission on Higher Education, 1947. Vol. III; p. 48. ORGANIZING HIGHER EDUCATION.
[3] *Progressive Education,* February 1948; p. 41.

[65]

security for the great masses of every color, every creed, every nationality. It should be a world in which national sovereignty is utterly subordinated to international authority ° ° ° (*Pp. 15 and 17*)

There would be no question as to the power of this authority:

The majority machinery of the United Nations, UNESCO, or any similar organizations created in behalf of world order should be so greatly strengthened that no member country, including the Soviet Union and its satellites, can conceivably refuse to abide by its own power-backed decisions. (*P. 117*)

These proposals—coming from their several directions—become ominous when read in conjunction with the Unesco publications *Towards World Understanding.*°

And this is what your children are being taught—in our own tax-paid schools.

° *Publisher's Note:* When his documentation was presented to the House of Representatives, Mr. Shafer at this point cited the Unesco program and documented its parallel with that of the rest of the movement. These remarks are omitted as the Unesco publications are the subject of Part III of this work—THE FLOOD.

"The people of the United States.—May they ever remember that to preserve their liberties, they must do their own voting and their own fighting."
William Henry Harrison, shortly before his election as the ninth President of the United States.
A Condensed Memoir of the Public Services of William Henry Harrison. 1840.

PART II   The Movement
TIDES   In America's Schools

18. THE RISE OF AMERICAN OPPOSITION

The record clearly documents the movement in America's schools, and confirms that its basic views are progressively being enlarged.

Responsible investigation is a right and a duty. It is the way of progress, of self-improvement. It is our personal safeguard against all that is harmful or subversive.

Leadership

In 1949 the superintendent of public instruction of the State of Michigan, Dr. Lee Thurston, created a commission on educational policies for this very purpose. The Commission included educators and representatives of the public. It undertook to appraise public criticism of the schools, to encourage legitimate discussion, and to establish mutual understanding between school leaders and the public whom they serve.

In a communication to the school administrators of the State in 1951, the Commission said:

In our American way, the supreme judge of the merits of the public school is the people. In the last analysis they pronounce the verdict.

I cannot commend too strongly such undertakings, or the spirit reflected in the statement.

Whence this leadership?

Inasmuch as there is a movement to make the schools of America into agencies of "social change", into promoters of socialism, collectivism and/or the welfare state, people have every right to inform themselves of the fact, to discuss the movement, to oppose it, to brand it as subversive, and then to see that educational authorities and members of the teaching profession are held strictly to account for their part in it.

[67]

To deny this is to deny citizens the right to "pronounce the verdict" upon their own schools. To hold that a man or woman lacks the right to thoroughly investigate this movement, on the grounds (as has been said) that he or she does not possess the "educational competence", is to state that neither possesses the competence of citizenship. It is to state that neither has the judgment to determine what he desires his society, his schools, or even his own son or daughter, to be.

I can think of no premise more outrageous.

The very fact that this is a minority movement, some of whose advocates already have abandoned its views, brands it for what it is. A procedure hardly can be dignified as *education* when it involves the promotion of social theories which are shortly discarded as false. Otherwise, schools become mere mirrors of prevailing social fads—and our sons and daughters the intellectual victims of those fads.

Friends within the profession

I would like to emphasize one fact which, by the very nature of this documentation, has yet to receive recognition—the fact that the movement has, and from the very outset has had, vigorous opponents within the teaching profession. Let me cite one or two, beginning way back years ago when few discerned the import of a program then in its early making.

Immediately following Dr. Counts' address at the 1932 Baltimore convention of the Progressive Education Association, a Short Hills, N. J., teacher, Ellen Windom Warren Geer, raised these questions:

⁂ Shall we indoctrinate [young Americans] with social theories which seem sound to us today, but which, by the time our children are able to accomplish anything for their furtherance, may be hopelessly outdated, and the adherence to which will have incapacitated them for open-minded recognition of that fact? Or is there a higher courage in remaining faithful to the hitherto untried experiment of developing a courageous openmindedness in the belief that so equipped, the new generation may be able, after they leave us, to cope with a changing civilization, only dimly foreseen by us, with far more wisdom than we can hope to attain ourselves? What course is truly "progressive"?[1]

No effective rebuttal has been forthcoming in twenty years.

The distinguished historian, James Truslow Adams, said of the *Call to the Teachers of the Nation:*

I do not see that the teachers of America have any right to set up as a "powerful organization", free from all influence outside—except for being guaranteed tenure and adequate compensation by the economic order which otherwise they are free to flout—to say precisely what the future society must be and to train the youth of the nation to believe solely in the teachers' Utopia.

My experience with the graduates of the public schools is that they have never been taught to use their minds or to learn the use of intellectual tools. It seems to me that there is a task calling for all the abilities of such teachers as we yet have, rather

---

[1] *Progressive Education,* April 1932; pp. 265 ff.

Q

than shattering this world to bits to mold it nearer to the Teachers' Union' desire—even if the Union could agree on a desire.[2]

John L. Tildsley, associate superintendent of New York City schools, saw what this movement would lead to back in 1938. He wrote:

Does Mr. Counts really believe that when he has won over the teachers to his revolutionary program, the parents, most of whom are opposed to the program, will continue to support the teachers who (against the wishes of the parents) are making converts of their children for an industrial system that never has been operated successfully anywhere?

Dr. Tildsley offered this counsel:

The supreme need of America today is neither an immediate democratic collectivist society nor more complete academic freedom. * * * It is the creation of a highly intelligent, social minded, self-disciplined, efficient body of citizens and a supply of thoroughly trained, courageous, strong-willed, potential leaders and administrators. * * *

His warning came too soon for general acceptance, and he seemed to sense it. Nevertheless, he deplored the Frontier Thinkers'*

seeming complete indifference to the steady deterioration in an ever accelerated degree in the quality of public elementary and secondary education in this country. * * *

Tildsley questioned indignantly whether a person holding the views now documented "has a moral right to enroll himself as a teacher of children or as a teacher of teachers-of-children." He charged that the leaders of the movement

lose sight of the child as the center of the educative process and are not concerned with his growth, save in one direction, namely, his growth into an accelerator of a democratic collectivist social order. They view the child as collectivist-Futter to be utilized without regard to the effect on him of the collectivist-society-making process.[3]

Was the outlook of such teachers, in regard to the public, unobserved? Certainly not unanimously, even then. Ralph W. Robey, assistant professor of banking at Columbia University, was explicit:

A lot of educators in this country look upon their profession as a closed guild. They feel that no one but a professional educator has any right even to make a suggestion as to what our schools are teaching. It is time they got that idea out of their heads.[4]

Gradually, a realization of the seriousness of the school situation started moves for its correction.

Penetrating criticism of AEF policy was presented by two directors of that organization in 1948. Lester B. Ball, an AEF vice-president and superintendent of schools at Highland Park, and Harold G. Shane, vice-president

---

* Frontier Thinkers was the name assumed by supporters of, and contributors to, The Social Frontier.

[2] Progressive Education, October 1933; pp. 310-14.
[3] The Social Frontier, July 1938; pp. 319-22.
[4] Directly quoted by Benjamin Fine in The New York Times, February 22, 1941; pp. 1, 6.

[69]

and board member of the AEF and superintendent of schools at Winnetka, Ill., wrote:

❋ ❋ ❋ It appears from study that a particular doctrine or body of dogma has been established, which presumably is to be accepted for implementation by members of the Association. It does not seem that this acceptance of a "line" or "position" is compatible with the progressive tradition.

In the policy ❋ ❋ ❋ sharp criticism is directed at the present American economic organization, without any comparable attempt to analyze the strengths of the system. Nowhere in the document is a scholarly effort made to evaluate the strengths of a capitalistic organization, or to point to ways in which it might be improved. Instead, emphasis is placed by implication upon the strengths of a more socialized economy, which presumably has no weaknesses worthy of mention. ❋ ❋ ❋

The two Illinois superintendents observed (perhaps with Britain's example in mind) that progressive educators

must avoid being duped by those who would use the liberal movement in American education for ends other than the orderly advancement and achievement of the ideals of free peoples.[5]

At a Barnard College forum, New York City, in February 1952, Francis M. Crowley, Dean of the Fordham University College of Education, flatly declared:

The progressive social philosophy of education generates confusion and fosters disintegration. The school should not be used as an instrument to agitate for the overthrow of existing society.

Finally, Willard B. Spalding, Dean of the College of Education at the University of Illinois, refuses to attribute mounting opposition to "self-seeking groups and individuals". He refuses to accept the assertion that opponents are "kept alive by subversive right-wing groups in order that they might strengthen their own treasuries or have some theme which they could use in their literature."

On the contrary, Dr. Spalding believes that whereas progressive education originally was concerned with "the development of the science of education", it has "somehow got off the track." He believes that dogma has been substituted for scientific inquiry, and states that he "is proud to be one of many" who left the Progressive Education Association and the American Education Fellowship because of this substitution.

Referring to the increasing condemnations of "progressive education", Dr. Spalding frankly concludes:

Why do they persist and why are they so widespread? I submit that perhaps the major reason for this is the abandonment by the progressive education movement of its early search for a science of education. ❋ ❋ ❋

Some of us feel that the progressive education movement has been captured by a group who are more concerned with changing society than with improving the quality of instruction in the classrooms of America. I think that change in the direction of the movement, because of this change in leadership, has been unfortunate for America as a whole.

---

[5] *Progressive Education*, April 1948; pp. 110-1.

In the long run, we can only eliminate [the criticisms of our educational system]
* * * by eliminating the conditions which cause them."

A job for each community

I believe the elimination of the program documented herein is a joint concern, a joint enterprise, of ministers of the Gospel, of educators, of public school officials, and of sovereign citizens and their own locally-created organizations.

I do not look to repressive legislation. Nor do I look to indiscriminate denunciation, to witch-hunting, or to high-voltage name-calling, to accomplish the result.

Rather, I believe that the key to the elimination of these conditions lies primarily in their exposure to public knowledge; in fearless discussion of the movement which has created the conditions; and in dynamic public cooperation between every interested and concerned citizen in America.

Many educators—very likely the overwhelming majority—will come out against this movement the instant they are assured they do not stand alone. After all, isn't that characteristic of most of us?

Then—may I make a suggestion? Form a compact group in your own community; get folks to study—seriously—this and other documentations; then form a clear campaign of action within that community. Study the school laws, the election laws—and give yourselves a specific time to make your local schools American. Generously so, yes—but American, to the core.

Our young citizens must, and they can, again have the clear opportunity to base their lives upon the *principles* of true education. As one man has said:

"Let's give them a foundation of something from which they can start to work. * * *

"I've been a teacher for seventeen years and I get awfully sick and tired of having students come up to me without any foundations at all.'"

Then, as your program succeeds, join with other communities to make the program statewide. A nationwide program can follow.

I believe this activity should be inaugurated in every community in the Land. I believe it should be pursued dynamically, and without delay.*

---

* Suggestions for locally-organized committees are to be found in the Appendix, pages 172-3.
ᵇ *Progressive Education,* November 1951; pp. 42-50.
ᵀ Ralph W. Robey, assistant professor of banking at Columbia University. Quoted by Benjamin Fine in *The New York Times* of February 22, 1941. (*Pp. 1* and 6)

"* * * A teacher works in a sensitive area in a schoolroom. There he shapes the attitude of young minds towards the society in which they live. In this, the state has a vital concern. It must preserve the integrity of the schools. That the school authorities have the right and the duty to screen the officials, teachers, and employees as to their fitness to maintain the integrity of the schools as a part of ordered society, cannot be doubted. One's associates, past and present, as well as one's conduct, may properly be considered in determining fitness and loyalty. From time immemorial, one's reputation has been determined in part by the company he keeps. In the employment of officials and teachers of the school system, the state may very properly inquire into the company they keep, and we know of no rule, constitutional or otherwise, that prevents the state, when determining the fitness and loyalty of such persons, from considering the organizations and persons with whom they associate."

Adler et al. v. Board of Education of the City of New York. 342 U.S. 493. Mr. Justice Minton, Opinion of the Court. March 3, 1952.

PART III
THE FLOOD   Introduction

19. THE STRATEGY IN OPERATION

The scope of this movement is being steadily broadened, even while its tenets are denied by those who should know better—if, indeed, they do not.

Its ideology is found not only in schools and colleges but at our great military institute, West Point itself. There, future officers study such texts as this:

Nationalization of the production of certain raw materials can be used to conserve supplies or to build up domestic production. The movement of capital can be controlled so as to channel it into the production of desired materials. The performance of Soviet Russia testifies as to the public effectiveness of such measures when used to improve the state's raw materials position.

Considered alone, this is socialist-communist doctrine. Considered in connection with the movement documented, it appears as a logical detail of that movement's plan.

The quotation is taken from page 43 of Raw Materials in War and Peace, a volume published in 1947 by the United States Military Academy, Department of Social Sciences.

The volume is a product of that very "area of study" which the progressive educators selected in 1934 for their classroom strategy and plans— the "area" of social sciences.

Furthermore, the volume is

used as a textbook * * * throughout the administrative agencies of the Government.[1]

---

[1] Hearings No. 38, House Subcommittee on Mines and Mining, February 1948; p. 224. STRATEGIC AND CRITICAL MATERIALS AND METALS.

[72]

The University of California

How does the strategy work in practice? Let us examine an actual case.

In stating that teachers should "deliberately reach for power and then make the most of their conquest", the movement employs every means at its disposal to have its partisans gain academic control of schools. It is their contention that a segment of the faculty could, and should, tell the Regents of a university what to do.

This is no fancy. It happens.

Take the controversy at the University of California. Contrary to widespread publicity, the issue was not over a loyalty oath; it was over wording. That simple matter obliged the Board of Regents, and committees of the Faculty and Academic Senate, to prolong discussion for more than nineteen months.

The entire procedure exemplified the tactics and strategy of a minority group which adamantly followed the progressive education line.

Regent John Francis Neylan stated the matter clearly:

It was perfectly obvious to him that a small cohesive group had started the agitation and it spread from them to a minority in the [Academic] Senate.[2]

The faculty oath—already nine years in successful operation—was to be reworded. The dispute centered around the new word-form. The Committee of the Academic Senate—with full powers—agreed on the new wording. The agreement was made with the Regents of the University, *i.e.*, with their principals and employers, the people of the State of California. The date was September 30, 1949.

That agreement was broken on November 7, and the procedure was not unique:

[The action of the Academic Senate is] clearly a repudiation of the exact agreement which was arrived at on September 30 * * *

PROFESSOR HILDEBRAND: It was partly the fact that it was 7 o'clock and dinner time and some [300] of the members of the Senate had left.

REGENT NEYLAN: We have been advised that was the exact fact, and also advised that there was wide-spread feeling that this had been adopted more or less as a matter of sharp parliamentary procedure. Nevertheless, it stands as the act of the Senate. Apparently on November 7 the Senate again repudiated its committee. Previously on June 24 it was repudiated. Again the Senate repudiated the acts of its representatives.[1]

This tactic is employed in all parliamentary bodies where a minority is determined to rule. The minority simply sits out a meeting until few are left, and then it goes to work. The tactic will be instantly recognized by

---

[2] Transcript of *Excerpts of Minutes*, Regents' Meeting, September 30, 1949; pp. 2-3.
[1] Transcript of *Excerpts of Minutes*, Joint Meeting of the Regents' Committee, the Faculty Committee and the Committee of the Academic Senate. January 4, 1950; pp. 2-3. (Before recess)

many members of parent-teachers associations, and there is a simple way to stop it. The way is this: You move that the meeting be adjourned until *x* hour or date.

If your motion is adopted, nothing can happen until such time.

Here, then, a militant minority not only challenged a policy that had been in effect nine years, one which had been adopted by other colleges of repute, but it dishonored the acts of its own representatives, and by methods at least suspect.

One exchange illustrates the attitude of those who so quickly cry "academic freedom" in relation to their own "inherent rights":

REGENT NEYLAN: The situation is this. * * * For nine years we have never heard any opposition, and now to tell the public that this faculty, which has been conscious of this policy for nine years, now refuses to agree with it—

Here the speaker was interrupted by a member of the committee representing the Academic Senate:

PROFESSOR DAVISSON: Why do you have to tell the public? * * * [4]

A dramatized account would end at this point. But there was instant rejoinder:

Regent Neylan replied: This situation is dedicated to truth, and on this policy the statements made to the public will be truthful and complete.

Judge Neylan was yet to learn that a compact minority can beat others to a deadline. A slanted story "leaked" to the press; the Regents were vilified throughout the State and even beyond; and then the pressure was directly applied.

Who—and what—was behind this?

Letters were received by the president of the University from members of the faculty at Berkeley and at Los Angeles. These letters, all practically identical, intimated that one consequence of dismissal of the few professors who refused to sign the newly-worded oath would be that

The American Association of University Professors would hold an investigation and the University might eventually be included in its list of "censured administrations."[5]

A little research establishes the identity of this AAUP.

The American Association of University Professors was founded in 1915 by Professor John Dewey of Columbia University, father of the progressive education movement. Its claimed membership at the University of California was only 295—yet this tiny minority might place a great university on its list of "censured administrations".

Further, this American Association of University Professors "investigates" academic situations; it relates those situations to its version of

---

[4] *Ibid.*, p. 6. (Following recess)
[5] Transcript of *Excerpts of the Regents' Executive Session*, February 24, 1950; p. 1.

academic freedom and tenure; and—through its national Council—it acts.

What is its position regarding communists on a teaching staff?

* * * [Regent Neylan] felt that the policy of the AAUP was the issue that the Board was facing, and which it had been facing right along. In this connection, he read a resolution which had been adopted by the Mills College* Chapter of the Association prescribing, in the name of academic freedom, non-discrimination against Communists for the mere fact that they are Communists, and proposing, also in the name of academic freedom, that members of the Association be represented on the governing boards of universities.[6]

The internationalists sent George Catlett Marshall to China to propose the same sort of thing to Chiang Kai-shek. (Chiang was not to rid his régime of communists; he was to form a coalition cabinet and take them in.)

Why, particularly, did such vast publicity attend the controversy at the University of California? Why was this publicity slanted, as clearly it was? The reason is:

This was the first distinguished faculty in the country to repudiate the policy of the American Association of University Professors, which opposed the exclusion of Communists [from the faculty].[7]

The Regents of the University had dared defy the program of a militant teaching minority, organized for just such ultimate purpose.

Who were the spokesmen of this minority?

There were several, of whom two in particular seem worthy of mention. One is Monroe Emanuel Deutsch of the American Association for the United Nations, and member of the AAUP. Deutsch is no "irresponsible member". He is vice-president and provost emeritus of the University.† On August 22, 1950, Deutsch circulated a pamphlet in which he said:

The reputation of the University will drop to an all time low. There will be the customary investigation by the American Association of University Professors, followed by a devastating and well-publicized report. The University of California will be black-listed and all good men will be warned to avoid it. * * * The same dry rot that has virtually destroyed the University of Texas, following a similar episode, will set in in California.

Is this, or is this not, a threat?

The second individual worthy of mention is Professor Ernst Hartwig Kantorowicz. Born in Posen, Poland, he arrived in the United States in 1940 and was given sanctuary at Berkeley. His contribution to the controversy at his host University was a pamphlet in which he refers to the

* A women's college near Oakland, Cal.

† *Who's Who in America*, Vol. 27, 1952-3. The volume also lists Deutsch as San Francisco area chairman of the Commission to Study the Organization of Peace, a project of the Carnegie Endowment. Dr. Frank P. Graham held the comparable position in North Carolina. Dr. James T. Shotwell headed this Commission.

[6] Transcript of *Excerpts of Minutes,* Regents' Meeting, June 23, 1950; p. 4.
[7] *Ibid.*

"vested rights of a professor which cannot easily be attacked or ignored without assailing, at the same time, certain fundamental rights of society. This", says Professor Kantorowicz,

was true in Imperial Germany; it is also true in this country, and the Regents of the University of California will have to learn a lesson, whether they like it or not. (P. 33)

Here there is no question at all. Threat it is.

A responsible spokesman of the Academic Senate of a great university threatens, in the specific name of the American Association of University Professors, literally to force the Regents into a course of action demanded by the militant members of that Association. A professor, graciously received, joins in the attack upon his hosts. The Regents, in full session, are faced with an ultimatum that, if they do not submit to a given course, the university will be professionally ostracized.

Kantorowicz, a member of the American Historical Association, was received at the Institute of Advanced Studies shortly following his attack. He quickly went to Princeton. His pamphlet, even more quickly, disappeared from circulation.

The entire procedure substantiates the documentation presented by Congressman Shafer, and the deductions made therefrom.

Here is the strategy of the movement in operation.

The activity of the American Association of University Professors is no new thing. As long ago as 1933 this Association came in conflict with the governors of Rollins College, Winter Park, Fla.

Rollins presented its case in the college *Bulletin,* stating:

"The following study will demonstrate" that the report of the *AAUP Bulletin* of November 1933 "convicts both the minor committee which investigated the College and drafted the report and the major committee which approved it, of attempted coercion, if not inviting in a form their own bribery, of misrepresentation, if not defamation of character, of bias and prejudice if not malice, and of the suppression of evidence."

The *Rollins College Bulletin* ended its summary of that case as follows:

"We do have an earnest wish to demonstrate that the Association [the AAUP], through its official control, has usurped powers not granted [at that time] by its charter; has pursued recklessly lines of procedure coercive in character rather than persuasive; has ridden ruthlessly over established college government; has not been guided by rules of procedure known to itself or others; has extended license to irresponsible Committees and thereby encouraged false, unjustifiable and uncontrollable methods of procedure and has deprived itself of control against malicious prejudices, false rules of evidence and publications designed narrowly to escape libel."

This description of the American Association of University Professors was published in 1933.

The parallel between the case of Rollins College—twenty years past—and that of the University of California, may be studied from the source of the quotations: *Rollins College Bulletin,* Vol. XXIX. December 1933, No. 11.

"So long as doubts such as these were wildish pebbles in the petulant waves that gnaw ceaselessly at any foundation, perhaps only because it is a foundation, no great damage was done. But when they began to be massed as a creed, then they became sharp cutting tools, wickedly set in the jaws of the flood. That was the work of a disaffected intellectual cult, mysteriously rising in the academic world; and from that same source came the violent winds of Marxian propaganda that raised the waves higher and made them angry."

Garet Garrett: *The People's Pottage.* 1953. (*Pp. 5-6*)

PART III
THE FLOOD

The International
Movement

20. THE THIRD "CALL"

The first *Call to the Teachers of the Nation,* in 1933, and the second "call"—that of the American Education Fellowship—in 1947, have their clear present parallel.

There has been issued a much broader "call". No longer confined to the schools of America, this "call" is designed to cover the world.

For years the groundwork was laid—in libraries, schools, textbooks, and among a minority of the teaching profession in these United States. Upon this groundwork is now being erected a mammoth structure, one whose design may well have been planned from the first. Out of this structure is to come not only a global indoctrination of pupils, of students, of adults and of the teaching profession, but it is to house an organization which will enforce that indoctrination upon each.

The plan is a matter of record.

Even so the plan will be denied. Weasel words will attempt to cloud its meaning. Against these disclaimers is posed demonstrable fact.

In 1947, not only did advocates of this movement add world government to their official goals, there is in actual operating existence an organization which is sponsoring groups to give it form and substance.

Furthermore, some of these groups were already operating when the American Education Fellowship published its official policy in 1947—high-placed denials to the contrary notwithstanding.

[77]

Two questions

Again there is a plan. This plan is not local; it is not confined to nations within themselves. It is not confined to the schools of America. It is international. It embraces the entire human race.

And the authority which is intended to emerge from this plan is no mere commissariat of education at Washington, D.C. The authority is to be worldwide.

In the process of its creation two facts emerge, crystal clear. They are these:

Americans are to accept and pay the commissars; even while

Americans are to be molded into "citizens of the world"—by the infinity of the commissars' global will.

These statements will be documented.

The documentation is precise, and consists of a series of small volumes published by the United Nations Educational, Scientific and Cultural Organization. By 1952 the number totalled eight.

They raise two personal issues. These are:

Will you permit the UN to do such things to your child?

Will you permit the UN to do such things to you?

"* * * one can truly understand UNESCO only if one views it in its historical context [and] viewed in this way it reveals itself as one more step in our halting, painful, but I think very real progress toward a genuine world government."

Milton Eisenhower, addressing the closing session of the first day's conference on UNESCO at Wichita, Kans., December 12, 1947. *The Kansas Story on Unesco.* Dept. of State Publication 3378. Int'l. Org'n. and Conference Series IV, United Nations Educational, Scientific & Cultural Org'n. 7. March, 1949. *(P. 23)*

PART III
THE FLOOD

The International
Movement

21. SOME SUGGESTIONS ON TEACHING ABOUT THE UNITED NATIONS AND ITS SPECIALIZED AGENCIES

Towards World Understanding. Vol. I. Unesco. Paris. 1948.

The Unesco series projects the movement into the field of international politics and of power.

Volume I presents the conclusions of a number of seminars, each sponsored by Unesco, specialized agency of the UN. The first seminar was held in the pleasant English countryside in 1948.

Its report introduces a plan.

A program is outlined to implement that plan.

This program is to be introduced in the schools of UN's member states. One may favor it; one may be opposed. In either event, all of us should know what the program is, and what it means—to ourselves, to our children and to our homes.

The program has "two main approaches":

1) The development in pupils of an attitude of mind favourable to international understanding, which will make them * * * ready to accept the obligations which an interdependent world imposes.

2) The dissemination of information * * * presented so as to stress the interdependence of the modern world, the development of international co-operation and the need for a world community * * *

The text is addressed to the teaching profession, and it reads:

One of the chief aims of education today should be to prepare boys and girls to take an active part in the creation of a world society based on peace and security and a fuller life for every human being.

As the Introduction states "the general objective is clear"— it is the great contemporary effort * * * to move towards a world society.

Nothing could be more explicit.

[79]

The "great contemporary effort"

How is this to be done? The Unesco seminar states:

One of the chief aims of education everywhere is to develop those qualities of citizenship which provide the foundation upon which international government must be based if it is to succeed.

Again, how? Teachers should

try to develop in the pupils a sense of association—of belonging to the United Nations and of pioneering in the development of a world community.

Thus does query at once arise: How does a "world society", a "world community", or a "foundation upon which international government must be based if it is to succeed", keep faith with what advocates of the UN Charter said in 1945? Was not every implication of "international government" categorically denied?

Certainly such classroom instruction is no "open covenant, openly arrived at", as Woodrow Wilson once proposed to the ribboned diplomats at Versailles. And two questions must be asked:

Are we witnessing something new, which stems logically from a limited, first intent?

Or have supporters of the UN been deliberately deceived throughout the years?

Debate on the UN Charter by the Senate of the United States evoked from proponents no such goal as "international government". It was by others that the charge was hurled. And this charge was vehemently denied, equally by Senators and by advocates of the Charter who had been so closely allied to the new internationalist order since the year 1933. The denial was accepted by millions who hoped that here might be an organization to bring some peace and goodwill among men. This denial was unanimous, and largely sincere.

That was in the year 1945.

What happened? Within thirty-six months a specialized agency of the UN was quietly confounding its warmest advocates. It was planning to indoctrinate every young person in America, through American schools, in the "foundation upon which international government must be based if it is to succeed".

Program for parents

The statement appears on the very first page following the Introduction of the Unesco publication. Of course, it should reflect the burden of what is to follow. That it does is quickly confirmed. Nor does its confirmation lack an element of surprise.

The surprise is found in a phrase heretofore unknown—a phrase of but three short words:

United Nations system.

It is the word *system* that intrigues. What is its meaning? And what does it imply?

The meaning is implicit throughout all eight volumes here reviewed. And the parallel of that *system* to the program of the progressive educators in the United States differs little save in the detailed magnitude of its scope.

How completely the "United Nations system" interlocks with the objective of bringing children to "a sense * * * of pioneering in the development of a world community" emerges with great clarity as the text unfolds. And, as children are oriented to the program, the idea that parents might expect some say in the matter is not neglected.

This is to be taken care of by orienting the parents themselves.

That means they are going to orient you.

Program for the children

Techniques are to vary at different age levels, and there are several methods of approach. One is that schoolchildren be taught examples of "international cooperation" which may be likened to the works of the UN.

As one example, the seminar cites the Universal Postal Union and there is apparent at once a wide discrepancy between indoctrination and fact.

You be the judge of this statement:

The Universal Postal Union came into being on July 1, 1875. Its purpose was to improve worldwide mail service, and by voluntary agreement to establish equitable rates and rules. The purpose was achieved. It then was maintained with outstanding success. No one ever heard of the UPU. It worked.

But in 1947 the UPU revised its organization to permit operation as a "specialized agency" of the United Nations. On the seventy-third anniversary of its successful being, this affiliation became complete. The date was July 1, 1948.

The UPU was immediately listed as the largest of UN's agencies, though it operates on a tiny budget—perhaps the smallest of all. In 1952 the figure was $342,900 for the year. Its permanent staff numbers seventeen.[1]

Presented as an example of "international cooperation" which may be likened to the works of the UN, the UPU antedates such affiliation by exactly seventy-three years.

To teach children otherwise seems not unlike saying to them that the decades of successful operation of the Bell Telephone System is an example of government ownership at its best.

As I say, you be the judge.

---

[1] UN Press Release *UPU/5 SA/67*, February 9, 1950; and *SA/127*, May 8, 1952.

Let us examine another approach: What constitutional ideology, if any, does the text reveal? It says:

In many countries a comparison can be made between the written constitution of the nation and the Charter of the United Nations. * * * The idealism of youth should be appealed to * * * [and] The social studies (geography, history, civics, etc.) provide particularly good opportunities for courses of this kind.

This allusion to constitutions immediately calls to mind three major "comparisons". These are:

Britain, which has no written constitution; the Soviet Union, which has had six; the Swiss Confederation, whose constitution is modelled after our own.

No mention is made of the Constitution of these United States—although it is the oldest written constitution in the world. In fact, the Document is unmentioned in the entire series under review. Such modest place as it may have in teaching the United Nations *system* is "a comparison between the written constitution of the nation and the Charter of the United Nations."

It is subordinate.

Thus is illustrated a technique which becomes more and more apparent as the Unesco publications are reviewed. And one is faced with a mounting question, which is this:

Are America's young citizens to be molded into some predetermined pattern—or are they to develop as individuals, schooled in basic truth?

A Model Plan

Plans are outlined for the training of new teachers and for the retraining of those presently in the profession. The Unesco seminar discusses this under the heading

Education for a World Society: The Education and Training of Teachers.

According to the plan, the teacher is to be selected and trained, and for a particular job. He is to express an ideology, and only one. The report states:

Unesco is working to assist countries to examine their own text-books and teaching materials with a view to improving them as aids to international understanding. A Model Plan for the Analysis of Textbooks* has been drafted. After it has been checked by experts in different countries, Unesco will suggest to its Member States that they review their own text-books in the light of the recommendations. The importance of including information, where appropriate, on the United Nations and its Specialized Agencies is stressed.

Isaac Leon Kandel had already written, in the *NEA Journal* of April, 1946:

Nations that become members of UNESCO accordingly assume an obligation to review textbooks used in their schools.

---

* This Model Plan is outlined in *A Handbook for the Improvement of Textbooks and Teaching Materials as Aids to International Understanding.* Unesco. Paris, 1949; pp. 69-90.

This "obligation" exists even though

For the present there is no provision for the scrutiny of textbooks in the UNESCO Constitution on the assumption that they are matters within the domestic jurisdiction of the member nations in which the Organization is prohibited from intervening.[2]

Notwithstanding the "assumption" which "for the present" governs the measure of a nation's jurisdiction, here is a Model Plan. It provides that governments review textbooks.

This means what? It means socialized education. How else can a "Member State" review textbooks "in the light of the recommendations"?

Moreover, this means censorship and propaganda on a global scale. Back in 1922 the International Federation of League of Nations Societies called their own project *Propaganda Through the Schools*.[3] The Unesco project is precisely that—without the frankness in the title.

The global mechanism, preconceived

As recently as 1935 the Institute of Intellectual Cooperation, a creation of the League of Nations, presented to various nations an agreement on the teaching of history. But what happened in 1935? "The United States considered it impossible to sign because of the fact that in that country public education was not under control of the Federal Government." In 1933 and again in 1936 Conventions received our Government's blessing, "but because nearly all educational matters are left to the various States, [the American Government] was unwilling to enter into any agreement which it might not be able to execute." Switzerland gave a similar reply, for similar reasons.[4]

Then a new kind of internationalism was made the vogue. Within twenty years our citizenry is faced with the proposal that "experts" issue "directives" to America's schools. Who are the proposed "experts"?

The answer is implicit in the caption which follows in the Unesco publication:

The Importance of Directives from Educational Authorities.

And who are to be the "educational authorities"? The reply is found in the 1947 *Report* of the President's Commission on Higher Education:

The role which education will play officially must be conditioned essentially by policies established by the State Department * * * and by ministries of foreign affairs in other countries * * * in carrying out * * * the program developed by UNESCO * * *[5]

Thus less than two decades of the new internationalism has produced a philosophy of collectivism from which, calmly announced, comes the

---

[2] *Cf.* page 65.
[3] *Handbook;* p. 27. (*Supra*)
[4] *Handbook;* pp. 19-20, 108 and 117. (*Supra*)   [5] *Cf.* page 65.

"rôle which education will play".

That rôle is set forth by the words of mandate, *must* and *will*.

Here is the mechanism, preconceived.

History is to be rewritten

Nor is the program a dream in embryo. The Eleventh International Conference on Public Education, held at Geneva, Switzerland, the end of June 1948, based its discussions upon the initial draft.

Convened by Unesco and the International Bureau of Education, the Conference considered these propositions:

That one of the chief aims of education today should be the preparation of children and adolescents to participate consciously and actively in the building up of a world society ° ° ° [and]

That this preparation should include ° ° ° the formation and the development of psychological attitudes favourable to the construction, maintenance and advancement of a united world ° ° °

Following its discussion, the Conference submitted

to the Ministries of Education of the various countries the following recommendations:

1. That all teaching should help to develop a consciousness and understanding of international solidarity;

2. That life in all educational institutions should be so organized as to ° ° ° interest young people in the problems of the world of tomorrow;

3. That a sense of duty towards the world community be developed ° ° °;

° ° °

6. That as this instruction is new and complex ° ° ° teachers ° ° ° should be specially trained to carry it out both by direct and indirect teaching as an integral part of all education;

° ° °

10. That textbooks of different countries be re-examined as often as possible, with a view to eliminating the passages that would be likely to lead to misunderstanding among nations, and to incorporating materials that would lead to fuller appreciation of world co-operation;

° ° °

So education is being recast in a rôle strikingly similar to that played by court historians in bygone days. No longer are men and women to be reared, capable of taking advantage of the lessons of history. History itself is to be rewritten. This is to be done by new court historians, but on the model of the past.

The purpose is determined by those who engage the court historians.

The spectre over the schools

At this point in reading the Unesco publication one is conscious of the feeling that a type of being is extant upon this planet, anonymous and unknown, yet wise beyond our ken; infinite in his expert knowledge—yet finite in his hand upon our children's fate.

This feeling is not unmixed with a presentiment that the chronicle of human existence is to be re-done—expurgated here, embellished there—by sages anonymous, themselves available only to Unesco and to the international *élite*.

When young people become mothers and fathers of a succeeding generation, they are to docilely mimic that which the present omniscients have decided they may learn—and nothing more.

All other material will have been eliminated by the experts.

Then—if the movement is not stopped—

The role which education will play officially must be conditioned essentially by policies established by the State Department * * * ministries of foreign affairs in other countries * * * [and] UNESCO.⁶

Another aspect of this future is no less clear:

For the present there is no provision for the scrutiny of textbooks in the UNESCO Constitution on the assumption that they are matters within the domestic jurisdiction of the member nations * * *⁷

Global authority is not provided—for the present.

This parallels the thinking of Theodore Brameld when he urged the AEF to

push for recognition by the United Nations of the need to lift UNESCO above its present purely advisory status.⁸

In his *Ends and Means in Education* Brameld further stated:

The majority machinery of the United Nations, UNESCO, or any similar organizations created on behalf of world order should be so greatly strengthened that no member country * * * can conceivably refuse to abide by its own power-backed decisions.⁹

And there it is—the global mechanism, preconceived.

The American teacher becomes a cog of the collectivist machine. The citizen becomes a robot in a Plato's Republic.

That is the spectre over America's schools.

The spectre can be denied, and it will be denied. The spectre can be "explained".

But it can not be explained away.

It is there.

Compared to the program, the textbook purges of Adolf Hitler dimly echo—like the tinkle of a forgotten toy long since broken by some child at play.

---

⁶ *Cf.* page 65.
⁷ Isaac Leon Kandel, in the *NEA Journal*, April 1946. *Cf.* page 65.
⁸ *Cf.* page 56.   ⁹ *Cf.* page 66.

"Now I am under the necessity of telling you that our right to self-government and the very integrity of the Republic is threatened as never before in its history by the so-called International 'Bill of Rights Program' of the United Nations."
    Hon. Frank E. Holman, past president of the American Bar Association, in an address at Los Angeles, Cal., May 26, 1952.

PART III   The International
THE FLOOD   Movement

22. THE EDUCATION AND TRAINING OF TEACHERS

Towards World Understanding. Vol. II. Unesco. Paris. 1949.

The second Unesco volume is entitled *The Education and Training of Teachers.* Three seminars discussed the subject, again in the English countryside. Karl W. Bigelow, professor of education at Teachers College, Columbia University, was director.*

Unesco arranged these meetings; Unesco suggested the topics; Unesco published the report. Of the thirteen lectures given during the sessions, four concerned Unesco and its work. The Director-General of Unesco and the Assistant Director-General of Unesco gave two of these lectures when the seminar began.

Nevertheless, Unesco registers disavowal that the views expressed are its official own.

Willard W. Beatty, president of the Progressive Education Association, made a similar careful disclaimer when the original *Call to the Teachers of the Nation* appeared in 1933.[1]

Unesco's earlier distinction

Already the sponsor of these seminars enjoyed a certain distinction, once removed. This had been achieved by Britain's Julian Huxley when he landed in the United States for one of his lecture tours. As his ship docked in New York, Huxley was interviewed by the press. During the course of that interview he said:

I hope Japan will not back down and that you will be at war with her next week.

---

* *Who's Who in America,* Vol. 27, 1952-3, lists Professor Bigelow as a member of, or consultant to, the General Education Board (social studies); American Association of University Professors; Progressive Education Association; American Council on Education; N.E.A.; and Unesco. As of November 1951 he was also on the U.S. National Commission for Unesco, together with, among others, Willard Givens and Pasadena's ousted superintendent, Willard Goslin.

[1] *Cf.* page 20.

Huxley's hope was expressed on December 5, 1941. Two days later, at Pearl Harbor, his hope was fulfilled.

Just over five years later Huxley was Director-General of Unesco, specialized agency of the UN. He was a member of the Colonial Bureau of the British Fabian Society.

All textbooks to be revised

The seminars' views in this second volume reveal further parallels to the program of the progressive educators in the United States.

There is reference to "the old untrustworthy examination system", and to the "great need to depart from the logical, systematic theory of the past". No hesitancy in departing from logic and system is observable to a reader of the Unesco publication.

With solicitous regard for the relationship between child and teacher, the latter is to be humanized. The *lacunae* left by the regrettable inadequacy of teachers in general and of American teachers in particular are to be filled.

And the few who are so solicitous for the many suggest reference material for the humanization. Eight of the volumes listed bear the imprint of the American Council on Education. This is the organization whose former committeeman, Dr. Lewis Mumford, urged the "universal policy" and global income tax in 1951.[2] It was the American Council on Education which "at the request of the United States National Commission for Unesco has published a summary and evaluation of work on textbook improvement" in America.[3]

The interests of the American Council on Education are further suggested by an

extensive survey * * * undertaken * * * with funds granted by the National Conference of Christians and Jews. This study involved the analysis of 267 elementary and secondary school textbooks * * * as well as a number of introductory college texts, and children's books * * * to discover how national textbooks dealt with cultural groups and intergroup relations in the United States.[4]

Another project deals with the "treatment of the Soviet Union in United States school textbooks" and here "The material selected for examination comprised 117 widely used social science textbooks."[5] Still another project is an "over-all study of the work done in the United States in the field of textbook revision".[6]

---

[2] *Cf.* page 64.
[3] *A Handbook for the Improvement of Textbooks and Teaching Materials as Aids to International Understanding.* Unesco. Paris, 1949; p. 43.
[4] *Ibid.*, p. 52. (Published as *Intergroup Relations in Teaching Materials.* American Council on Education. 1949.)
[5] *Ibid.*, p. 52. (Described briefly in *Public Opinion Quarterly.* Winter, 1947-8; pp. 567-71.)
[6] *Ibid.*, pp. 52-3. (Published as *Textbook Improvement and International Understanding: I.* James Quillen. American Council on Education. 1948.)

A further activity

involved the examination and evaluation of material on the Far East appearing in 180 widely used United States elementary and secondary textbooks.[7]

The evaluation was prepared in collaboration with the Institute of Pacific Relations.

Is this acceptable reference material for the teachers of your children?

Removal of a stereotype

The seminar discovers that

It is not clear why men and women become teachers.

It reports that

Teaching, like any other occupation, brings with it certain frustrations.

One of these "frustrations" springs from the teacher being "psychologically isolated" from the rest of the community. The seminar says so. It says the teacher "is isolated because the community isolates him". Therefore, he "must live within the teacher stereotype".

The seminar is moved to suggest steps to deal with the matter. Global educators will remove the stereotype. This, according to the world psychiatrists, is "one of the major tasks in social education".

Perhaps other seminars will suggest removal of further "frustrated stereotypes", now "isolated" as bankers, baseball players, housewives and social workers. But, the internationalist? Not so. He, assuredly, can be no stereotype. He is to be neither frustrated nor eliminated.

On the contrary, millions more of him are to be produced.

When regimentation is benign

The seminar observes that in many countries teachers are still under supervision which is "excessive, arbitrary, and autocratic". Therefore

What we must establish is a situation in which teachers feel free to experiment, to share in policy making, and to contribute to a co-operative effort.

While teachers' unions are not openly advocated (as elsewhere they are), abundantly clear is a pattern—which "we" must establish—wherein workers help run the factory, the second baseman helps to pitch, the watchman at the bank helps advise on loans, and the conductor confers with the orchestra in timing his downbeat.

The seminarists make it clear that there is to be a tremendous pool of experimentees.

The goal is "world understanding". These two words, or similes thereof, occur so frequently as to become not only a major *motif* but the dominant

---

[7] *Ibid.*, p. 51. (Published as *Treatment of Asia in American Textbooks*. American Council on Education and the American Council, Institute of Pacific Relations. 1946.)

[88]

theme. The verbal counterpoint offered is not convincing, for this is what it says:

> What happened in the totalitarian countries was that training replaced education.

And Volume II is entitled *The Education and Training of Teachers!*

The conclusion is a natural one: Collectivism is benign—when applied on a global scale.

As *The Social Frontier* has said:

> It all depends on who does the regimenting and the purpose the process is intended to serve.`

The teachers' "special responsibility"

The seminar speaks of nationalism. Again there is reference, and again the reference will enjoy no unanimous approval from parents of small fry now attending America's schools.

The reference is Bertrand Russell. This British authority was once appointed to the faculty of New York University. The appointment was withdrawn following legal action on the part of a Brooklyn mother and housewife, who charged:

> That the said Bertrand Russell * * * is a person who, for many years heretofore, had advocated and still advocates sex relationships among students attending Colleges and schools; and has advocated and still advocates that such sex relationships should be encouraged among students of schools and colleges, and that such sex relationships, without the formality of marriage, would be of benefit, intellectually and morally, to the said students * * *

> [That these activities] are repugnant to the accepted standards of good conduct, and constitute a danger and a menace to the health, morals and welfare of the students * * * "

> [That Bertrand Russell] was tried and convicted in March 1918 for a malicious libel on the American Troops while they were in England as the overseas expeditionary forces of the United States. He was sentenced to prison in England for this offense against the United States to serve a term of six months in prison.¹⁰

In rendering decision, the Court (Mr. Justice McGeehan) stated that Russell's appointment was "an insult to the people of the city [and] * * * in effect establishing a chair of indecency * * *."¹¹

Here is a man to whom the Unesco seminar refers as author of source material for the instruction of American teachers. In the reference cited by the seminar, Russell deplores that history is taught in such manner as to "serve to keep alive a bigoted nationalism".

` *Cf.* page 23.

" *In the Matter of Jean Kay* vs. *The Board of Higher Education of the City of New York.* Petition of Jean Kay. New York Supreme Court. March 18, 1940. (Pars. 11 and 17)

¹⁰ *Ibid., Papers on Appeal.* Affidavit in Support of Motion. Folio 132.

¹¹ New York Supreme Court, *173 Misc. 943.*

Observe, too, the semantic procedure, for it has been effective. The word *nationalism* is given a modifying adjective. Are nationalism and bigotry complementary? By no means. Add the adjective *bigoted,* and the meaning is not nationalism but chauvinism. And nationalism and chauvinism are not synonymous at all. Yet that is what the inserted adjective conveys.

No one seems to have thought of a term to express "bigoted internationalism".

The program requires a "better teaching of the social studies". The reason is expressed by the seminar itself:

In social studies courses, special emphasis is placed on the purpose and functioning of the UN and its agencies.

Therefore, say the seminarists,

* * * teachers of these subjects have a special responsibility.

The three Rs

The responsibility is to be discharged in a most objective and most truthful way—a claim which I think you will find open to question.

There is no suggestion, in the proposed classroom studies of the UN and its specialized agencies, of, say, UN's conduct of America's tragic crusade on the Korean peninsula, or of its 1947 "partition" of Arab lands to make way for other people whose ancestors never lived in the Near East at any time in history.

Such items are not found in "accepted" textbooks, written, recommended or revised.

How about the three Rs? The seminar states:

Therefore, we regard it as a matter of first importance for social and international living that educators should be more concerned with the child, and the healthy development of his body and mind, than with the content of the various subjects which go to make a school curriculum.

When your son or daughter goes to school, you are not to examine a curriculum; you are to examine educators. They, soon enough, will have been properly trained. From them your child will absorb "international understanding" and "world-mindedness"—albeit *in corpore sano.*

You must not be too concerned with "the content of the various subjects" offered by the school. The seminar says:

Because of failure to adopt a wise approach to child growth and development, the primary school still tends to function as if it were an institution for the abolition of illiteracy * * *

Yet parents are becoming alarmed that progressive education does not abolish illiteracy but creates it. Employers are increasingly shocked at the results of two decades of "education" under the progressive experiment. Many a graduate is not receiving what otherwise his schooling would justify —even in terms of the internationalist dollar of fractional worth. (The statement may be confirmed merely by mentioning the point to a few employers.)

"Democracy" in school administration

But experiment there is, and experiment there shall be. This will include:

Substantial reduction in the number of subjects in the curriculum. * * *

Increased opportunity for students to evaluate and criticize all aspects of the work, including the efficiency of tutors. * * *

In general, a tendency to abandon rule from above in favour of democratic co-operation between staff and students. * * *

The faculties are to judge the Regents; the students are to judge the faculties. Who is to judge the students is yet to come.

There is to be a

Greatly increased use of camps for both educational and social purposes.

As John Maynard Keynes, British apostle of deficit finance, once remarked, "This is a great [financial] gain."* In education, the gain is "social". The individual disappears.

The kind of institution recommended by the Group is one in which * * * all members, students and staff alike, take part without artificial distinctions or discrimination.

An M.D., a Ph.D., an LL.D. becomes an "artificial distinction"; professors must not unduly stress their degrees, for that implies "discrimination". All of which is called "democracy" by some; by others it is recognized as Marxist technique.

An article in the May 1937 *Communist* illustrates this. Its author, Richard Frank, first refers to the "broad legislative program for federal aid to education" then being launched by the American Federation of Teachers. Then he shows how "democracy" should work:

* * * a fundamental demand of any popular movement around the schools should be democratic administration of the school system by elected representatives of the parents, teachers and students. * * * The inclusion of students on school boards* * * is of the utmost importance. * * * it will give the students * * * a thorough training in democratic procedure. It will give them practical democratic experience. (*Pp. 442-3*)

Both Marx and Lenin referred to "democracy" as the necessary stage through which you passed on the road to the communist state.

More Marxist parallel

Students with the necessary educational and personal qualifications should be admitted, irrespective of sex, colour, class, or creed, and should if necessary be supported by government grants.

This reference is identical with a part of the manifesto of the First Communist International in 1864.

The "government grants" are assumed as a matter of course.

---

* Keynes was addressing the House of Lords on the British plan for "the future economic government of the world." Snow: *Government by Treason;* p. 25. (THE LONG HOUSE, INC.)

What is meant is that you will continue to pay.

The report is concerned lest the student not get "a realization of what is meant by good citizenship." A laudable goal—but it seems dimly possible that what constitutes "good citizenship" will be determined, not by citizens acting wisely or not, but—by the political authority which grants the funds.

It will determine the definition, on the citizens' behalf.*

Courses in history, geography and economics

can help to throw light on such matters as standards of living, economic rivalries, living space, labour problems, minority questions and large-scale economic planning, none of which are matters of purely national concern.

This view is expressed, and sometimes by nearly identical language, in almost every major project set before the UN, its subsidiaries and its operational affiliates.

The viewpoint parallels that of the Marxist International.

The Total State

The global concept of education and The State is expressed as

° ° ° the economic valuation which governments place on education ° ° °

Here is the tradition of centuries—The State (here called "governments"). The founders of the American Republic once broke that tradition. The Constitution of 1789 not only broke the tradition, it created one which was the exact opposite. Education was freed *from* the state. And thenceforth American education depended, and entirely depended, upon the value placed upon it by the citizen himself, each within his community.

There was a corollary, too, now seldom remarked: Classes—as permanent classes—began gradually to disappear. "Three generations from shirtsleeves to shirtsleeves" became an American axiom. A "classless society" actually was developing. With each citizen educated to take his chances on profit and loss, there could remain no permanent class. "Class" disappeared in exact relation to one's ability to achieve the "class" to which he aspired —or to maintain his position, once achieved.

The process is being reversed.

Take the seminar's program for what it calls "underprivileged children". What is to be done with them? They are to be taught by teachers drawn from "underprivileged groups". Such teachers have a "special sympathy for the children of such groups."

This is the class concept of the collectivists in operation.

The seminar strongly urges increased salaries and pensions for teachers. Certainly few people will object to this. (The average salary for teachers in

---

° "It is hardly lack of due process for the Government to regulate that which it subsidizes".

Wickard, Secretary of Agriculture, et al. v. *Filburn.* 317 U.S. 111.
Mr. Justice Jackson, Opinion of the Court. November 9, 1942; p. 131.

[92]

1961 was $5,389.*) But what does the proposal mean? Does it mean more internationalist dollars? Or does it mean a higher real wage—which is something quite different. How can this latter be brought about? By teachers—and other citizens—helping to make the dollar sound once again. And the only way to make the dollar sound is to stop global crusades. It can only be made sound by ending policies which require that paper currency be printed, and that bank-credit money be created, as the fictitious way of "paying" for them. Stop the crusades, and the dollar will depreciate no more.

No other "remedy" touches the cause. The road of a spurious internationalism is the road of inflation, bankruptcy and the Total Collectivist State. Indeed, some assert precisely that to be the plan.

The Marxist sees this, and sees it clearly. He is working tooth and nail to continue it. The internationalist approves identical means: the fatal debt and spending of his global crusades—even as he decries the ends.

President Truman's seizure of the steel mills in April 1952 was a clear case in point.

The owner—whether director or holder of one share—found himself being deprived of his rights because of internationalism—war. He, and his property, were taken over by Executive Order 10340, April 8, 1952.

The worker—whether foreman, puddler or roustabout—found his rights threatened, because of internationalism—war. Even as he demands more internationalist dollars he is surrendering to The State the power to fix his wages, the power to determine the conditions of his employ, and the ultimate power to determine when and where he shall work. He, and his labor, are being taken over—the warning being Executive Order 10340.

This is exactly what will happen to every teacher in America—if and when he lets himself be organized for the global plan. He, too, will face a future Executive Order 10340. Under the "progressive" program, that Order will be made to stick.†

And there is but the single cause. That cause is internationalism—war.

This is the final tragedy of "one world", now being taught in the Nation's schools.

Such discussion is not present in the Unesco seminar report.

---

* The figure is from the National Education Association.

† The collectivist doctrine has distinct implications in "federal aid to education". Its advocates deny that federal control would ensue. Do they not believe that government *should* control the use of its citizens' tax-paid funds?

And where does the "government" get its funds if not from the very same taxpayers who—it is claimed—cannot raise them locally?

Nor is the claim that *federal* funds are needed to build 600,000 classrooms in the coming decade equated with our State and local governments' average construction of better than 68,000 new classrooms a year. Indeed, the latter have met a rise in primary and secondary school enrollment of 20% by increasing available classrooms 30%.

Educational ration-cards, in book form

The third seminar relates that, in training teachers,

A general programme of instruction should be provided, * * * and taught by staff members who are enthusiastic believers in the need for better international understanding.

No one quarrels with the need. The question is:

Does the United Nations and/or Unesco reveal principles which, according to its own symposium, justify acceptance of the "general programme of instruction" foreseen?

Is the answer so unanimous that we should all graciously accede to the program described?

The UN and its specialized agencies are to be dramatized by at least two publications. One is a simple textbook for students; the other is a detailed handbook for instructors.

* * * Unesco is urged to forward copies of such publications to every teacher-training institution in its Member States, and, in addition, to maintain a permanent mailing list to which future material may be sent as it becomes available.

This will give the global teacher "a new social outlook" and make him a "citizen of the world". The material, at the same time, will

help practising teachers * * * make themselves better citizens of the world.

The Marxist International publishes an identical goal.

This process would be "seriously jeopardized", says the seminar, by

The feelings of frustration and sometimes of fear which teachers who find it professionally unwise to express certain political or religious views may experience.

Whether, under the global régime, a teacher or anyone else might feel it "professionally unwise" to view affairs in a manner other than in the Unesco, or internationalist, manner, is not made clear*—until you study elsewhere the provisions of the Genocide Convention and the Universal Declaration of Human Rights.

It is clearly intended, however, that the new generation of Unesco-Americans shall avoid

An attitude of intellectual jingoism and a conviction of the superiority of their own culture * * *

As recently as 1946 even the most ardent internationalist disclaimed all idea of "world government". It was an ectoplastic nebulum, a spectre of "The Enemy". It was, in other words, a bogey. This bogey was conjured up by "Isolationists"—meaning the advocates of political Neutrality. Yet

---

* It will be clear enough to many citizens of Indiana. Frank Hamilton, of Indianapolis, received a fellowship to study in England. When he returned, he stated publicly that Britain's socialism wasn't working so well. The U.S. Office of Education promptly sent him a letter of chastisement. Resentment was immediate and widespread, so the officious Washington bureaucracy formally apologized—doubtless determining to tread more warily for a while.

Unesco seminars are discussing, and Unesco is publishing, methods of indoctrinating young people with

"those qualities of citizenship which provide the foundation upon which international government must be based if it is to succeed". [The seminar has taken this quotation directly from Vol. I, p. 6.]

So, the seminar immediately resumes,

When pupils reach the adolescent stage and are able to grasp clearly the ideas and concepts involved in the work of the United Nations, more direct methods can naturally be used.

This indoctrination—first indirect, then direct—of children and adults repeats, chapter and verse, the program of the Progressive Education Association, the American Education Fellowship and other advocates of the collectivist movement in the schools.

Well, we've been taken in. Many a man is revising views which he held for years—and one respects a man who is big enough to change his mind. More than a few Senators openly regret their eager acceptance of the Yalta, Tehran and Potsdam agreements, the Italian "peace" treaty, and other tragic bits of paper of which internationalism was the cause. Even the UN Charter is losing its hypnotic hold. As Senator Pat McCarran of Nevada stated seven years after his affirmative vote:

When it is stated that the Senate will never vote for a bad treaty, I will confess that I voted for what I now consider a bad treaty, that I will regret all the days of my life, and that was when I voted for the United Nations.[12]

And, while global educators write the History of Mankind*—under Unesco supervision—even they may encounter difficulty in purging this grim fact from our "poor or out-of-date textbooks".

However, these celestial minds—in earthly beings—are thorough if nothing else. Carefully selected are their textbooks; carefully selected are their teachers; and carefully selected are the references which they provide. Not incorrectly, they observe that

inaccurate or incomplete bibliographies could seriously retard the training of teachers and could have an adverse effect on international understanding.

How accurate and complete are their own bibliographies will become clear in the section to follow. For the fact emerges that the celestial minds will permit to appear only those documents which have the imprimatur of themselves.

Such references are to be our educational ration-cards, in book form.

---

* This project is being financed by grants-in-aid from Unesco. Julian Sorell Huxley, Director-General of Unesco during 1947-8 and member of the Fabian Society, Colonial Bureau, was named in 1950 as one of an international commission to oversee the work. The six volumes may run to 3,000,000 words. Huxley's associates on the $600,000 project include Ralph E. Turner, of Yale; A. L. Kroeber, formerly of the University of California; and Bertrand Russell.

[12] Senate Committee on the Judiciary, *Hearings on S. Joint Res. 130.* Official transcript, original; p. 232. May 22, 1952.

"* * * We are dealing with a slippery collection of escapists who get most of their ideas from the National Education Association * * * aided by several of the rich foundations in the nation * * *

"[UNESCO] is an international organization that should be forced to keep its nose out of American school business * * * The National Education Association also ought to stick to its knitting and quit trying to remake America in the image of the United Nations."

Fulton Lewis, Jr., in his syndicated column. September 19, 1952.

PART III   The International
THE FLOOD   Movement

23. A SELECTED BIBLIOGRAPHY

Towards World Understanding. Vol. III. Unesco. Paris. 1950.

The third volume is *A Selected Bibliography.*

It was published by Unesco. The references are "selected". No doubt, then, of its sponsorship. This time, the views expressed are Unesco's official own.

This is the first bibliography published by Unesco on education for international understanding. It is not intended to be exhaustive, but has been drawn up to give teachers and leaders in adult education suggestions for useful books, pamphlets and articles.

These references are for adult education. They are—via your mentors —for you.

They are to be "useful". Useful for what? Useful to whom?

Peruse the *Selected Bibliography.*

"Opposite" camps . . . identical ends

Absent therefrom is all criticism, all question, all argument—however scholarly—which raises the slightest intellectual eyebrow at the proposed amalgamation of all nations into one great glistening whole. Present are seventy pages, and five hundred and fifty titles for the guidance of "teachers and leaders in adult education"—via the UN, of course.

Were this but the delightful adventure of some mutual admiration society, a cherubic panorama of terrestrial peace-to-come, the whole thing might be dismissed as naïve internationalism à la Coué.

That is not what it is.

Examination does not reveal the "Better and better each day" of the charming Frenchman of a generation ago. Here is reference-indoctrination far more parallel to the ideology of M. Joliot-Curie, French Marxist of the present day.

[96]

The selections are a curious mixture. Individuals and organizations widely believed to be on opposite sides of the collectivist fence are found, in this *Selected Bibliography*, to be reference authorities for a common end.

Global "peace" . . . by perpetual war

For example, the list contains seventeen publications of the Carnegie Endowment for International Peace. The titular founder of this Endowment was Andrew Carnegie, a man who made his money in America and left great sums of it to propagandize Americans. This is no personal statement of the reviewer; it is the statement of Carnegie himself. His autobiography contains both the statement and the plan. The 1893 edition, now extremely rare, bore the title *Triumphant Democracy*. In the final chapter Carnegie outlined his great design—to amalgamate the Republic with Britain's Empire.

The Carnegie objective was similar to that of Cecil Rhodes, and Rhodes outlined his own plan in seven separate wills. The first will stated his goal as "* * * the ultimate recovery of America as an integral part of the British Empire * * *" The seventh will, signed on July 1, 1899, established the Rhodes Scholarships. Two of these went to each State in the Union, and provision was made for one hundred annual awards.*

Does this lead us somewhere? The evidence is not lacking that it does, for in 1935 the League for Industrial Democracy could state that "* * * the Student L.I.D. * * * feels particularly proud that the last annual batch of [96] Rhodes Scholars contained six members of the L.I.D."[1] Clearly, members of the Student L.I.D. were regarded as several thousand times more suited to the avowed purposes of the Rhodes Fund than were American university students as a whole!

Again it is impossible to ignore the unfailing parallel in these tides "mysteriously rising in the academic world".

Some fifty years after Carnegie's autobiography first appeared, the Carnegie Endowment for International Peace for the first time made its presidency a paid position. The purpose was to obtain for that office the services of Alger Hiss. In this the Endowment was successful.

Listed among its publications is *Three Years of the United Nations*, an appraisal and forecast co-authored by John Foster Dulles, Paul Henri-Spaak and Alexandre Parodi. All three are great exponents of the new internationalism. Dulles was made chairman of the Board of Trustees of the Car-

---

* Aydelotte: *The American Rhodes Scholarships*. 1946. Also, *American Oxonian*, April 1944-January 1945. (*Who's Who in America*, Vol. 23, 1944-5, lists Aydelotte as a trustee of the Carnegie Foundation for the Advancement of Teaching since 1929; chairman of the educational advisory board of the Guggenheim Foundation since 1925; a trustee of the World Peace Foundation since 1927; a member of the American Historical Association and the Council on Foreign Relations; and an honorary member of the American Association of University Professors.)

[1] *Thirtieth Anniversary Report. 1905 . . . 1935*. The L.I.D. (*Cf.* Bibliography, page 174)

negie Endowment at the same meeting where Hiss was made its president.[2*]

Dulles is also the chief architect of the Japanese peace treaty. This is no treaty between the United States and Japan; it is an agreement between Japan and the United Nations. It contains deliberate steps toward the very world government which, in the Senate debate on the UN Charter, was denied to high heaven by every sponsor and proponent thereof. None was better known than Senator Arthur Vandenberg of Michigan, who said:

> In a word, we have not created a super-state. We have not organized a "world government". We have not hauled down the Stars and Stripes from the dome of the Capitol. We have simply agreed to cooperate effectively with 49 other sovereign states in the mutual pursuit of peace and security.[3]

These highly debatable matters are not discussed in the Unesco publications, nor are they presented for others to discuss.

In the *Selected Bibliography* one finds, as publisher of recommended reading, the World Peace Foundation of Boston, Mass. This is one of the many early peace foundations now supporting instruments of war. The UN, by the very articles of its Charter, and the North Atlantic Treaty Organization (NATO), by the very terms of its being, guarantee not peace but war. Each guarantees that every local war, by its being, is potentially global war —and Korea is an acute example of the fact.

---

* The date was December 10, 1946. Hiss took office on February 1 of the following year. On May 14, Edward C. Carter, longtime director of the Institute of Pacific Relations and its affiliate, the American Council (IPR), wrote a letter to O. E. Hansen. He said:

"* ○ ○ for over a year representatives of the IPR have been engaging in extended consultations with representatives of the FPA [Foreign Policy Association], Carnegie Endowment, Council on Foreign Relations, World Peace Foundation, etc., working toward a far greater coordination of effort with a view to a much wider national service.

"○ ○ *

"The man on whom we are all pinning our greatest hopes for advancing the whole cause of interorganizational coordination and cooperation is Alger Hiss ○ ○ *

"○ ○ *

"○ * ○ [With Roland Redmond of the American Geographical Society, Hiss proposed] securing a common office building for several research organizations on a property immediately adjacent to the United Nations here in New York. * ○ * There are several other concrete cases of interorganizational cooperation on which we are working for a common end."

Two weeks later, May 28, Carter wrote to Brooks Emeny, president of the FPA:

"As a concession to the Council on Foreign Relations, the World Peace Foundation, the Carnegie Endowment for International Peace, and the IPR, I am inclined to think that if you want to get the maximum number of organizations in under your umbrella, you will be wise to consider calling the new organization the American Institute of International Relations or the American Institute of World Affairs rather than attempting to woo these organizations into becoming subordinate to the FPA."

Hearings, Part 8. Subcommittee of the Senate Committee on the Judiciary. January-February, 1952; pp. 2817-9. INSTITUTE OF PACIFIC RELATIONS.

[2] Dulles was also chairman of the Rockefeller Foundation and of the General Education Board. (*Who's Who in America,* Vol. 27, 1952-3)

[3] *Congressional Record,* June 29, 1945; p. 6985.

[98]

The Fabian Socialists

Next, take the Fabian Socialists. In Britain, this small group first infiltrated the old Liberal Party; it gradually indoctrinated the latter with Fabian views. It then proceeded to kill the Liberal Party, and took over—all in the name of "Labour." Fewer than 3,000 member Fabians engineered this progressive *coup*, and a clear present parallel is visible within both parties in the United States. During this entire period the Fabian Society of Britain was in active touch with the Intercollegiate Socialist Society and then with its successor, the League for Industrial Democracy.

Those who have felt that the new world order calls for internationalism but never, never socialism, are confronted with socialist imperial Britain, a result, and with parallel procedures in our own Country clearly visible to all but the inveterate ostriches, and the most naïve.

They are also confronted with Unesco's *Selected Bibliography.* Here, as recommended reading—for "teachers and leaders in adult education"—is *The World Parliament of Labour,* a study of the International Labour Organization written by R. J. P. Mortishead of the I.L.O. and published by the Fabian Society, International Bureau. This latter was organized "To prepare the ground for an international socialist policy in international affairs."[4]

In other words, the Fabian Society is bracketed by Unesco as educational reference authority alongside the publications of the Carnegie Endowment for International Peace. Again is suggested the common ends—however each side debates the means.

This view, and its documentation, is not represented in Unesco's *Selected Bibliography.* It has no part in Unesco's plan for the training of "teachers and leaders in adult education".

The view does not possess that singular type of "objectivity" required by the ruling *élite.*

Threads of ideological communality

The threads of ideological communality do not lessen as the *Selected Bibliography* is brought under scrutiny.

The National Council for the Social Studies, NEA, has a number of publications listed, among which is *International Organizations After the War,* by M. Lerner, E. Lerner and H. J. Abraham. These gentlemen are quite unknown for non-internationalist views. The National Education Association is listed, with publications on the UN and "international understanding". The NEA is a recipient of foundation funds.

Among authors is Britain's Julian Sorell Huxley, the man whose hope for our war with Japan was so quickly, and so tragically, fulfilled. The Foreign Policy Association is well represented. The FPA, like the Institute of Pacific Relations, has long received funds from the great foundations,

---

[4] *Cf.* page 3.

including those of Rockefeller and Carnegie.*

* The statement is easily substantiated.

There is, for example, the testimony of Edward C. Carter, trustee of the IPR, on whose farm at Lee, Mass., were found 75 file drawers, each containing some 3,500 documents—250,000 items in all. These were discovered in a barn whose walls were covered with maps of the U.S.S.R. In 1951 Carter, under oath, testified:

SENATOR WATKINS [of Utah]: * * * [Frederick Vanderbilt Field] was the financial angel for IPR, was he not?

MR. CARTER: Not financial agent.

SENATOR WATKINS: Angel. He was helping all the time.

MR. CARTER: He was a minor cherub. The main support came from the Rockefeller Foundation and Carnegie Foundation and large American business corporations. * * * [Dr. Philip C.] Jessup [of Columbia University] was chairman of the American IPR in 1939 and 1940.

INSTITUTE OF PACIFIC RELATIONS. Senate Committee on the Judiciary. *Hearings.* July 25-August 7, 1951; pp. 31-2.

Jessup also was a director of the Council on Foreign Relations from 1934 to 1942 and Field was a member for ten years beginning with 1940.

Annual Reports of the Executive Director, Council on Foreign Relations. 1940-1949.

From 1925 through 1950 the total income of the IPR was $2,536,600, of which 50 percent came from the foundations (chiefly the Rockefeller Foundation, Carnegie Corporation and Carnegie Endowment).

Statement of W. L. Holland, executive officer of the International IPR and the American IPR. *Hearings,* Senate Committee on the Judiciary. *Report No. 2050,* July 1951-June 1952; p. 4.

The American Council, IPR, is "Cited as a Communist front which received funds from the American People's Fund, another front organized and directed by Frederick V. Field as a repository for funds to be distributed to Communist enterprises." The Council also has received Carnegie and Rockefeller funds.

Guide to Subversive Organizations and Publications. House Committee on Un-American Activities. March 3, 1951; p. 16.

California Committee on Un-American Activities. *Report,* 1948; p. 168.

The foundations often evince a singular choice of field workers. For instance:

"The name of Guenther Stein, member of the Sorge Soviet espionage network and in 1950 expelled from France for espionage, nowhere appears on formal listings of IPR trustees, employees or committee members. Nevertheless, he wrote at least 18 articles for IPR publications, spread over the years 1936-47; acted during the war as Chungking correspondent of the IPR; was praised by Owen Lattimore (while Mr. Lattimore was editor of [the IPR quarterly] *Pacific Affairs*) as 'by long odds the best economic journalist in the Far East'; and was in frequent and close communication with many leading members of the IPR family."

INSTITUTE OF PACIFIC RELATIONS. Senate Committee on the Judiciary. *Report No. 2050.* July 1951-June 1952; p. 140.

A tabular breakdown of Carnegie and Rockefeller grants to the IPR, from 1929 through 1949, is published in the *IPR Hearings,* Senate Committee on the Judiciary (Vol. XIV, 1952; pp. 4850-1).

The Rockefeller *Review for 1950 and 1951* lists these further appropriations: American IPR, $60,000 (*p. 103*); Pacific Council, IPR, $50,000 (*p. 104*); Foreign Policy Association, $20,000 (*p. 104*); Council on Foreign Relations, $45,000 (*p. 117*); American Council on Education, $166,000 (*p. 106*) and $31,616 (*p. 123*); General Education Board, $5,001,625 (*p. 123*).

Do these facts lead one to unalloyed confidence in the *educational* associations (such as the National Citizens Council for Better Schools, formerly the National Citizens Commission for the Public Schools) whose funds come so substantially from the same foundations?

Nor do those responsible for the *Selected Bibliography* find the slightest hesitancy in placing books from the Soviet, the Foreign Policy Association, the NEA and the Carnegie Endowment in the same ideological list with others by the Church Peace Union and Harold J. Laski. The lifetime work of Professor Laski was, to say the least, Fabian in its whole, left in the extreme, and by some claimed to have been outright Marxist. He was long a member of the Executive Committee of the Fabian Society. He it was who said, of the *Conclusions and Recommendations* of the American Historical Association's Commission on Social Studies:

> At bottom, and stripped of its carefully neutral phrases, the report is an educational program for a socialist America.[5]

The research director of this report was Dr. George S. Counts, and the report itself was made possible by a grant of $300,000 from the Carnegie Endowment. The Church Peace Union was founded and endowed in 1914 by Andrew Carnegie.

Unesco lists a work on "cultural relations" by Isaac Leon Kandel, published by Teachers College, Columbia University. Kandel was born in Romania. He is a member of the NEA, has written for the Carnegie Foundation for the Advancement of Teaching, and is a Council member of the American Association of University Professors.[6]

Unesco follows this listing with a work by Walter Maria Kotschnig, who was born in Judenburg, Austria, and came to the United States in 1936. He is

> one of those inevitable émigré professors who has been in this country less than 10 years and who is now prepared to take over the formation of the crude, untutored American mind * * *

Kotschnig attached himself to the Office of Education in Washington, D. C., and forthwith produced a plan not essentially different from the one advanced by Harold Rugg in 1942. The plan was

> subjected to analysis by members of the staff of the Commissioner of Education and this analysis reveals his whole proposal to be superficial, self-serving, and worthless * * * a wholly un-American device of propaganda.[7]

The Department of State took Kotschnig under its wing and sent him to represent its policies within the United Nations.[8]

These are the authorities offered by Unesco as guides for the "orientation" of yourself and your child.

Missing . . . the greatest human Document of all

These references—for "teachers and leaders in adult education"—proceed from a single position, which is this: In the new internationalism lies

---

[5] *Cf.* page 30.
[7] *Congressional Record,* March 6, 1944; p. A1124. Memorandum from John T. Flynn.
[6, 8] *Who's Who in America,* Vol. 27, 1952-3.

all wisdom, all good, and all hope for the future of the world.

That means the "present" for those men and women who, as children, are now attending your community schools.

It means a further thing: A self-appointed snobocracy, having led our people and Nation into perpetual war (in pursuit of perpetual peace), is indoctrinating every man, woman and child in America by deliberately manipulating our teachers, our schools, and the reference materials employed by each.

We are footing the bills.

Unesco's *Selected Bibliography* proceeds from "international understanding", through what is being called "genocide", to education for global citizenship. And the threads that hold together this coming of an enforced Millennium are clearly to be discerned. They range in persons from a Julian Huxley, a Harold Laski, a Rt. Hon. Ellen Wilkinson,[9] to a Kandel and a Kotschnig. They range in organizations from the National Education Association, through the Foreign Policy Association and the entire progressive education movement; the National Union of Teachers; the World Peace Foundation, and an ideological infiltration of top levels of many of the finest women's organizations in America.*

The material has one great burden throughout—internationalism. It is the burden of Unesco's *Selected Bibliography,* as it is of the entire series under review.

The announced intent is to inculcate an "attitude"—among adults and in the classroom—which is being called "world understanding". The purpose is described as "peace".

This is to be achieved by a perpetual state of war.

And by no means is the garden of propaganda devoid of charm. It is gaily decorated, and festooned with verbal banners which are three:

Understanding, peace—and freedom.

The one great Document of Freedom in all the world, the Constitution of these United States, is mentioned not at all.

---

* This infiltration was excellently treated in the Crain-Hamilton title, *Packaged Thinking for Women,* a little book which now is unfortunately out of print.

[9] Ellen Wilkinson was an early member of Britain's Independent Labour Party, and union organizer. She joined the Communist Party on its formation there in 1920 and was a member while on the Manchester City Council in 1923. She resigned from the Party upon her election to Parliament on the Labour ticket in 1924. She was Minister of Education in the Attlee Cabinet from 1945 until her death, February 6, 1947. (*Who Was Who 1941-1950.* Black. London; p. 1277. *The Annual Register. 1947.* Longmans, Green. London, 1948; p. 568.) For years she was on the Executive Council of the Fabian Society, and is the same Ellen Wilkinson who lectured in American cities under the auspices of the League for Industrial Democracy.

"The [United Nations] Charter is, in the main, a translation of this Russian [Soviet] system into an international idiom and its adaptation to an international community. * * *

"This plan has no sense unless it means * * * a world police state * * * for if it is not meant for that purpose, it certainly can serve no other, as has repeatedly been shown in these pages * * *"
    Salvador de Madariaga: *Victors Beware* (pp. 270-72).
    London. 1946.

PART III   The International

THE FLOOD   Movement

24. THE UNITED NATIONS AND WORLD CITIZENSHIP
Towards World Understanding. Vol. IV. Unesco. Paris. 1948.

Another Unesco seminar was held at Adelphi College, Garden City, N.Y. Its report outlines more of the program intended for our youth. The report comes from six individuals, all teachers. They are from Afghanistan, Chile, France, the Lebanon, Thailand and the United States. Dr. Laurin Zilliacus, of the U.S.A., chaired the group and was editor of the report. Unesco warns the reader that

The opinions expressed in this pamphlet are the views of the authors, and are not necessarily those of Unesco.

The title is *The United Nations and World Citizenship*.

Here is no hit-or-miss program. The reader is confronted with the "system". How is this "system" to be built? The answer is found in the report. This is concerned with the

many ideas on methods of presenting the United Nations system in the schools[.]

A reader also encounters what the legal mind calls *assumpsit*. This means that from the very outset the premise of the whole is assumed.

What is assumed? This:

In the world of today, no part of mankind can live in isolation from the rest. International war can no longer be confined to two or a few nations or even to the nations of a particular region.

Here is the weakness of *assumpsit*. Alternative is ruled out. So—

One world or none is thus the choice given us by military reality.*

Thus, the seminarists—Unesco's ineffable six.

----

* *One World or None* was used as the title of a propaganda film produced in 1947 by the National Committee on Atomic Information, with technical assistance from the Federation of American Scientists and narration by Raymond Gram Swing. (*Hearings*. Senate Committee on the Judiciary, April 1951-March 1952; p. 52. Communist Tactics in Controlling Youth Organizations.)

[103]

The official policy statement of the American Education Fellowship offers an identical "choice"., *i.e.,*

❂ * # atomic war # ❂ # and enforceable international order # * #

and, in exact parallel to the Unesco seminar, states that it, the AEF,

should become the clearest, most purposeful educational spokesman for [such enforceable world order.][1]

The "choice" at the least is debatable, yet it is adopted *a priori* for the teaching of our children. Its adoption lends more than slight credence to what the seminarists say of themselves in their own third paragraph:

In the opinion of the writers of this report, we educators do not commonly know as much of the facts of world affairs as we should; nor have we given them enough thought.

With an insouciance little short of sublime, they go on to declare that

World machinery is required; and human beings with the right outlook are required to utilize it or to insist that it be utilized.

The reader suspects that here is a doctrine of infallibility, self-proclaimed.

The bright spot . . .

However, there is a bright spot. The seminar says there is a way for peoples (nations) to get along together. This way differs from the one presently being pursued.

The six teachers declare:

A suitable term for it would be "transnational co-operation", that is, the co-operation of groups or individuals *across* boundaries to exchange views or solve common problems. Experience has shown that *transnational* co-operation generally results in fruitful agreement. The same cannot always be said of international (intergovernmental) "co-operation". The reason would seem to be that the participants in transnational co-operation generally have a common aim in a limited sphere of human affairs. National representatives, on the other hand, representing the foreign policies of their governments, frequently have conflicting aims in much wider spheres. Transnational co-operation may yet prove to be the way to prevent *international* war.

The seminar refutes its main *assumpsit;* it presents an alternate course —one which would be enthusiastically welcomed by every "Isolationist" in America.

The skeptical reader, however, will suspect a "catch", for this alternative would mean collapse of the plan to force the will of a super-government upon the individual wills of the parts thereof. It would be the death warrant of the UN.

It also would mean the recovery of America's political Neutrality, and a return to inter-nation-al law. This is world law which becomes such by and with the consent of those to whom it pertains, and within the explicit scope for which each part of that law is framed.

---

[1] *Cf.* page 56.

[104]

Such, formerly, was the Law of Nations, an evolution of the peaceful settlement of Man's problems upon this planet, enforced and enforceable of his own free will.

With the advent of interventionism, the Law of Nations became a parchment of the past.

Global educators—those who "do not commonly know as much of the facts of world affairs as we should"—might reasonably take upon themselves a study of the seminar's transnational remarks. In them lies the germ of peace.

It is further suggested that the global educators undertake this study in simple and distant quietude, as befits a type of scholarship to which they might modestly aspire.

. . . and the "catch"

Volume IV continues:

The Charter describes the machinery of the United Nations, and the aims and principles to which the member governments have pledged themselves and their peoples.

Notwithstanding this "pledge", the seminarists blandly observe that

there is a growing demand that foreign policy shall not only serve the interests of the people but that its *conduct shall be brought under the control of the people.*

Here the internationalists reach heights in semantic tongue-in-cheek—and the main catch is yet to appear.

The seminar notes the tendency of an individual—any individual—to identify himself with the grandeur of his ruler, potentate or nation. This tendency, it says, is

perhaps the most difficult of all the old concepts to bring up-to-date.

The seminarists will bring the tendency up-to-date. With great accuracy they say:

Today we frequently find governments pursuing the vested interests of small but powerful groups while proclaiming—perhaps even believing—that they pursue national interests. And we commonly have the mass of citizens accepting this fraud.

Now, look again at that statement. Carefully put the word *internationalists* where the word *governments* now appears. See what you have. Does not the statement come very close to the truth? Does it not turn, and pointedly turn, at the very policies now in vogue?

Be careful, however, that this be done in the quiet of night, and alone. For you are challenging a "new" potentate, global in scope. Be wise, speak not openly, that historians may not fail to some day record of us—even as the Unesco seminar records of our feudal forebears:

They regarded their ruler's increased girth as their own, even while they were being ruined or slaughtered to achieve it.

The exponents of global theory now return to the idea of transnational cooperation. Their balloon soars, shining with verbal iridescence. And then it goes pop! The reason is found in the philosophy of global collectivism from which there is offered no escape.

The totalitarianism is explicit: Transnational organizations might be given powers not only to draw up plans in their respective fields but to bind member governments to carry them out ⚬ ⚬ ⚬

And what then? The seminarists reply:

It would be a beginning of functional world government ⚬ ⚬ ⚬

And so one finds that the Unesco seminar and Dr. Theodore Brameld are as one:

The world of the future ⚬ ⚬ ⚬ should be a world in which national sovereignty is utterly subordinated to international authority ⚬ ⚬ ⚬

The majority machinery of the United Nations, UNESCO, or any similar organizations created on behalf of world order should be so greatly strengthened that no member country ⚬ ⚬ ⚬ can conceivably refuse to abide by its own power-backed decisions.[2]

Here is the long-anticipated catch.

But will you permit these things to be taught your child?

That for which men die

Now comes surprise. It takes a form which a hopeful reader might interpret as rivalry within the UN itself. Unesco, says the report, concerns itself with

the real interests of the people—food, clothes, shelter, working conditions, leisure pursuits, education, scientific and cultural progress, and civil rights.

And what about the Security Council? Read carefully, as the Unesco seminar proceeds:

From the point of view of "We the people" these are realities, the preoccupations of the Security Council [are] illusions—illusions of grandeur, power, prestige.

And, says the seminar, in the very next sentence:

Unfortunately, although men live meagrely on such illusions, they die profusely for them.

Back in 1920, no Borah, Lodge, Poindexter, Reed or Hiram Johnson did better than that!

Another fait accompli?

The seminar, in conclusion, recommends

The introduction into school time-tables ⚬ ⚬ ⚬ of new methods ⚬ ⚬ ⚬ for co-operative planning by the teachers, and ⚬ ⚬ ⚬ realistic adaptation to actual conditions in the schools.

This introduction of "new methods" was not lacking in interested cooperation. For two years evidence had been taken

---

[2] Cf. page 66.

from nearly a thousand experts on world affairs, school teachers, professors and administrators, and the cost of their inquiry ran to $26,000.

The organizations which sponsored the study were the Association for Supervision and Curriculum Development, NEA, the National Council for the Social Studies, NEA, and the Associated Committee on International Relations. And who first asked that the study be made at all? The Executive Committee of the National Education Association.*

The question is this: Is the program being openly submitted for acceptance or rejection by the people of these United States? Or, under interested guidance, is it suddenly to burst upon us, another *fait accompli?*

Missing . . . Liberty's basic prerequisite

One may laud the fact that the "High Contracting Parties" of the old League of Nations have been made to disappear, as the seminarists point out. But with vast correctness they state that this

Verbal victory does not guarantee victory in fact. * * * The emergence of the words, "We, the peoples" is no more than a promise.

Promise it may be. Yet one is not unconscious of a temptation to suggest that the substitution is mere semantic paraphrase.

Power remains.

One may laud the observation that

The psychological basis for a world society would surely be better expressed by the phrase "We the people", thus recognizing that the unity of mankind is fundamental, whereas subdivisions and their governments are secondary.

An enormous discrepancy is there, however, and it is found in the assertion that

The emergence of the words, "We, the peoples" is no more than a promise.

No American conscious of his heritage could accept this premise. He would immediately delete the *s* from *peoples.* Then, unlike the global educators, he would consult history. And the words of his reply might go something like this:

Why do you ignore the greatest step ever taken in the governmental process of Man—a step taken only by those who founded this Republic? Great as are your names, you have not brought to your own peoples the vital personal Freedom upon which all governments *by consent of the governed* must rest.

When, for the first time in the recorded annals of Man the words *We the People* did appear, they served to introduce the Preamble to my own Constitution. They are far more than a "promise" to me; they are basic to my life. For this is what they mean: The sovereign ruler vanished; I, a *citizen* sovereign, emerged. In all of history none other prospered as did I.

I was free.

---

* Published in 1948 by the NEA under the title *Education for International Understanding in American Schools, Suggestions and Recommendations.*

Free, I intend to remain.

"A new method of thinking has arisen", wrote Thomas Paine. And thus was a people's own self-government attained.

This, it is submitted, is first to be achieved by you and your associates, within your separate lands.

Such is the enormous discrepancy to be observed.

Sovereignty, under the Old World philosophy—now planned to be taught in all our schools—once again is becoming a vested interest, as it was in the days of feudal lords and kings. Title is being assumed by a self-perpetuating world *élite*.

"We, the peoples" simply pay, obey and die—as of yore.

Therefore a suggestion may be advanced, and it is this: That the quintessence of meaning which pervades the American Constitution of 1789 be included in all that certain educators "do not commonly know of the facts of world affairs"—and that the global mystics discover the one National Charter on all this earth which finally enshrined the sovereign individuality of Man.

Nowhere in *Towards World Understanding* is the slightest reference to this basic prerequisite of citizen-liberty to be found.

"O! ye that love mankind, stand forth. Freedom hath been hunted round the globe. Europe regards her like a stranger. England hath given her warning to depart. Ye that dare oppose not only the tyranny but the tyrant, stand forth!"

Thomas Paine, in *Common Sense.* 1776.

PART III

THE FLOOD

The International

Movement

25. THE DRIVE FOR TOTAL MIND-CONTROL

Four distinct procedures are now in focus. These are:

1) The program of the progressive educators. This is the drive for social-reconstruction-through-the-schools;

2) The program of the global authoritarians. This is the drive for world-collectivism through the thought-guidance of parent, teacher and child;

3) The drive of the Unesco-ites for the collaboration of the child himself;

4) The program of the global collectivists outlined in the Unesco publication, *A Handbook for the Improvement of Textbooks and Teaching Materials,* 1949. This is the drive for total control over the human mind.

Item *3* found expression in *Towards World Understanding,* Volume II:

Again, and very obviously, both in our institutions which prepare teachers for their work and in the schools where their work is done, we must win our students' support for those international authorities whose concern is the maintenance of peace. (*P. 24*)

The *Handbook* referred to in Item *4* states:

As already indicated, Part I of this handbook incorporates the historical material to be found in *Looking at the World Through Textbooks,*[1] a document prepared by the Preparatory Commission of Unesco and issued just before the meeting of the first Session of the General Conference of Unesco in November, 1946. (*P. 59*)

In other words, less than eighteen months elapsed before those who denied all idea of "world government" were publishing a work consciously devoted to that end.

---

[1] *Document C/9;* Unesco. Paris, 1946; pp. 18-24.

[109]

The involuntary experimentees

The *Handbook* suggests that colleges and universities

Consider education for international understanding in establishing entrance examinations and requirements. (*P. 129*)

It recommends that educational organizations

Urge the improvement of textbooks and, if necessary, bring organized pressure to bear against highly undesirable books. (*P. 130*)

The *Handbook* recommends that educational organizations

Protect the academic freedom of the individual teacher so that controversial issues can be considered objectively in the classroom. (*P. 130*)

The *Handbook* urges "lay organizations" to

Give organized support to the use of objective textbooks and to the protection of academic freedom. (*P. 131*)

It urges that "private international organizations" undertake

The establishment of an international commission of scholars and educators to examine textbooks on request and to give them the stamp of approval if they meet certain standards. (*P. 132*)

Who is to determine the "objectivity"; what is the peculiar nature of that "objectivity"; who is to determine the "certain standards"; and, now, who is to give textbooks the "stamp of approval", is pretty clear.

And these people—and their associates—brook no discussion of the most controversial issue of all: The global movement which they promote!

So another conclusion is justified, and it is this: There are to be two kinds of men upon this earth—

1) The great mass of "common" men—to whom are issued directives;

2) The closed international *élite*—who issue the directives.

This prospect is not stressed by members of the closed *élite*.

These gentle men and fierce

In startling brilliance here shines great light. And that light reveals to us a most amazing scene. Strange people move about within it—people who have no single face, but two; others have but one, though this single face has two sides. And these people frown, and smile—look in two opposite directions and say two different things—in one split second of time.

One face, with its ever friendly mien, faces one direction—and there are seen its friends: "progressives", "social scientists" and Unesco-ites, demanding the right of analysis and of revision exclusively for themselves.

But—their other face; their other eye; their other voice! These face another way—toward all who examine curricula, textbooks, teachers and boards of education; toward all who raise their voices in effective protest at the collectivism and internationalism which is being taught young Americans in schools where real Americanism properly should be taught.

How you are expected to tremble in your boots at the slightest glance or sound! No more are you to confront your teachers, superintendents or school board, to demand that your youngster's mind be exempt from planned indoctrination; that it enjoy its own development—as befits a freeborn man.

You have been stamped as "educationally incompetent"—by the "progressives" who make the stamp.

Not only is analysis of textbooks meritorious—when done, of course, by them—but their friends are to "bring organized pressure to bear against highly undesirable textbooks", *i.e.*, against those which answer in the negative their own measure of the text: "does it serve our purpose?"

Selah! It is marvelous—this sight which stands revealed!

Action by private citizens

Thus, the grand experiment—upon millions of involuntary experimentees.

Great foundations, great endowments, support such people, organizations and aims. Yet there is a strange absence of other endowments to make possible the publication of alternatives to which, presumably, millions of our citizens would subscribe. While private industry cannot compete with subsidized, tax-free "government" operations—and pays counsel to say so—the same private industry somehow seems to feel that the opposition can employ competent writers in direct competition with internationalists who are heavily endowed. Private industry is silently acquiescing in its own demise, by a remarkable prevalance of checkbook paralysis.

Nevertheless, discussion is becoming more open each day. In the process, individual citizens are doing a whale of a job—by themselves.

These people have an old-fashioned belief—that one should

> Render unto Caesar the things that are Caesar's,
> and unto God the things that are God's.
>
> *Matthew XXII, 21; Mark XII, 17.*

"Yet this government never of itself furthered any enterprise, but by the alacrity with which it got out of its way. It does not keep the country free. It does not settle the West. It does not educate. The character inherent in the American people has done all that has been accomplished; and it would have done somewhat more, if the government had not sometimes got in the way."

Henry David Thoreau: *Civil Disobedience.* 1849.

PART III
THE FLOOD

The International
Movement

26. IN THE CLASSROOM WITH CHILDREN UNDER THIRTEEN YEARS OF AGE

Towards World Understanding. Volume V. Unesco. Paris. 1949.

SECTION 1: THE PROBLEM IN GENERAL.

Enter, now, the proposed American school. Stand invisible, if you will, behind a teacher whose duty and responsibility it formerly was to properly instruct the junior citizens of the Republic. Among those youngsters facing you is your own.

Witness, in this Volume V, what is to go on. The volume is entitled *In the Classroom with Children under Thirteen Years of Age.*

You will be watching "progressive education", as developed on a global scale.

Another seminar reports. It had been held at Poděbrady, Czechoslovakia, in the summer of 1948. Attention was concentrated on

education in the classroom as a means of developing international understanding.

"The views expressed are not, of course, the official views of Unesco," the reader is informed. Unesco, however, again sponsored the seminar and published the report. Miss Hazel Gabbard and Miss Rebecca Simonson represented the United States of America. Three of the ten countries sending delegates were in 1948 within the orbit of the Soviet.

Why you are unfit to rear your own child

On the fourth line of the first page appears this statement:

Before the child enters school his mind has already been profoundly marked, and often injuriously, by earlier influences; * * *

Four type-lines after the semicolon, and in the same sentence, eight final words name the source of those "earlier influences" which are so "injurious". These the child

has first gained, however dimly, in the home.

[112]

There is no mistaking the meaning. The seminar means the home; it means the American home; and it means you.

The same thought was expressed by Marx and Engels as

bourgeois clap-trap about the family.

Your "misdirection of human effort"

Members of parent-teachers associations may suspect from the program that the "parent" part of their association is quietly being removed. The mind of the young person, already and often injuriously marked by ideas he "has first gained, however dimly, in the home", is to be weaned from those ideas. It is to become internationalized. The report says so:

* * * these earlier years may be indispensable to the education of children for world citizenship.

The American Education Fellowship's phrase is "enforceable international order".[1]

It is highly important, too, that we realize how this program parallels the legislation for Universal Military Training presented to Congress in 1951. The bill, *S. 1*—known on Capitol Hill as the Marshall-Rosenberg bill— was so drawn as to elicit the following among admissions of fact during the extensive hearings which were held:

The bill provided for eventual compulsory *non*-military service for all 18-year olds who could not qualify even for limited-duty under UMT. Mrs. Rosenberg stated:

"At this moment the President has no plan which we want to submit'* * * [because] we would have to ask you to so materially amend, for instance, the pension laws' * * *'"

as to cover the allocation and employment of such non-military youths in the collectivist scheme of things. The number of these young men was estimated at from 100,000 to 150,000, but "it may go a little higher", said Mrs. Rosenberg.

Introduced into the UMT hearings was a Declaration of Manpower, adopted at Atlantic City, N.J., on January 10, 1951 by the Association of American Colleges. This Declaration urged.

"adequate and immediate comprehensive planning to insure the constructive utilization of the ability and training of all college women."[4]

The Marshall-Rosenberg bill included provision for the selection of students, for the designation of their courses of study, for Government financing of their studies, and for direction of their ultimate occupations.[5]

Lastly, the hearings revealed that a Federal Security Agency program for the care of children of employed mothers was "already in the mill".[6]

Here is developing a perfect situation, tailor-made. In the classroom, the child is purged of the "injurious influences" which parents have put

---

[1] *Cf.* page 56.

1951 Hearings references:	2	3	4	5	6
Senate, on *S.1*. Pages:	51-3	193	464-5	51-3,497	55-6,113,158-9,556-7
House, on *H.R. 1752*. Pp:	—	—	—	88-9	47-8,115,348-51,664

—however dimly—into his youthful mind; gradually, the son or daughter becomes indoctrinated—through "uncoerced persuasion"; the mother is drafted into "national service" while her child is cared for by the FSA; and 18-year olds either go into military service or have their studies and employment arbitrarily defined for them.

No young American is to be free from the moment he reaches his eighteenth birthday, and even—as we shall see—from birth.

Yet it is claimed that we are "fighting communism"!

The world collectivists proceed concurrently to

help the child become internationally-minded * * *

The result, at maturity, is to be "world-citizenship".

Publicity highlights "national service". Nothing is said of national socialism.

The plea is for "international cooperation". But, as with UMT, not one Unesco spokesman breathes the slightest hint of socialism, national or worldwide. This delicacy is paralleled in the policy statement of the American Education Fellowship.

"Socialism", to the planners, is a naughty word.

Implicit, however, is the control of thinking in the home itself. "Citizenship in a world society" is the "ideal to be pursued", and it is to be pursued "whether in the home" or anywhere else. True, the youngster is to assimilate knowledge "to nourish his interests". But who is to determine his interests is not his parents—yourselves—nor yet he.

His interests have been predetermined.

Further, the very essence of the American Constitution is subtly attacked. The attack is indicated by a mere adjective, itself the unique selection of the makers of this report. The adjective is *selfish*. For, say the internationalists,

With that kind of education they [your children] will be protected against selfish individualism and indiscriminate sociability, both of which are a misdirection of human effort.

Individualism may become selfish, and of course it often does. That is not the point. The point is individualism. The American Bill of Rights enthroned the individual; it dethroned the collective. And here the internationalists, precisely as with *bigoted* nationalism, employ a semantic twist to cloud the truth: They would re-enthrone the collective—personified in themselves.

So your child is to be taken from your care and placed under the benign governance of strangers. They, in their infinite wisdom, will protect him against your "misdirection of human effort".

The home is literally to be uprooted. It is to gyrate in cosmic space, a process guided and hastened by the new *élite* who themselves will make the typhoon.

[114]

Wandering in the wreckage, your child may be discerned. He may be altered, to be sure; he may show signs of others' gentle care. But he will have passed

in a progression of loyalties which will enable him later to reach the climax of membership in the world community.

You still may recognize him by his birthmark, or by his physical shape.

This means what? *"Only such a school as we envisage * * *"*

This "membership in the world community" is to be achieved by a new type of school, called the "integral" school. This new *intiger vitae*

embodies the best of the traditional school as well as the ideals essential to the school of today—[and] is able, of course, to impart that knowledge of the Three R's which has for centuries constituted the curriculum of the traditional schools.

Permission is accorded that the global child be able to read, write and add.*

This "integral school"

is far better able than the latter to familiarize the child with the social geography of his time, and to foster in him * * * the obligations of a world citizen.

The "integral school" will do this to the child

in such a way that he is conditioned for liberty under laws freely adopted.

How young people are by global authority to be "conditioned" for liberty is found by objective study of the entire Unesco series, here reviewed.

In the American's Bill of Rights it is a matter of just eight hundred and thirty-three words.

This Charter of Freedom has no part in the collectivist plan. It is too simple, too magnificent. It is basic, not an illusion. And, as another seminar put it,

Unfortunately, although men live meagrely on such illusions, they die profusely for them. (*Vol. IV; p. 15*)

Thus, in addition to the direct application of force (war), the *élite* is to bring to bear a most ancient art, newly rediscovered. Formerly, its tool was the court historian, retained for a noble's pay. Now it is to be the public school, retained on "government grants".

The method is being subtly employed—by sages anonymous of the great *élite.*

From gentle "uncoerced persuasion" the program is to culminate in

Only such a school as we envisage * * *

The process is still called education.

---

* Dr. Edgar A. Waugh, professor of political science at Michigan State Normal College, Ypsilanti, seemed to suggest otherwise in addressing the thirty-fourth annual convention, American Federation of Teachers, AFL, at Grand Rapids. He said:

"If either personality development or spelling has to go, let it be spelling."

The New York Times, August 22, 1951; p. L25.

The "social sciences" will be made worldwide

Conversion begins in the kindergarten. There, the teacher will correct many of the errors of home training * * *

From that point the teacher will gradually prepare the child for membership * * * in the world community.

Curricula are not only to be altered—a process known as "slanting" by editors—but coeducational subjects are to be seriously reviewed. Coeducation, it appears,

does not recognize that some subjects, such as mathematics, require separate teaching methods for boys and girls.

Women mathematicians, it seems, have been achieving degrees in spite of the exasperating presence of young men. Their daughters need not be so exposed. In the new world school, science will be classified by gender. There will be Math *M* and Math *F.*

All subjects, and all science, can play some part in developing the "world outlook". So much depends on the teachers. With them,

There remain certain general attitudes to be created if we are to achieve success in making our children world-minded. * * * it is the teacher's attitude towards the world society which has the strongest influence on the pupil's mind.

The proper attitude will be created. As Kenneth D. Benne wrote in 1949:

* * * teachers and school administrators * * * [must] come to see themselves as social engineers * * * They must equip themselves as "change agents".[7]

The "social studies" again are named. And the reason is clearly expressed:

These studies seem to us inseparable, at least up to the age of 13, from education in social-mindedness.

This is precisely what is causing concern, mounting to alarm. Many hold that self-reliance, initiative, character—even basic knowledge of the high meaning of our form of Government—have disappeared with the stressing of "social studies" and "social-mindedness" in our schools.

To the world *élite,* this concern of people does not count. The "social studies" are to be imposed worldwide.

The "error of perspective" will be rectified

The seminarists urge that histories be purged of "nationalist prejudices", and here is a point upon which many will concur. First to be determined, however, is—what "prejudices"? Who is to determine them? Is it to be an Arnold Toynbee, with his *Study of History?* Is it to be a William L. Langer of Harvard, with his *World Crisis and American Foreign Policy?* Both are subsidized publications; the first by the Rockefeller Foundation for

---

[7] *Cf.* page 58.

over $200,000 (via the Royal Institute), the second for $139,000.* What "prejudices" were eliminated in the Langer-Toynbee volumes? What others were put in?

In many schools these texts are required reading, and your sons and daughters have been absorbing "history" and other subjects—according to the gospel of, among others, Langer, Toynbee, Henry Steele Commager, James T. Shotwell and the great foundations.[8]

The seminar has therefore raised this issue: What criterion is to determine the "prejudices" to be taught your child? And the seminar will answer with a clarity that is complete:

does it serve our purpose?

In geography, the seminar asks: Does not learning about one's own environment and then proceeding to learn about the world lead pupils

to the mistaken conclusion that what is nearest to them is the most important, and what is remote is relatively insignificant?

The process—and the result—is to be reversed. And so a map is to be always before the pupil, and this is to be a global map. The seminarists report:

This seemed to us so important that we were led to hope that Unesco might persuade a publisher to prepare a world map that would really touch the child's imagination.

This map—which might or might not express the official views of Unesco—is to be so designed that when

the child began the study of national geography, he would be already partly immunized against an exaggerated sense of the importance and beauty of his own country * * *

Having proposed an identical program vis-à-vis the home, the seminar now declares that geography teaching must immunize the child

---

* Rockefeller Foundation, *Annual Report*, 1946; pp. 33 and 188-9. In the *Annual Report* for 1947, the following may be noted: The *Kinsey Report* was financed (*p. 116*); Toynbee's *Study of History* received $50,625 (*pp. 41, 211-2*); "Another grant went to the American Council on Education for an emergency investigation of methods of textbook revision" (*pp. 260-1*); and $1,500,000 was allotted to the General Education Board, this being the sum conditionally granted each year to renew an operating fund of $7,500,000 originally appropriated in 1946 (*p. 268*). According to its 1951 *Annual Report* (*p. 439*), between 1946 and 1948 the Foundation provided $10,500,000 for the General Education Board to continue its work through 1953. The 1951 *Report* also lists a gift of $402,600 to the Institute of International Studies at Princeton.
     Nor has another angle been overlooked—that of the rising opposition to the entire movement. This, too, is being cared for. In 1949 there was organized the National Citizens Commission for the Public Schools, now called the National Citizens Council for Better Schools. Who finances it? During the first two years of its operation, it received $548,000 in grants and contributions. $537,000 of this sum came from the Carnegie Corporation and Rockefeller's General Education Board. On the Advisory Panel was Willard E. Goslin, former Pasadena superintendent. (*N.C.C.P.S. Publication No. 3*. Summer, 1951; p. 19.)
x 'A glance through *Who's Who* will confirm these associations.

against that error of perspective which is at the root of jingoism and nationalism.

Immunized against the beauty of his native heath, your child is to be encouraged

in an interest in all that is remote and strange; and to engender such an esteem for "theirs" as will counteract the excl¨¨ive regard for all that is "mine".

But wait. See, now, this new teacher in person; the teacher who faces your children in class. He will listen to the youthful questions, and

In answering them, the teacher should speak the language of the naturalist or of the ethnologist or of the economist, as the occasion requires. At a¹¹ times he must speak the language of the poet ⁰ * ⁰

How is this paragon to exist? On "government grants". These you are to provide.

Recess and vacation periods will not be lost. They will

be used to cultivate their world-mindedness * * * A child taught thus will ⁰ ⁰ ⁰ ⁰ gradually lose those habits of prejudice and contempt which are an impediment to world-mindedness.

God and human nature are to be made over—though this is not necessarily the official view of Unesco.

There will be global court historians

The seminar moves on to history. It states:

School textbooks have, as a rule, been written with so little objectivity and integrity that history, as generally taught up to now, has been an obstacle to international understanding.

Truth in the statement there is. But does the seminar propose that archives be opened, that an era of Great Enlightenment now begin? It does not. Does the seminar suggest, however remotely, that the ancient Assyrians' court historians were prototypes of the court historians of the present huge foundations—and of the internationalists momentarily ruling the world? It does not.

What, then, does the seminar suggest? It does not suggest; it demands. What it demands is that historical literature be revised—under Unesco auspices.

It proposes global court historians, infinitely wise.

How is the revision to be done? It, says the report,

should carry much further the elimination of events which, from the world-education point of view, have no value, such as the endless catalogues of wars.

Only that is to remain which Unesco declares suitable for adult or for growing child.

Only that is to remain which answers Unesco's question, self-proposed:

does it serve our purpose?

The identity of the "our" remains in the celestial undisclosed.

The Document unrecommended

The text announces that children

should study the history of their own country only in relation to its part in the development of the whole of humanity.

Local history, State history, American history—all are secondary.

Recommended are certain charts. Some will illustrate

the construction of the Pyramids and the Parthenon, the expedition of Alexander; Buddha and Confucius; the Vikings, the Crusades, Magna Carta, Christopher Columbus, the American Declaration of Independence, the French Revolution, the Red Cross, the League of Nations.

Absent is all reference to Him Whom we call the Prince of Peace— by those who talk of "peace". And absent is all reference to sixty long centuries of struggle for the Rights of human beings. The one instrument of self-government in the whole of history to embrace the teachings of Jesus Christ, and to implement those teachings in its creation of the sublime sovereignty of Man, the individual—is mentioned not at all.

That is the Constitution of these United States.

A delicate process of self-capture

That pupils should learn a·language other than their mother tongue is suggested. The study, however, no longer

mainly for utilitarian purposes, should now be incorporated into basic education for a quite different reason, namely, to modify the child's attitude toward foreign civilizations.

The seminarists pursue their thought to the ultimate of self-capture.

The teaching of a language, it appears, might begin as early as the kindergarten. From·the age of 10 your child should be taught, at least partly, in this second medium. Certain risks are acknowledged. Perfection involves long and careful study

which will always remain beyond the reach of the majority of pupils. * * * Yet how can these pupils be identified in advance?

The wise men answer:

These questions raise a difficult problem.

And there they are. The seminarists' process of self-capture is complete.

[119]

"When our people are free from poverty and want and malnutrition, it will be time enough to begin to plan to permanently suckle the world at the expense of the American taxpayer."

Chief Justice John Marshall.

PART III

THE FLOOD

The International
Movement

27. SOME SUGGESTIONS ON THE TEACHING OF GEOGRAPHY

Towards World Understanding. Unesco. Volume VII, Paris, and Volume X, Paris, 1951.

The ideological threads which have now clearly emerged make it unnecessary to examine these two volumes in detail. The disclaimer that they represent the official views of Unesco is duly recorded.

Geography as a means of indoctrination

The following are verbatim quotations from the first half of Volume VII.

This handbook is an adaptation of a document prepared at Unesco's request by a small group of French geographers to assist geography teachers in primary and secondary schools. (*First sentence, first page*)

[It is] a handbook designed for members of the teaching profession in every country. (*P. 3*)

✿ ✿ ✿ what is to be stressed here is its rôle in developing a "world Sense" in children (*p. 15*) ✿ ✿ ✿ leading [the pupil] beyond his limited local horizon to see his country and himself in relation to the world. In this way, geography helps to break down the isolation in which men and nations have been prone to live. (*P. 16*)

Geography should thus act as a corrective to exaggerated nationalism and mistaken chauvinism ✿ ✿ ✿ (*P. 16*)

[As for one's own country, such teaching will make men] better able to judge its importance and worth and its actual or potential rôle in the world. (*P. 16*)

Two wars ✿ ✿ ✿ have made the "isolation" of any country a dead letter. (*P. 17*)

✿ ✿ ✿ the geography teacher should point, in passing, to international pacts and international organizations intended to help in solving complex problems of economic interdependence and international solidarity. [Such knowledge] postulates world-mindedness, the attainment of which is a major aim of Geography teaching. (*P. 18*)

Thus, Geography teaching can and should ✿ ✿ ✿ train children more thoroughly ✿ ✿ ✿ by giving them a world outlook and making them citizens of the world ✿ ✿ ✿ (*P. 18*)

[120]

* * * many young people are uninterested in, or even skeptical about, moral teaching, especially at the present time, when it is so rarely carried into practice in modern society. Unconsciously reflecting the superficial opinion of their elders * * * (P. 19)

It is probable that Geography can contribute as much as any other study to training for world-mindedness. (P. 19)

In order to produce a body of public opinion favourable to world co-operation, we must mould the minds of the future citizens of the world, directing them towards a geographical, and hence universal, attitude. (P. 20)

[On a theme of world authorities and Point 4:] The subject of "conservation" will thus arise naturally and, with it, discussion of the remedies for waste and of international agreements designed to settle conflicts. (P. 32)

* * * we must not be afraid to give an objective explanation * * * of the influence of cartels and trusts on the system of free interchange and the community interests of men. (P. 33) [Only political cartels are good.]

Thus they [the children] will come to understand the important part played by national and international organizations set up to deal with problems arising out of the inter-dependence of nations. (P. 33)

Geography can and should be a training in international understanding and tolerance. (P. 37)

To sum up, the geography teacher should have a truly international outlook * * * (P. 38)

He [the pupil] should take with him, when he leaves school, a permanent interest in Geography, combined with a lasting desire to increase his knowledge and to make himself ever more conscious of his rôle as a citizen of the world. (P. 47)

So much for Volume VII. For some reason it is no longer in print.

Volume X, entitled *A Handbook of Suggestions on the Teaching of Geography,* appeared in 1951. The following are excerpts.

The present volume does not attempt in any way to take the place of the previous publication, but is designed to complement it.* * * It is addressed to teachers of geography in both primary and secondary schools and to educational authorities in all parts of the world. (Pp. 3-4)

One of its purposes is

to provide a training in world citizenship or, in other words, to create a spirit of international understanding and good will. (P. 7)

Volume X appears to a reader as a watered-down exposition of the purposeful teaching of geography which is advocated in Volume VII. The reader is more than a little impressed by the similarity of this treatment to that accorded the original Brameld draft before the American Education Fellowship released its final statement of policy in 1947.

While the text is largely devoted to details of study, and to excursions and exercises more or less concerning geography, by no means is the thread of indoctrination withdrawn. How this thread intertwines can be seen from a few quotations.

* * * naturally the value of social studies courses as one means of helping to integrate the children's knowledge was discussed by the participants [of the seminar]. (P. 11)

All children will be found to have some prejudices caused by the home or neighborhood atmosphere. ʰ ʰ ʰ where necessary they must be corrected and good attitudes developed or strengthened. (*Pp. 12-3*)

Around 11 or 12 years of age ʰ ʰ ʰ A broader canvas for geography than that offered by local studies will now be appreciated. (*P. 17*)

At this stage ʰ ʰ ʰ the child * * * may gain some appreciation of the interdependence of peoples around the world ʰ ʰ ʰ and against this background the child may be asked to remember that many of the world's peoples suffer from hunger, and that the United Nations and its Specialized Agencies are trying to alleviate the suffering. Other world problems, for instance, how to make adequate provisions for shelter, clothing and health for all peoples, may be approached from the same positive angle. (*Pp. 18-9*)

Thus they [the children] can to some extent discipline themselves in order to cooperate towards a desired end, which is excellent social training. (*P. 22*)

ʰ ʰ ʰ before 15 years of age, world problems * * * may sometimes be introduced incidentally, or quite frequently form a motivating idea for a lesson. Mention of the work of the United Nations can, for instance, be referred to where it seems to be relevant. (*Pp. 24-5*)

After the age of 15 the adolescent ʰ ʰ ʰ tends to find everything around him old-fashioned and in need of reform and is often perplexed by the contradiction he finds among adults between ideals and reality, or between the principles he has been taught to affirm and adult behaviour. (*P. 25*)

The home country is not, of course, neglected, but is considered in its world setting. (*P. 26*)

ʰ ʰ ʰ a Current Affairs course in the U.S.A. for 17 or 18-year old pupils illustrates the kind of questions which need to be considered geographically and historically:

(1) The wise use and development of the world's system of communication and transportation.

(2) The factors, geographic, political, economic and social which encourage a United Nations world rather than a world of many isolated units or a world of two camps.

(3) The development of ways and means of assisting underdeveloped areas. (*P. 27*)

[The seminar] therefore, considered it most important that where possible teachers should link their geography lessons or their social studies course with reference to the work of the United Nations. (*P. 27*)

The research technique recommended here implies a purpose and a plan prearranged by the teacher. If geography is to be taught for international understanding or for any other specific purpose the teacher should have in mind a complete plan progressively worked out. (*P. 30*)

* * * it is particularly regrettable when children generalize about other peoples and other nations. ʰ ʰ ʰ Not only should geography teaching discourage such statements, which children may pick up from their parents or the newspapers, but it should also train the pupils to accept no generalization which is not based on adequate knowledge. (*P. 35*)

If he [the teacher] is conscious of the educational value of geography ʰ ʰ ʰ He will ʰ ʰ ʰ underline the common effort of people all over the world to satisfy their primary needs. In this way he will help to arouse the children's sympathy and a genuine desire to understand other people's problems. ʰ ʰ ʰ In the back of his mind would be the desire to see that his pupils had some emotional appreciation [which] also could be unobtrusively introduced at suitable stages in the lesson. (*Pp. 36-7*)

In addition the geography teacher should never allow to go unchallenged statements from his pupils which reveal a supercilious feeling of national superiority. * * * Where some undeniable element of superiority exists in one country over another, it can be shown in discussion that this ought to be a source of responsibility towards other poorer countries, and not, as so often happens, a source of conflict. (P. 37)

Pages 39 to 72 inclusive are given over to suggested exercises for pupils. The result of one such exercise was that

The children soon discovered the name and shape of their school building. (P. 40)

This exercise was for children 12 years of age!

Appendix B of the volume complains that teachers of geography have not been trained in teaching at all and even their knowledge of the subject itself is very sketchy. This applies particularly to primary school teachers. In these circumstances, it is not surprising that most of them do not have a broad world outlook and do not realize that geography has an important contribution to make to the development of good national and world citizenship. * * * secondary school teachers are good geographers but tend to be poor teachers. (P. 73)

Five conclusions are listed, and the first of them is this:

Students and teachers in service need to understand why geography teaching should have an international purpose and to be shown how all school subjects and the social life of the school can affect the attitudes of their pupils towards other peoples and towards the need for world co-operation. (P. 74)

The indoctrination is clear. The face of the globe is to be remodelled —by Unesco's plastic surgeons.

Volume X has a 9-page bibliography. Among the publishers and titles listed are the following:

Publisher	Volumes listed
American Association for the United Nations	1
American Council on Education	2
Federal Security Agency, U.S. Office of Education	4
National Education Association	3
National Council for the Social Studies, NEA	3
Progressive Education Association	1

"But if ye have bitter envying and strife in your hearts, glory not, and lie not against the truth."

James III, 14.

PART III
THE FLOOD

The International
Movement

28. IN THE CLASSROOM WITH CHILDREN UNDER THIRTEEN YEARS OF AGE

Towards World Understanding. Vol. V. Unesco. Paris. 1949.
SECTION 2: THE CRUX OF THE PROBLEM

The world-minded child is to be brought into being by a group called "we." In both world-child and adult "we" will develop great "objectivity", and to this "objectivity" the Unesco seminar now refers. By its function in the global program, the "objectivity" is clearly defined.

It is ethereal detachment from things earthly.

Here, for instance, is how it works:

Limited government—by direction and consent of the sovereign governed —was first established by the founders of the American Republic. Hence, it can not be studied with objectivity. Unlimited government—where "Verbal victory does not guarantee victory in fact"—can be studied with objectivity.

To teach the former might cause "jingoism and nationalism". To teach the latter will create "world understanding". Thus your child, first "immunized" against early evil influences of the family (yourselves), then

immunized against an exaggerated sense of the importance and beauty of his own country * * * will gradually lose those habits of prejudice and contempt which are an impediment to world-mindedness.

He will proceed

in a progression of loyalties which will enable him later to reach the climax of membership in the world community.

That is "objectivity".

It is to be introduced into our Nation's schools.

[124]

Missing . . . the greatest drama in the history of Man

Nowhere is even mentioned the stupendous human drama which is mankind's struggle from serfdom unto Freedom. No textual footlight illumines that stage upon which the Egyptian, Ptahhotep, took rush in hand to write immortal hieroglyphs on ancient *papyri;* nor yet that other stage, far more recent, whereon a man called Thomas Paine inspired men's souls with words writ upon a drum—a drum which, next day, would be rolled for those who died that that for which he wrote might live, and be attained.

Nowhere is there the slightest inkling that that struggle of sixty recorded centuries is itself the most moving and beautiful story in the evolution of Man.

Nor is the splendor of its human culmination, in the Constitution of the American Republic, referred to even with slight or distant bow. Yet that Constitution chartered Man's self-government of Man.

In theory, and in practical essence, it is the beacon of that spiritual Liberty which all men seek, and without which there is but existence, not life.

Individual, it is the antithesis of the collective; personal, it is the antithesis of The State; spiritual, it is the antithesis of the global mechanism now proposed.

Its Charter, and its Trusteeship—by right of inheritance yours and mine— was American in its physical setting even as it is American in its unique spiritual being. For here was achieved Man's sovereignty upon this earth, in clear acknowledgment of and reverence for, Him from Whom came his own guidance and inspiration.

All this is supremely clear in the Constitution of these United States.

It is the oldest written Constitution in the world.

In its stead is this

In the new "integral" school, our children will not learn this thing because it will not be stressed. Our children are to be taught only the internationalists' opaque interpretation, which is a

comparison * * * between the written constitution of the nation and the Charter of the United Nations. (*Vol. I; p. 8*)

This is in line with the rise (since Freud) of a questionable art, that of exaggerated self-condemnation. Not particularly noticeable abroad, the art has flourished in many American circles. It has been made fashionable for us to ignore—even to decry—all objective appreciation of the Republic's true historic rôle in the winning of Freedom upon this earth.

Nowhere is the effect more tragic than in the classroom teaching of our children.

Despite the "objectivity" urged by Unesco seminars, the fact remains that in one part of the world, and only in one part, did Man achieve his sovereign Right to freely live; where he made the police-force of government his servant and not his master; and where he wrote into the Charter of his Nation clauses which were to forever ordain that the relationship of himself to his state would not be reversed.

The Unesco seminars imply that other men, from other climes, can make all of us "citizens of the world" before they have created primary citizenship within their own fair lands.

Their postulate is put so glibly that it defies belief. Yet it is there.

An "objectivity" most uncanny

The very "objectivity" of which these people speak is not overwhelming in the several texts. Yet the globalists are to educate "objectivity" in our children. This requires of their teachers

a knowledge of the laws of child psychology.

Now, if there are "laws" of child psychology, the sixth volume of the series is going to reveal to parents what, if anything at all, the experimenters know about them.

Careful, indeed, are the seminarists to point out that children

cannot be given too many exercises of the sort calculated to put them on their guard against all forms of auto-suggestion and hetero-suggestion.

Only the auto-suggestion and the hetero-suggestion of progressive internationalism are to be absorbed.

The youngsters are to have a lot of fun. There are to be jamborees, trips, visits and all manner of juvenile junkets. These are to be paid for later (with interest and handling charges) out of their incomes as eventual grown-ups.

This fact is not announced.

But the program is to achieve "our aim of world understanding". It is to

eliminate * * * the nationalist ideology which has poisoned international relations since the beginning of the nineteenth century.

Wars just never occurred before the beginning of the nineteenth century!

There is to be an "international auxiliary language" to facilitate correspondence between children of various countries. What happens to this juvenile shorthand as your child grows up, is not divulged.

Several scientists are named in connection with "examples" of international cooperation. No Americans are among them. The report says that

the name of Einstein can be reserved for later.

A "Museum of human co-operation" is suggested—under the auspices, of course, of Unesco. The seminar feels that

it would be desirable to publish a book describing the museum and illustrating the exhibits, so that teachers in the remotest places could to some extent give pupils the benefit of its work.

Into how many of the 2,796 languages of the world this "book" should be translated is left to future budgets.

Disregard for fact seems almost uncanny. The seminar says:

It is to be hoped that soon the evolution of international politics will again permit the teacher to tell his pupils that war has been outlawed, as it was during those moving years of the League of Nations.

Here is "objectivity" with a vengeance!

War "again" outlawed! And as it was during those "moving years" of the League of Nations!! The number of years not being specified, a reviewer may use reasonable judgment. Let us take the first five years of the League's existence, 1920-1924. Here are the wars, big and small, which comprise the record of those five years:

1918-1920 Campaigns against Soviet Russia. Russo-Polish war.	1921 Panamanian-Costa Rican border dispute. Peruvian-Chilean war. Mutiny of sailors of Kronstadt.
1918-1921 Civil war in the Soviet Union; war in White Russia and struggle for the Ukraine; war in White Russia and the Baltics; campaigns of Deniken and Wrangel in the Caucasus and Southern Russia; war in Siberia and Eastern Asia.	Outbreaks in Egypt. Arab-Jewish riots in Palestine. 1921-1930 Allied occupation of Düsseldorf, Duisberg, and Ruhr. 1922 Chauri Chaura insurrection in India. Attempted rising of Macedonians.
1919-1920 Russo-Persian war. Polish-Czech Teschen conflict. Latvia invaded by Russians. Finnish-Russian War. French-Arab fighting.	Upper Silesian rebellion. 1922-1924 Kurd insurrection in Iraq. 1923 Abortive communist insurrection in Bulgaria. Insurrection in Memel.
1919-1921 Irish revolution.	Coup in Lithuania. Rebellion in Tripoli.
1919-1922 Graeco-Turkish wars. Polish-Lithuanian dispute over Vilna. Riff war in Spain. Morocco revolt against Spain.	Italo-Greek Corfu incident. Hitler's beer hall Putsch in Munich. Civil war in southern Ireland.
1919-1924 Italo-Yugoslavian Fiume trouble.	1923-1924 Rebellion in Mexico. Franco-Belgian invasion of the Ruhr.
1920 Nejd-Asir war. Revolution in Mexico. Monarchical Putsch in Berlin, Spartacist rising in Ruhr. Arab insurrection against British in Iraq. Russo-Japanese war.	1923-1925 Military coup in Spain. 1924 Communist rising in Estonia. Revolution in Albania. Revolts in Brazil. 1924-1925 Nejd-Hejaz war. Military revolts in Ecuador.
1920-1926 Civil war in China.	1924-1927 Riff rising in Morocco.

Source: Legislative Reference, Library of Congress, Washington, D. C.

This was war "outlawed" during those "moving years" of the League of Nations.

And the surrealist picture unfolds to the tune of an "International anthem", now proposed.[1]

---

[1] In Indiana, schoolchildren have been singing this "anthem". *Cf. Appendix; p. 169.*

How your children are "infected" at home

The seminar admits, even as did the American Education Fellowship, that there are obstacles to the program. Among them are "family pressures". The seminarists regret that many parents prefer to see their sons and daughters associate with

only a small number of people "of their own sort".

The seminar states:

Under such conditions world-mindedness is indeed not given much opportunity to develop. When the only child or the two children thus brought up enter school they are ill-prepared to become members of the group formed by the class.

This is directly traceable to

the narrow family spirit of the parents.

So, when the family, and its training, conflicts with the new "society", and its purpose, the course is simple: Remove the influence of the family.

The report is nothing if not specific. You—or friends of yours—have heard that something of the sort was planned. You—or friends of yours—could not believe it. It *is* unbelievable—yet here is the substantiation.

The seminarists proceed:

The family may, in fact, * * * cultivate attitudes running counter to the development of international understanding * * *

This must be tolerated no longer for, if tolerated,

the way to world-mindedness is obstructed. Even a rapid survey in kindergarten and elementary schools is enough to show that in every country such summary opinions are frequently all the children hear at home about other nations and civilizations.

And the seminar concludes:

For the moment, it is sufficient to note that it is most frequently in the family that the children are infected with nationalism by hearing what is national extolled and what is foreign disparaged.

I heard no such thing as I grew up—did you? But I did hear some good things about my own Country—in what seem to me to have been happier days, before it was made unfashionable to speak or hear such things.

Inasmuch as

so many men and women [are] incapable of appreciating the worth of anyone not belonging to their class, confession, political party or country

a program must be developed by others more responsible:

The school can do little if parents infect the child with that sclerosis of the mind

which makes such attitudes possible.

The "infection"—the mental sclerosis—comes from yourselves. This form of cerebral *rigor mortis* is apparently hereditary.

Thus, the global diagnosticians.

[128]

Parents are to "admit the error of their own accord"

Only during the last years of school is it possible to discuss some of the problems that will bring home to boys and girls the decisive influence for good or evil that parents can exert on their children. When dealing with children below the age of 13 the educator will acquit himself most effectively of his duty in this respect by always setting the children an example of behaviour inspired by wisdom and love.

The internationalist educator is to replace father, mother and home.

Teachers will meet with parents, and it will emerge that troubles

often will have been caused by an educational error committed by the latter.

This much achieved, there remains one further step:

The only road to success lies in getting the parents to admit the error of their own accord.

You will confess to your mental sclerosis. FK off

The "poisoned air" within your home

With this admission, the global educators will

be able to rely on the vigilance and discrimination of the parents in allowing their children access to only such books, films and radio programmes as are best fitted to awaken taste and judgment, a sense of morality, social awareness and world-mindedness.

Thus, in sum, is our youth to be "conditioned for liberty"—with your collaboration.

And how about parents—how about you? Why, you are to be "conditioned" as well. At the happy parties which the mentors convene, mothers and fathers are

brought by talks with the teacher to admit, in theory, that their narrow family spirit * * * threatens the integration of their child in the school.

When I was growing up, my fellow-students took care of that.

Thus only in its attention to applied detail does the program of the internationalists differ from that in Dr. Counts' *Call to the Teachers of the Nation*:

* * * any program of education designed for the coming generation, if it is to be successful, must march hand in hand and be closely coordinated with a program of adult and parent education.[2]

The seminar had said, "We shall come to nationalism later on." This it now does. It states that

education in world-mindedness can produce only rather precarious results

so long as a situation is permitted to endure where

the child breathes the poisoned air of nationalism * * *

Isaac Kandel's phrase in the *NEA Journal* was

The poison of aggressive nationalism, injected into children's minds * * *

Theodore Brameld's phrase was "diseased nationalisms".[4]

---

[2] *Cf.* page 40.　　　　[3] *Cf.* page 65.　　　　[4] *Cf.* page 55.

And whence this "poisoned air"?

it is frequently the family that infects the child with extreme nationalism.

Your home, now so stultified, will be air-conditioned. An all-wise cabal will purify its "poisoned air"—by means of global fission.

The mechanism is most unique. It is to be operated exclusively by the world cabal.

One might call this mechanism the cerebral cyclotron.

The solvent

The plan includes methods to combat "jingoism". This will end "nationalist wars."

A scholar might remark that nationalism itself is a phenomenon only of the past hundred and fifty years—a point upon which this seminar agrees.

Like the progressive educators, the seminar urges wide professional cooperation. And, precisely as did the AEF, it states:

These organizations already exist within most countries, and on the international level there are such bodies as the International Federation of Teachers' Associations and the International Federation of Secondary Teachers. These organizations should take the offensive.

Teachers should

besiege the authorities with material demands in the manner of a trade union.

This also parallels the program of the AEF.

The seminar finds that, of the obstacles to "Education for world-mindedness",

The principal one certainly is nationalism.

By what alchemy an American internationalism is to absorb the na-tionalisms of Europe, and the inevitably *rising* nationalisms of the Far East is obscure. And it becomes more obscure with each passing year.

The seminarists suggest that

Education for world-mindedness ⚬ ⚬ ⚬ is a political problem even more than an educational one.

This we may grant, if we grant it solely in immediate terms. Give "education"—as planned by the movement—another school generation o two, and the problem is solved.

The proposed education is the solvent.

To "usher in the revolution"

Meanwhile,

the present position of teachers does not, in general, permit them to intervene in th field of politics with the requisite authority.

The situation needs change, and the internationalists will change i

The new teacher can then enter the field of politics "with the requisite authority".

World-minded educators, trained for the job, thus will

deliberately reach for power and then make the most of their conquest.

They will make the world over, unto their own image and likeness.

And there will be drafted at least two charters. The seminar describes them:

a Children's Charter should secure for all children such education as is summarized in this report, which alone can create the atmosphere in which development of world-mindedness is conceivable; [and]

a Teachers' Charter should secure for all members of the teaching profession the liberty to provide such an education by the means they decide upon, as well as the right of access to commissions and councils responsible for the organization of public education.

Young men and women are to have nothing to say about their education. They are to receive "such education as is summarized in this report". Parents are to have nothing to say about it. They will have been brought

by talks with the teacher to admit, in theory, that their narrow family spirit * * * threatens the integration of their child in the school.

The global teachers, selected and trained, are to enjoy complete "academic freedom", and are to proceed with the program

by the means they decide upon.

This is the plan for our schools.

These are the means

which alone can create the atmosphere in which development of world-mindedness is conceivable * * *

Only

a school reorganized to this end and equipped with everything that is indispensable to its effort * * *

can crown the program with success.

The seminar concludes:

the activity of the school cannot bring about the desired result unless, repudiating every form of nationalism,

all nations amalgamate into one great glistening whole.

The program

may usher in the revolution (the expression is not too strong) * * *

This phrase is not my own. It is taken from page 57, three pages before the end of the instant report.

Employed in the text in a subsidiary sense, it is clearly applicable to the whole.

How many Americans will quietly acquiesce?

[131]

"But if any provide not for his own, and specially for those of his own house, he hath denied the faith, and is worse than an infidel."

1 Timothy, V, 8.

PART III
THE FLOOD

The International
Movement

29. THE INFLUENCE OF THE HOME AND COMMUNITY
ON CHILDREN UNDER THIRTEEN YEARS OF AGE

Towards World Understanding. Volume VI. Unesco. Paris. 1949.

SECTION 1: THE STUDY OF CULTURAL CONTINUITIES

Volume VI is the result of another seminar held at Poděbrady, Czechoslovakia. Again the text

is in no way an official expression of the views of Unesco.

Nonetheless, Unesco sponsored the seminar, as it sponsored the others. Unesco published the conclusions, as it did the others. And the Introduction states:

Unesco is proud to have this opportunity of publishing a statement by a great American anthropologist, who during her life made an outstanding contribution to the development of understanding among peoples.

This statement which Unesco is proud to publish takes up the first nine pages of the forty-four comprising the report. Its author is Dr. Ruth Benedict, professor of anthropology at Teachers College, Columbia University, New York.

Synthetic "popular" lines

During Dr. Benedict's professorial lifetime, her views met with no spontaneous approval on the part of all who delved into them. Some of the delvers did not remain silent. Strange things happened to them.

Yet, by the very magnitude of its impact, the strangeness has become the norm.

This is what happens; and here is how it works:

1) A general "line" is first established, and it is this line which must be followed if life is to proceed on the even tenor of its ways;

2) Individuals, organizations, speakers, books, etc., are selected for admittance to the closed circle which has established the particular line;

3) All who question the theory, the line or the course determined, are given the silent treatment, or are smeared. In academic circles, they are not "accredited". Elsewhere they are not "accepted". In other words, they are beyond the pale. If, nonetheless, someone begins to make himself heard and felt, he is classed as "controversial";

4) Now the line is "popular", and the internationalists go merrily on their way.

To deviate from that line is to sin. As sinful people and sinful views are to be shunned, those who voice objection to the line are classed as sinners, and are shunned.

These things happen to thinkers outside the closed cabal, however sound and documented be their thinking. These things happened to delvers who were less than pleased by Dr. Benedict's views.

You may think whatever you like—but you are ostracized if you say it out loud.

This is the essence of mind-control. Its result is called "unity".

That this "unity" is synthetic matters little.

Documentation does not matter at all.

The intellectual baby-food

For long professional years Dr. Benedict's activities, utterances and writings followed requirement *1*. Her close associations entitle her to recognition as a working member of the cabal, or caste, fulfilling requirement *2*. All who took reasoned exception to her work were put in class *3* by the hierarchy effectively in control.

And so Dr. Benedict's efforts were made to fall under item *4*.*

The result, though peculiar, has long been fashionable in the best circles. That which is "controversial"—if it follow requirement *1*—is monopolized by the ruling caste. The members of this caste are "untouchables". They are Brahmins. Their views are "accepted", and without ques-

---

* Again the singular leanings of key personnel is suggested by sworn testimony:

"A very important picture listed here [by the Young Progressives of America, December 27, 1948] is *Brotherhood of Man*. This was produced by the United Auto Workers, CIO, and is a color cartoon based on the pamphlet *Races of Mankind* by Dr. Ruth Benedict and Dr. Gene Weltfish. She is a leader of the Congress of American Women, and has sent greetings to Soviet women on the anniversary of the Russian Revolution." (*Hearings.* Senate Committee on the Judiciary, April 1951-March 1952; p. 53. COMMUNIST TACTICS IN CONTROLLING YOUTH ORGANIZATIONS)

tion. Professors, college presidents and ministers of the Gospel find themselves—wittingly and unwittingly—giving voice to detail or to generality of the "accepted" line, victims of thought-control.

The "unity" then spreads to parents, clubs, associations and civic leaders. It becomes "enthusiastically adopted" everywhere.

This mental baby-food is typical of the scholastic diet prescribed for millions of young Americans, from the grade school through the university.

The result is an alarming decrease of independent thought.

Tyranny, suavely applied

Now, a second treatment exists which is the precise opposite of the first. Whereas the first treatment is applied to things, the second is applied to human beings. It is applied to those who would objectively examine what has been made "popular", and how it was so made.

They are removed.

The procedure is especially effective in silencing independent historians and revisionist writers. They are decreed "controversial". And, as they must be suppressed, they are suppressed. This is what happened to Charles Austin Beard.

If they are in academic circles, one of two things happens to them:

1) Professorships, or "Chairs", become distant and remote; or

2) They are given an opportunity to climb on the foundation gravy-train by "changing" their views. Then, as happened in the cases of William L. Langer and Carlton J. H. Hayes, their "new" views are published and widely praised.

Normal public fora—columns, press notices, the lecture hall, radio, old line publishers—are closed to a potentially effective critic. He becomes the victim of organized blackball.

What is the result, predetermined as it is?

Controversy—on vital issues—is made impossible. Take just one example: Foreign policy. When has a clear, nationwide debate on foreign policy taken place? Not once in thirty years.

The reason is precise, though odd in one respect. The court historians, abundantly subsidized, are entrenched behind a line of verbal sharpshooters located in the press, the radio, the screen and the pressure brigades. Among the last-named, that with the most diverse personnel is the cult of interventionism.

The essential peculiarity within this pressure group lies in the purport of internationalism itself. For years—however baleful its results—the theory of internationalism was sincere devotion to peace. This has changed, and the change is painfully slow in being recognized.

[134]

The transition from the former internationalism of peace to the present one of war may be roughly dated from the Kellogg Pact to "outlaw" war, with the accompanying hoax which pretends that war is "aggressive"—or that it is not. Henceforth, every local war carried within itself the fatal germ of global conflict. Gone is the older, peaceful philosophy; present is that of the "saviour with the sword".

This change in the character of internationalism should be recognized. It is the nationalists who now oppose intervention by military force.

This is a fundamental thing, and the internationalists have not permitted it to be discussed. The reason is suspect, for the cultists can not defend their new internationalism against it—the suspicion being that many an interventionist knows it.

Nor is the alternative posed by a world "grown small" that of global war or global peace, however the latter be "maintained". The clear challenge is to *localize* conflicts which are inevitable. Segments of the world are adjusting themselves to evolutionary change. This does not call forth an international fire brigade running hither and yon, putting out blazes with hook and ladder, and an omnipresent global pump.

Canute with a light blue banner is nonetheless Canute. And the tides of the affairs of men are as plainly inexorable as were those which the classic example could not stay.

The rise of nationalisms from Morocco to China illustrates the point. Rising, they are. Inevitable, they are. Successful, they will be; indeed, successful of inherent right. And local wars are going to occur as these nationalisms rise. But intervention can—and, if not stopped, will—make of these local wars the global conflict which humanity could avoid.

Meddling in family quarrels—as infant states, prematurely or not, demand the right of equal status with foster parents—serves but to widen quarrels, costs and deaths.

While this fact of internationalism is painfully seeking recognition, whatever might upset the calculated unanimity with which "the people" joyously "accept" the interventionist program sees little light of day. Easy slogans are employed, such as these: "National unity will be impaired"; "national defense will be endangered"; it is wrong in "times of emergency".

The result is that the people no longer control the policies of their own government, at home or abroad.

In other words, the American's own Government—which he still can determine—is slowly becoming the Charlie McCarthy of a global ventriloquist.

Uncontrollable by him, he is by it controlled.

Hence "unity"—in place of the discussion of constructive alternatives.

[135]

Mussolini did it. Hitler did it. Stalin did it.

What it is is tyranny. The American version has simply been more suavely applied.*

There shall be no "controversy" . . . it is sin

No incidence of this suave tyranny is more poignant than the "uncoerced persuasion" of our youth.

The purpose is being described as the advent of a dovelike Millennium. And there is intended to be no controversy about it.

This concept, with its silence, smear and pressure brigades, has been an unfortunate addition to the national scene. It has completely reversed the American procedure: Open, frank discussion of public affairs. And it is a technique of the collectivist machine. This technique, new within living memory, is the opposite of that now applied to an "unmentionable" personal disease. This latter is now subjected to early diagnosis and often

---

* This is illustrated by three moves, each interlocking with the other. The first one failed; the second is in operation; the third includes mechanisms in operation and others being promoted.

The first move began in 1946 during the years when millions of people were hoping for a new Millennium. State Legislatures were presented with resolutions which called for a Convention to propose an amendment to the Constitution in order that the United States might become a party to "world government". The resolution, in its various forms, was known as the "Humber" resolution, from one of its chief backers and advocates who, incidentally, had been a Rhodes scholar. Twenty-three Legislatures passed such resolutions—with a notable absence of discussion or publicity. The Convention might well have become mandatory had it not been for the tireless work of citizens who made it their business to seriously investigate the matter and then to document results. Twenty Legislatures consequently rescinded. This was the move that failed.

The second move is causing Congress to pass "laws" to accord with the "spirit, undertakings and commitments" of the UN Charter. This clearly subordinates the American Constitution not only to that Charter but to its *implications*—with no man knows what limit. This is being accomplished without the sovereign consent of those whose Constitution it is.

This second move also embraces a network of alliances—military, social and economic. The North Atlantic Treaty Organization is one of these. Another, SEATO, embraces Southeast Asia. NATO not only is a pact for war, its terms reveal further steps to "world government". Already, under its terms, the men and women of our Armed Forces—*and* their "civilian component"—can be accused by foreigners and tried in foreign courts. They have no recourse.

The third move includes the Genocide Convention, Universal Declaration of Human Rights, and International Trade Organization. The ultimate consequence, or intent, is to be world collectivism. Under the Genocide Convention—if adopted—a citizen of Boston or Tulsa could be haled before a tribunal in Kiev, tried for an "offense" committed in Seattle, convicted, and sentenced to penal servitude in Ceylon. No Right—formerly his by his own Constitution and Bill of Rights—could be invoked.

These facts—which you can readily substantiate by reading the actual "agreements"—are denied by advocates of the global movement, precisely as others deny the collectivist movement in the schools.

Manpower to enforce the program is to be supplied by these United States, under the proposed UMT.

This side of the picture is notably absent in the agenda for our Nation's schools.

[136]

cure, thanks to widespread understanding of the symptoms. The ills of the world are spreading, as the perfected technique of silence is applied.

Intellectually, the new internationalism has been turning back the clock.

The castle-cabal

What does the Unesco seminar say about these things?

Dr. Benedict propounds:

> Those who oppose international co-operation * * * blame the chaos of the world on the existence of differences between one nation and another; every difference is fresh evidence that other nations are evil and have evil intentions. Over and over again they stress that other nations must accept the virtues and practices with which they are familiar in their own culture before it is possible to make a peaceful world.

This statement does not stand up on examination. It was the internationalists who urged that we join the "freedom-loving allies" in their crusade(s). It was not the "isolationists", nor is it the "isolationists", who assert that

> other nations are evil and have evil intentions * * * that other nations must accept the virtues and practices with which they are familiar * * *

Quite the contrary. The "isolationist" has consistently said: Let other nations politically alone.

It is the interventionist who demands the enforcement of FEPC, local and worldwide.

But to gently suggest that internationalists, and their policy of intervention—on the documentable record—have themselves created the global beast-of-the-moment, is "controversial". And further, to gently suggest error in the mechanistic theory behind their global authorities—whether over dollars, casualties, or over the defenseless children attending your local school—is even more than controversial; it is becoming global lèse-majesté.

Against such affront, the castle-cabal turns all the fury of its silence, its invective or its smear.

A cosmic cradle . . . within, your cosmic child

Dr. Benedict's opening phrase is followed by her sequitur:

> This is an attitude which is centuries old. It has not made for world peace.

Again the statement crumbles upon examination. Did the Delian League of ancient Hellas bring peace? No. Did the Holy Alliance of 1815 bring peace? No. Did the Holy Alliance of 1919—masquerading as the League of Nations—bring peace? Again, no. Does the Holy Alliance presently masquerading as the United Nations, bring peace? The "holy" side may have a working majority in the global mechanism—bought and paid for, to be sure—but the veto is in the hands, always, of

[137]

other nations [which] are evil and have evil intentions.*

Dr. Benedict overlooks this. She says:

Now Unesco proposes that social scientists should take the lead in promoting a new attitude, and should study national differences even in such fundamental things as the way we bring up our children.

A cosmic cradle is to be created. In it will repose your cosmic child.

High priesthood of "understanding"

"Progressive education" is to be installed worldwide. And the immeasurable boons of the "social studies" are to be brought to all mankind.

These boons are not to be gradually achieved; they are to be enforced.

People must respect the cultures of others, the lady-consultant says. I thought they did, but apparently Americans do not; at least, that is the idea conveyed to a reader of the Benedict text. Nor is it possible longer to tolerate such a thing. Many attitudes must be rendered obsolete. For example,

An idea which is common in the United States may be used as an illustration of this fact: Americans have, because of their experience within their own country, an unshakable conviction that people, whatever their original nationality, can and will adopt American virtues and practices if these are made clear to them.

Dr. Benedict was referring to immigration. And a reader might reasonably observe that had she voiced such thoughts at an Immigration hearing before the Senate Committee on the Judiciary she would have brought upon herself all the charges of "bigotry" which the internationalists and pressure brigades—sole possessors of unbigoted views—could muster.

But, she adds,

As international policy, however, this American attitude is not merely inadequate, it is destructive.

Here she hits a very large nail resoundingly on its head. This is precisely the policy of the internationalists, clearly to be seen. As millions of Americans do see it, "social scientists" are to

take the lead in promoting a new attitude

and the indoctrination will enable Americans to "learn to understand" all other countries, cultures, people and aims.

America is to aid all "freedom-loving peoples" in the preservation of their "freedom"—herself gradually becoming collectivist in the process. Conversely, America is to deny the aspirations of the yellow, brown and

---

* The revealing function of the veto has not been widely remarked. It is not a question of procedure at all. It is a question of force.

Modification of the veto's use does not even imply that an altered mechanism—such as was adroitly discovered in the General Assembly—will make the machine to function. What the veto reveals is this: It demonstrates that in the United Nations there is no such thing as "international cooperation".

Only force remains—compulsion, or war.

[138]

black peoples—from Kamchatka to Ceylon—who, for weal or woe, are demanding the right to rule themselves.

This is to deny to others the right to their own futures, a right which has been a cherished American heritage since the signing of the Declaration of Independence.

That, in the process, America incur the colossal resentment of those millions who are yellow, brown or black, does not matter—internationalism is "popular"; it must go on.

The price

Thus is disclosed a gigantic pattern of consequences. This pattern is encroaching upon liberties embodied in the Constitution; it is preparing the Nation for the *Diktat* of a world collectivist state; and it is bringing upon Americans an onus unforgiveable—the resentment which colonials and exploitees have been nursing for centuries against *other* rulers across the seas.

Under the guise of "international cooperation", "collective security" and of "peace", the call is for greater and greater armed force. Meanwhile, the taxpayers' money is appropriated to keep in office political authorities abroad—some of them socialist, some Marxist, all collectivist to a degree.

> Therefore by their fruits ye shall know them
>
> *Matthew VII, 16, 20.*

On one side of the record is inflation-prosperity. On the other side are nearly five hundred thousand American military graves since December 7, 1941. And, while fathers and mothers *both* work to meet the costs of bare necessities, the minority revolutionaries reach out to take from them their young.

At no time, in the coming educational Millennium, do the teachers offer such analyses for acceptance or rejection by the students themselves.

Psychiatry . . . an "instrument to be used"

In the words of Dr. Benedict—stratospheric as are their flights—the Unesco publication now leads the reader into the real burden of Volume VI. This is what she says:

> The organization of emotions and attitudes in different countries is begun in the way the baby's physical needs are met. How and when and what and by whom the baby is fed; how he is taught to control elimination; how his motor development is restrained or encouraged; what inducements and threats are used to get him to sleep; whether or not there are taboos against touching his genitals; what habits of modesty are insisted on; and by what means, and how early the treatment of the boy baby differs from that of the girl—all these vary greatly in different European countries.

Clearly, these must be investigated.

Dr. Benedict propounds:

> Genetic study of different cultures is precisely this study of how the members of

each generation are conditioned "to become responsible participants" in the way of life which is traditional in the community into which they are born. The technical development of such study is possible today because of knowledge that has been acquired in several related sciences.

These "sciences"—to use the lady's word—include

(a) the study of the physical maturation of the child. * * *

(b) studies of human physiology. * * *

(c) medical studies in the field of psychosomatics. * * *

(d) psychiatry. * * *

Dr. Benedict states:

Modern psychiatry has revealed many of the fundamental dynamics of personality. It has been used for therapy, but its use in genetic cultural study is necessarily different; in such a study it becomes, not therapy, but an instrument to be used to promote understanding of cultural dynamics.

Out of this welter of words a meaning gradually appears. Here is no gentle suasion upon the relaxed and couch-borne patient, to reveal his inner soul. That is therapy. And more than therapy is required.

Modern psychiatry becomes an "instrument to be used".

To be used by whom—and for what? To be used by the great *élite*—"to promote understanding of cultural dynamics".

It develops that "cultural dynamics" begins early in life, and so modern psychiatry is to be brought into play. Its operators are to be those of infinite wisdom who understand "cultural dynamics". The end, asserted by the various seminars and their sponsor, Unesco, is "world understanding".

Upon whom is this "instrument" to be used? Upon the babe—laughing, squealing; bouncing, anaemic; tall, short; fat or thin.

The baby is yours.

What now happens becomes clear in—

VOL. VI, SECTION 2: AN OUTLINE FOR RESEARCH ON CHILD TRAINING IN DIFFERENT CULTURES

The Benedict statement is followed by another seminar report. It, of course, is "in no way an official expression of the views of Unesco." Unesco says so.

Yet Unesco sponsored the seminar, and Unesco published the report. And, as it is clear that it will be Unesco, or similar agency of internationalism, which will press the program into America's homes and schools, upon Unesco and its affiliates must be taken such action as may be determined by citizens of the Republic.

The "progression of loyalties"

No apology can be offered for lack of reticence in bringing you verbatim quotations from the text. It still may be your feeling, as you tiptoe in to regard your sleeping child, that he is your "Pride and Joy"—and not to be experimented upon by those who bore him not.

The source and purpose of the report are identified in the opening words:

The following memorandum was prepared at Columbia University as part of a project of research in contemporary cultures. * * * It lists a number of topics to be investigated and proposes various techniques which may be used in order to obtain the required information.

Upon the occupant of the cradle the castle-cabal now converge—to research and to experiment on a global scale.

It will be recalled with what frankness one seminar admitted that

we educators do not commonly know as much of the facts of world affairs as we should * * * [*Vol. IV; p. 5*]

Nevertheless, here is a plan to organize "child training". So the seminarists propose a global search for information on which to organize.

Mere clinical records are not for them. They will go to the source. From millions of children is to be built a compendium of results. These results will enable the global investigators—"scientists"—to organize child training.

Was it not "training" that another seminar termed the procedure of the Nazi and other totalitarian régimes? It was.[1]

Obviously there are good totalitarianisms and bad totalitarianisms. The difference is one: Who runs the show?

We need only to look carefully at the objective in whose name control is exercised.[2]

It all depends on who does the regimenting and the purposes the process is intended to serve.[3]

The real issue is * * * what forces are to do the planning, by what means are controls to be exercised, and for what purposes.[4]

That is just the point.

Your child is to be taken at infancy and brought up according to the dictates of "social scientists", now global in their sphere. When your child enters school, he is to study textbooks purged of some things and embellished with others—and the method is called "uncoerced persuasion". He will attend an "integral" school, to be thence graduated in a mold which has "conditioned him for liberty".

In the process, your child will have been freed of those "injurious influences" which he "has first gained, however dimly, in the home"; he

---

[1] Vol. II, p. 21. *Cf.* page 89.

[2] Professor Norman Woelfel, *Progressive Education*, May 1946; p. 266. *Cf.* page 60.

[3] *The Social Frontier*, June 1935; pp. 5-6. EDITORIAL. *Cf.* page 23.

[4] Professor John L. Childs, *Progressive Education*, February 1950; p. 118. *Cf.* page 58.

will have lost "those habits of prejudice and contempt which are an impediment to world-mindedness"; and he will have gone through "a progression of loyalties which will enable him later to reach the climax of membership in the world community".

This much is clear.

The fields of child-study are outlined

There remains to be seen what is planned for the cradle-occupant; what, by the internationalists, is to be done with him and with his being.

Here are some excerpts from the text:

1. TOPICS FOR INVESTIGATION.

(a) *Attitude toward having children*

What are considered the advantages and disadvantages of having children? What is the preferred size of the family? How is childlessness regarded? Are there devices for overcoming sterility? for limiting the family? Is there any arrangement for illegitimate children? for orphans? How is adoption managed?

(b) *Pre-natal period*

What are supposed to be the typical feelings of pregnant women? What changes in mode of life are introduced during pregnancy in relation to diet, marital intercourse, work, etc.? Are there special taboos or prescriptions for the mother to insure the well-being of the unborn child? Are any precautions to be taken by the father or other members of the family?

(c) *Birth*

Attitude of the mother, father, or others, toward labour pains? Are anaesthetics used? Who is present at birth? Where does it take place? Is the child separated from the mother after birth? What precautions or ceremonies are undertaken to ensure the well-being of the new-born child? Are there different attitudes towards boys and girls?

(d) *Feeding*

1. Nursing: How soon after birth is the baby first fed? Breast or bottle fed? How is the baby held during feeding? Is the baby fed when it cries or at fixed intervals? Do babies sometimes refuse to eat? If so, what is done? When the baby stops feeding is it taken as a sign that he has had enough or are efforts made to get him to take more? What is the mother's attitude toward nursing? Is it one of enjoyment, convenience, or fear that it will spoil her figure? How is the mother who has too little milk regarded? Is marital intercourse restricted during nursing?

2. Weaning: When is it effected? At a fixed age, according to the child's reactions, at the mother's convenience, or in relation to the birth of the next child? Is there any relation to the child's teething or biting? Is weaning sudden or gradual? Does the mother try to disgust the child with the breast? Are children given things to suck, for example, pacifiers (comforters)? If so, before or after weaning? Are children given objects on which to teethe? What is supposed to be the effect of weaning, if any, on the child? How is thumbsucking regarded?

3. Solid Food: Is it introduced before or after weaning? What solids are first offered? How are they given, by spoon, hand, or pre-chewed by the mother? Where is the child fed, with the rest of the family, or alone? Is the child fed when hungry or at regular intervals? Is there supposed to be a danger of the children's refusing to eat or not eating enough? How is this dealt with? What is the attitude towards over-eating?

What foods are considered specially good for children? bad? palatable? unpalatable? Are children rewarded with foods they like for eating those they dislike? Is food used

[142]

as a reward or punishment in other connections, for good or bad behaviour? Is the children's diet the same as or different from adults'?

At what age is the child supposed to feed himself? How long do adults continue at times to feed the child? What standards are there for table manners? When and how are they taught?

(e) *Elimination*
When is toilet training begun? Does mother praise good performance? Is the child scolded or punished for soiling or wetting? How early? Do adults express disgust over the child's dirtiness? How is the child trained; by being put on the pot or taken outside the house? When is toilet training supposed to be completed? Are there differences in bowel and bladder training? Do mothers demand promptness in elimination? Do they examine and criticize quantity and quality of the child's faeces? Up to what age? Is there supposed to be a difference in the ease with which boys and girls are trained? Do mothers worry about constipation, diarrhoea? What preventives or remedies are used? Is there a special toilet language for children? At what age are children taught to carry out elimination privately? Not to speak about it? Do adults refrain from performing eliminatory functions in front of children? How is breaking wind treated? Hiccoughs? Belching?

(f) *Motor development*
Do clothes at any time restrain movements? What reasons are given for clothing which purposely prevents movements, that is, swaddling clothes? What movable or stationary furniture is specially provided for the child? How much is the child carried, how, and by whom? How much free mobility is the child allowed? At what age? What supports are considered important? When does the child learn to crawl? Is he taught, encouraged, discouraged? When does he learn to walk? Is he rewarded for walking early?

What are the spacial limits for the children's motor activities inside the house? How are children warned away from dangers indoors (stoves, fireplaces, etc.) and outside (street crossings, possibility of getting lost, etc.)? Do the mothers show alarm, threaten punishment, or tell stories of frightening beings who will do something terrible to the child if he wanders off?

What are adult expectations about the children's sitting still? When and for how long? What kind of motor play is encouraged?

(g) *Sleep*
What is done if the child does not want to go to sleep? Are there inducements, threats, stories of bogey men, transfers to mother's bed? Does the child sleep in the parents' bedroom? In a room with brothers and sisters? In his own bed or with others?

(h) *Health*
What are considered the chief dangers to the health of the young child? Cold, wetness, dirt, over-eating, over-exertion, scratching self? What main precautions are taken to safeguard health? How is the sick child cared for?

(i) *Physical contacts, masturbation, sex play*
When and by whom is the child kissed, stroked, embraced, sat on lap, tickled, rocked, etc? What variations of such contacts occur according to age and sex? What restrictions are there on physical contacts? Is the child encouraged or required to kiss others?

When the child is bathed, is special attention given to the genitals, or are they specially avoided? Are there special children's words for genitals?

Is masturbation in children recognized as being common or exceptional? Are sex differences supposed to exist in this connection? What are the presumed effects? What deterrents are employed? threats? punishments? hand-tying?

[143]

Do children play sex games, such as "doctor", with each other? How are these regarded?

The alphabetical list goes on up through *t*. The headings range from *Clothing and self-exposure*, to *Sex distinctions, Sibling relations* and *Adolescence*. Under this last the text reads:

° ° ° Are the children treated differently according to sex? How and what do the girls learn about menstruation? from whom? What are the boys' chief sources of sex knowledge? How much emphasis is placed on chastity? What adolescent sex activities are common? Are they known or unknown, sanctioned or unsanctioned by the parents? Is romantic love for a remote object common? Are there confidences about early love? To whom are they given? Are first love objects likely to be of same age, or older, or younger? Are adolescents supposed to go through a period of "storm and stress"? Do they tend to become religious, irreligious? Do they tend to adopt radical ideas? to rebel against authorities? If so, against which authorities, home, school, political, literary? Is adolescence regarded as a happy or unhappy time? Is there a name for it? When is a young man or woman supposed to be an adult?

Means for "handling" your child's "resistance"

The seminar lists four general methods to obtain these data. The four methods are subdivided into more than twenty suggested means.

Ways are outlined for "handling resistance", that is, for "handling" your child's possible recalcitrance to becoming the experimentee of his global mentors. For example, there is imaginative play with dolls. Here, states the report,

the interviewer may suggest: "Let's have the little boy-doll do something naughty; what shall we have him do? And then what does his mother do?" etc.

Your child will be handed a boy-doll. The boy-doll will be made to do something. The something suggested is not "good"; it is "naughty".

One page later:

the interviewer may ask, "Did you ever hear of anything bad a boy did? Could we make something up?"

Not something "good"; something "bad".

While it is observable that the "interviewer" seems to be the one learning—and not the child—another thought persists in tugging away at the reader of the Outline. It is this: Is someone, or are someones, trying deliberately to create delinquency?

Were you to walk into the school while the "interviewer" was in the midst of such questioning, what would you feel like doing?

All data are to be recorded, classified and cross-classified. Eventually they are to assist in making everyone a "world-minded citizen". A global authority will have conditioned us all for "liberty".

Thus a gigantic experimental laboratory is planned. The children of the world—and the young people of these United States—are the involuntary experimentees.

[144]

You—their parents—are to be brought to happy acquiescence by the various programs of "adult education" outlined by the movement.

One phase is the elimination of "abnormalities" within your home. To them another Unesco seminar devotes the next report.

VOL. VI, SECTION 3: ABNORMAL INFLUENCES ON THE PSYCHOLOGY OF THE CHILD

Five individuals comprised the seminar. They came from England, France, India, Luxembourg and Norway. The chairman was Miss Agatha H. Bowley, subject of His Majesty's socialist imperial realm.

The report does not differ intrinsically from the others, for it maintains the theme of the great *élite,* which is this:

The State (meaning themselves) is to replace the family. It is to assume all love, affection and authority, an assumption which will be to the great and everlasting benefit of the child.

There is no escape from the meaning, from the intent, or from the conclusions to be drawn from meaning and intent. One finds that

Early relationships with the parents may be termed unsatisfactory or abnormal if they result in:

(1) over-attachment,

(2) domination,

(3) antagonism,

(4) jealousy (of one parent over the child's love for the other), or,

(5) rejection.

Clearly, The State can rectify these matters. When a child's "psychological needs are not satisfied", a World Authority can provide all things.

Rule of the collectivists: "does it serve our purpose?"

The Global State will at first finance itself by appropriating your earnings under the guise of taxes. It will appropriate your savings by inflation—which is a progressive capital levy on all. It will continue to shatter the value of those savings to "pay" for its crusade—inflation's sole and unique cause.

Thus financed into being, The Global State will substitute its collective love and wisdom for your own.

The State will now "revalue" its currency, and from this point it can permanently finance itself. This it will do by fiat control of money. It will take over every form of wealth—and substitute its collective ownership for your own.

Unless the policy called internationalism is stopped, this is its course. By no other means can the new internationalism perpetuate itself.

And this reversion to feudalism is being called "social reconstruction"—as taught in the Nation's schools.

The human product—your child, mind you—is to eminently satisfy the end in view. What happens to individuality, discipline, character, independence, and other honorable qualities of a free maturity—and what happens to the people and wealth of the Nation—is clear enough. To this there is one precondition:

That you calmly accept the criteria laid down, and which answer the demands of the collectivists. Those demands are one:

does it serve our purpose?

"Progressivism" . . . *on a global scale*

To accept the criteria, however, is to graciously surrender your child to the care of the omniscients—and yourself to The Global Collectivist State.

Your child will then be "conditioned for liberty". You will accompany him on his way.

He will be reared by "social scientists", and they will conduct the grand experiment.

Gradually good community citizenship is developed, and it becomes more possible to cultivate the qualities necessary for world citizenship.

Denied in 1945, begun in 1946, first published in 1948, the program of world government thus reaches into the school and home, to take from you your child.

The satisfaction of the child's basic psychological needs in his early family life is the most certain means of ensuring good personality development and of laying the foundation for world citizenship.

Unquestionably, as the seminarists remark,

Progressive methods * * * are of great value * * *

Thus the program for social-reconstruction-through-the-schools becomes the program of Global Government, itself to rest on force.

The program has been denied, and it is constantly being denied. The NEA, for example, stated in June 1952:

* * * There is no effort in the UNESCO seminars to draft binding conclusions or to prescribe a uniform way of teaching. * * * UNESCO functions as an organization of sovereign nations. It has not advocated world government, nor has the United States National Commission for UNESCO done so:[5]

Such denials can be continued until our children grow up. Then, through a genteel indoctrination called "uncoerced persuasion", there "world government" will be.

This is the program for your child, under the collectivism of the internationalists, however on the surface it may seem benign.

---

[5] *United Nations Information for Teachers* (UNIT), a publication of the United Nations Education Service sponsored by the Committee on International Relations of the NEA. Vol. I, No. 10. June 1, 1952; pp. 2, 3. (Now refer to top of p. 79.)

The first sentence of the final section of Volume VI reads:

The aim of this seminar is to formulate an educational program leading to world-mindedness.

The final sentence, thirteen pages later, states:

At present society is nowhere adequately shaping itself to the requirements of education, and nowhere does it provide all that children need and want.

Few, indeed, will fail to recall "little monsters" who *have* had all they "need and want." Yet this is a minor observation compared to what is derived from the text between these two sentences. Here is found the entire range of socialized education—as it is modeled and fashioned by international *modistes.*

And nowhere does the word *socialism* appear.

To utter the term would be to expose the standardized mannequin underneath.

The mother's "continuously sensitive presence and attention"

The thirteen pages describe a future little short of Utopia—for a close-knit ruling caste.

Realism in planning is needed more acutely than ever before, for citizens and parents outside the field of education are becoming dismayed over the enormous demands on them which educators are presenting in the name of child welfare. Children must not only be well fed and physically healthy; they must also be reared in happy homes, where marriage is successful, and where at least the mother subordinates her other interests to the needs of the children; where neighbours are as wise as the parents themselves; where words are introduced at the exact stage of development judged most propitious in vocabulary studies; where religion and other abstract phenomena present themselves in a sequence adapted to children's gradual comprehension of them; where the environment offers plentiful opportunity for the varied experimentation called "play"; where age mates appear on the scene precisely when needed; where sexual experiences occur in an automatic harmony equally beneficial to all who share in them. To fulfil such expectations it is clear that everything in the world would have to be changed, and, particularly, that the whole life of adults would have to be subordinated to the educational requirements of the next generation.

It took me several readings to fully grasp what that paragraph implies.

* * * However, it must be remembered that there is risk of a revolt, especially on the part of mothers, whose continuously sensitive presence and attention are now regarded as necessary to the emotional security of their children. After a period of emancipation, women may again come to feel in danger of being reduced to biological servitude.

Here is confirmed the purpose to remove the mother of the family and to substitute a benign omniscience for her own—despite the "risk of a revolt, especially on" her part.

As for "biological servitude", the hearings on the 1951 UMT bills (*S.1* and *H.R. 1752*) show how close American mothers have been brought to just that condition—by the policy called internationalism, now pursued.

[147]

Isn't this communism?

The great parallel

There is a great and underemphasized parallel to be observed in all this. The internationalist is a warm supporter of UN. At the same time he is convinced that he is opposing communism. Yet I wonder if he really understands communism? Oh, the internationalist sees its outward threat to his wellbeing, but has he studied Marxist strategy and dialectic?

Such a study is not easy; but it can reveal, clearly and without equivocation, a fact that is all too apparent to students of Marxism who oppose the program of the other world collectivism. What is that fact? It is that internationalism is producing the very conditions toward which every top communist has worked since the days of Marx. The parallel is explicit in communist writings since the publication of *Das Kapital*.

Many a good citizen has had the misfortune of being called "communist" because of this parallel between Marxism and the new internationalism.

Thus the world of "tomorrow" is becoming a reactionary world of yesterday. Was it not the new internationalist program which made the power of the Soviet, and which overnight began the feudalistic regimentation of our people to "deter and contain" the very power thus created?

Who can successfully deny that here the progressive educators are right? They, said Dr. Childs, believe

that there is an intimate connection between the domestic effort to achieve a more socialized economy and the world effort to develop a democratic system of collective security.[6]

Pursuance of that policy will bring the Police-State here. Reverse the policy called "collective security", and the threat of a socialized Nation will dwindle to the puny efforts of those who are socialists *per se*. Return to political Neutrality can end this collectivist "trend".

The Marxists are using the proletariat, and *both* internationalisms are using your child. Hence, the widespread movement in our schools.

In regard to home and schooling the Marxist parallel is clearly stated in the Communist *Manifesto's* reference to the

bourgeois clap-trap about the family and education, about the hallowed relation of parent and child * * *

Lenin laid down the rule that

Without drawing the women into social service, into militia * * * it is impossible to build a democracy, let alone socialism.[7]

These preconditions are exactly what interventionism has been bringing to our people. The 1951 UMT bills (*S. 1* and *H.R. 1752*) fitted perfectly into this pattern.

---

[6] *Cf.* page 59.
[7] Snow: AMERICA—*Which Way?;* pp. 75-80. (THE LONG HOUSE, INC.)

Silent Voices

So is documented the program of the Unesco seminars, in clear and striking parallel to that of Dr. Harold Rugg and the "progressive" educators:

Thus through the schools of the world, we shall disseminate a new conception of government—one that will embrace all of the collective activities of men.[N]

These words, like those of Marx, of Carnegie and of Lenin, indicate no prescience; they describe a plan. The program of the Progressive Education Association, of its successor the American Education Fellowship, and the program of the Unesco seminars, follow that plan with precision. Rugg spent years at Teachers College, Columbia University, and he was far from alone of his ideological kind. It was there, in the self-constituted realm of "academic freedom", where Dr. Ruth Benedict authored and thrived for so long.

Almost five hundred thousand military graves have been dug since December 1941. In 1951 there began a steady withdrawal of the Christian Crosses from those graves. Does this not bespeak the tragic futility of the "new social order"? Do not the facts speak for themselves?

"Everything in the world" must be changed

But the great experiment, called social reconstruction, is destined to proceed—until good citizens take time out to bring it abruptly to a halt.

In 1933, the *Call to the Teachers of the Nation* stated that "the school can scarcely hope to function effectively"

until society is already transformed * * * (*p. 23*)

Sixteen years later—far from being modified—the premise is enlarged. Volume VI of the Unesco series declares:

To fulfil such expectations it is clear that everything in the world would have to be changed * * *

Two clear alternatives are proffered:

* * * either educational principles must be made to allow for greater varieties of environment, or social conditions must be adapted to educational needs.

The seminar's first alternative enjoyed long and successful practice under America's decentralized, community control. It was precisely the hundreds of "varieties of environment" which made our school system unique—and the school system was in striking parallel to the unique structure of the Government of our Federal Republic.

But this American system is no longer "modern"; it is not "progressive"; and it is not "common". Therefore, something must be changed.

What is to be changed? In 1933 it was "society"—in 1949 it is "everything in the world".

[N] *Cf.* page 31.

"Everything in the world" is to be changed, but not by you. It is to be changed by global authority, Unesco preferred.

The result is to be millions of happy "citizens of the world", this planet at blissful peace.

The "peace" is to be attained—by perpetual global war.

It then is to be maintained by force.

Our children are to be trained to acceptance of the result.

Plato's Republic . . . on a global scale

In Britain, the Fabian Socialists first infiltrated the political mechanism. They then achieved power and liquidated the wealth of the people and of the nation. They next went on the American dole—as part of. "collective security". This subsidy of socialist imperial Britain was financed by the American taxpayer, and he was told that it was to combat socialism-Marxism!

In America's schools, the movement, the program and the strategy are identical with Fabian procedure. They are the tactics of the progressive education movement. They are the tactics of the movement for social-reconstruction-through-the-schools.

Small wonder that "progressive" educators see

an intimate connection between the domestic effort to achieve a more socialized economy and the world effort to develop a democratic system of collective security.

And now the global educators announce, through this Unesco seminar, that

If the educationists of the world joined forces, they should be able to demand of all governments

that the program be achieved.

For families, there are proposed

specific allowance schemes.

These allowances would come from the collectivist state. They will be taken, first, from you.

Neither bribery, dole nor socialism is mentioned in the text.

This seminar, like the others, foresees

freeing the child more and more from the family.

The mother will be "liberated":

Bearing in mind both the economic arguments in favour of expanding the labour supply, and the arguments for participation by women in gainful employment, an acceptable compromise solution would be to shorten working hours to about six hours a day for all those already employed and at the same time to increase the supply of labour by utilizing greater numbers of married women.

The homemaker is to be "utilized". Greater "production" is thus assured. Children are freed from the "injurious influences" with which you have heretofore "infected" them. Then they—your children—are to be subjected to the tender mercies of "social scientists", by them to be "conditioned for liberty"—according to a global plan.

As for the American home, it can be no more.

Collectivism will have been achieved.

While the program, apart from the *Selected Bibliography,* does not necessarily represent the official views of Unesco, clearly such views ultimately can be expected.

If, meantime, American citizens really are "conditioned for liberty", it is hardly to be expected that a whimper can be raised—from a father, a mother or a child.

The program of the collectivist movement in the schools will be complete.

Plato's Republic will be in operation—on a global scale.

The ultimate in internationalism will have been achieved.

"Let every man make known what kind of government would command his respect, and that will be one step toward obtaining it."

Henry David Thoreau: *Civil Disobedience*. 1849.

PART IV
THE TURNING
OF THE TIDES

Accomplishment
and Resolution

In a few short years the young people now attending school are going to run the Country.

What can be expected of them if they are taught what is outlined by this movement?

Is its philosophy to be further ingrained—or are the American Constitution and Bill of Rights to again provide the basic training of our youth?

*"How in the name of Heaven * * *?"*

At the outset of this book Congressman Shafer expressed certain personal views:

* * * I believe that a movement which arrogates to the educational profession— or to any other profession or segment of our national life—the awful responsibility of "social reconstruction", is subversive. * * * that a movement which urges teachers, or any other group of people, to "deliberately reach for power and then make the most of their conquest" * * * is subversive. I believe that a movement which * * * belittles old, inherited loyalties, and the truths and values established by ages of human experience, is subversive. [And] I believe that a movement and philosophy which aims to convert the public schools into agencies for the promotion of supernational authority or world government, and which urges the systematic eradication —beginning in the kindergarten—of nationalism, decreeing that nationalism and the loyalties which it involves must go, is subversive.

It is submitted that the documentation substantiates Mr. Shafer's concept, and that his use of the word *subversive* is correct.

The statement concluded:

I make no claim that the ensuing documentation is complete. I do claim, however, that the documentation is typical, and represents the basic premises and objectives of the movement—so stated by its own proponents.

I have attempted to identify my sources with painstaking care.

It is submitted that this promise is meticulously kept throughout the text.

One question remains: How can this documentation be employed to eliminate subversion in our schools?

As the Hon. William Jenner of Indiana put it in the Senate of the United States:

> I want to make one thing clear. This war against our Constitution is not being fought way off in Madagascar or in Mandalay. It is being fought here—in our schools, our colleges, our churches, our women's clubs. It is being fought with our money, channeled through the State Department. It is being fought twenty-four hours a day—while we remain asleep.
>
> How many of you Senators know what the UN is doing to change the teaching of the children in your own home town? The UN is at work there, every day and night, changing the teachers, changing the teaching materials, changing the very words and tones—changing all the essential ideas which we imagine our schools are teaching to our young folks.
>
> How in the name of Heaven are we to sit here, approve these programs, appropriate our own people's money—for such outrageous "orientation" of our own children, and of the men and women who teach our children, in this Nation's schools?[1]

In documenting the collectivist movement it has been felt essential to include references to matters other than education itself. This has seemed advisable for the reason that the drive for mind-control is no isolated phenomenon. It is not single in its aim.

It is part of a composite whole, one which is designed to completely alter what, with quiet and unassuming pride, five generations of free human beings have known as the *American* Way of Life.

This documentation brings the movement into the open where it belongs. Some will prefer the course proposed. That is their right. Others will rise against it, and that, too, is their American right.

What is your own position—and what are you going to do about it?

The spectacle seems to justify something more than an eyebrow gently raised.

The tide begins

> "* * * all power is inherent in the people, and all free governments are founded on their authority, and instituted for their peace, safety and happiness; for the advancement of those ends they have at all times, an unalienable and indefeasible right to alter, reform, or abolish the government in such manner as they may think proper."
>
> Third Tennessee Constitution, 1870. *Art. I, Sec. I.*

The attack upon our institutions has so far failed to attain the success which has crowned its efforts in many other lands. There are three great reasons for this, each dependent upon the other. These are:

---

[1] *Congressional Record*, March 20, 1952; pp. 2592-4. By permission, the Senator's original text has been slightly rearranged.

The protection of our substantive law, the Constitution itself;

The presence in public office of men and women in sufficient numbers to block the final implementation of the scheme; and

The undaunted courage of those citizens throughout the Nation who have braved business and social ostracism in combating it. From the first they refused to accept the facile claims of many in positions of trust. More and more, others are revising their early views as they see how their natural confidence was betrayed.

Each of these three factors has delayed the collectivist takeover, the disparate approach of which has often been but dimly visible in its parts.

With each new documentation the ranks of those determined to put an end to the movement visibly increase.

Protagonists of the American Way have begun to seriously penetrate the heavy curtain which heretofore they encountered. The first major break came in January 1950, when the sovereign State of Georgia adopted *H.R. 146.* This reversed the Commonwealth's former "world government" declaration, passed four years earlier. It stated that the "said resolution of 1946 be now repudiated and that the General Assembly of Georgia go on record as opposing the principles of World Federation." Informed Georgians had laid careful documentation before the often amazed men who had felt that the Constitutional Convention should be called. California quickly followed suit, the men of its Legislature convinced by the same kind of careful documentation, laid before them by citizens of the Golden State. Of the twenty-three Legislatures which passed the early resolution, twenty have now reexamined their position and reversed it.

Thus was turned the first grim legislative tide.[2]

Opposition is growing; in numbers, in documentation and in concrete results. The 2,700 schools participating in the UN essay contest in 1951 dropped to 2,600 within a year.

The Houston, Texas, school board forbade participation. The Los Angeles schools withdrew *The E in Unesco,* a UN manual, from use. The high school principal at Pawtucket, R. I., suspended a students' "Unesco Thinkers" society for asserted Marxist and atheist taint.

In the Spring of 1952 the Congress of the United States passed Public Law 495 (*66 Stat. 556*). Title I of this law is known as the *Department of State Appropriation Act, 1953* and much of the credit for its passage be-

---

[2] These States have rescinded: *Ala., Ark., Cal., Colo., Fla., Ga., Ky., La., Me., Md., Mass., Mo., N.H., N.J., N.Car., Okla., Ore., R.I., Tenn.,* and *Virginia.*

Delaware and *Michigan* have adopted resolutions opposing all forms of world government.

Three States which passed the Convention resolution have taken no further action: *Conn., Utah* and *Washington.*

This was the situation at the beginning of 1962.

[154]

longs to Senators McCarran and Jenner—upon whom descended in whole-
sale lots the pressure brigades described herein. Here is the key section:

Sec. 112. None of the funds appropriated in this title shall be used
(1) to pay the United States contribution to any international organization
which engages in the direct or indirect promotion of the principle or doctrine of one world government or one world citizenship; (2) for the promotion, direct or indirect, of the principle or doctrine of one world government
or one world citizenship,

Then came the outlawing of the entire Unesco program in the second
largest school system in the Nation. By unanimous vote, the Los Angeles
Board of Education took action in mid-January, 1953. The Board said:

"There shall be no official or unofficial 'UNESCO Program' in
the Los Angeles schools; and the presently inactivated Central Advisory Committee and UNESCO chairmanships are hereby permanently discontinued."

The subjects of human relations, which had been assimilated into the
Unesco program beginning in 1946, were returned to their traditional place
in the curricula of the Los Angeles schools.

Here is reversal, plainly to be seen.

The American Way

"The government of the Union, then, is emphatically and truly a government of the people. In form and in substance it emanates from them.
Its powers are granted by them, and are to be exercised directly on them
and for their benefit."

McCulloch vs. Maryland. 1819. Chief Justice Marshall,
Opinion of the Court. (Wheaton. IV, 316)

Other endeavors are helping to turn the tides, to return our sons and
daughters to that pride of individuality and of independence which was
once, and so thoroughly, characteristic of the Nation.

One of these endeavors began in New Orleans in October, 1948. Bill
Fischer, president of the Progessive Bank and Trust Company, came up
with an idea. He believed in America's youth. He laughed at the banter
which greeted him—and he went ahead, as so many of our forebears have
done in the past.

He went into the schools. He talked with small fry, with teachers, with
principals and administrators. He talked thrift. And the spark grew to
youthful fire.

Here was an old thing, made new. Here was character, and independence. Here was work! And did the young folks eat it up!! They
began to see earning, and saving, and independence—in relation to themselves. They asked for jobs, sought jobs, got jobs. Any kind of job; a big
job, a little job. For these they were paid, and Bill Fischer's idea bore
fruit.

Almost overnight his bank was being overrun with shavers, many no
more than eight years old, standing on tip-toe so the tellers might see them.

[155]

And there were older ones, too. Some of these have since been able to enter college because of the money *they* had earned and saved.

The first year 9,000 youngsters deposited a total of $37,000. Then the figures climbed. By the end of 1952 three-quarters of New Orleans' 100,000 school children had accounts, and 135 of the city's 175 schools were participating in the program. Some 20,000 deposits were being made a week, and the average was over a dollar per deposit. At that time—the end of 1952—these deposits (net, *after* withdrawals) totalled $1,108,624. This sum stood in the names of 75,000 individual boys and girls. Think of it!

The cost to the bank? Well, *this* bank has its own cost-system. And its president, Bill Fischer, has considered a factor not present in the questionnaire of bank examiners or of practicing CPAs. That factor is the character of future men and women.

And that was the essence of Bill Fischer's old-new idea.

Interest is paid at 2 percent. Each week there is a Bank Day at the schools. The youngsters bring in their passbooks and their coins, earned and saved. And these are put into individual envelopes, then into sacks, and taken to the bank. Next day the bank messenger returns with the passbooks, and all deposits have been recorded. Checks are honored from 1¢ up and, of course, are parent-endorsed.

And there is Bill Fischer and his bank, building self-reliance, building citizenship—in the young folks, where it counts. Future leaders, now attending the schools of New Orleans, are building these things within themselves.

Over in Searcy, Arkansas, there is another project, different and yet the same.

At Harding College, president George Benson and his staff have installed a Pilot-Plant in American Education. This brilliant adventure was begun in 1952. It is absolutely unique.

It comprises an educational curriculum based altogether on historic American principles. American history; the American heritage—and its contributions to all of civilization; American economics and business achievement; the American way of Government; the meaning of Freedom, and its never-ending struggle with statism and regimentation; the Christian Heritage; the traditions and ideals of these United States—and a host of other truly American practices and beliefs. In addition, the Harding "Pilot-Plant" will develop textbooks and teaching techniques for high schools and colleges.

Here is a living thing, one which can be made to spread, and spread— to clear the air of that synthetic defeatist propaganda which has been surrounding us like a fog.

Here *Americanism* is being pioneered—in the Land which bred the term.

Here is a new-found, academic tide.

The Republic

Louisiana and Arkansas. Two States; two cities; two complementary fields of work. And each and both are building minds, and character, and vigorous citizens, to the end that this Republic once again may take no second place in the demonstration of what Man may accomplish on this earth, by and within himself.*

Here is Freedom. Here is practice of those virtues which, limited but by human frailty, are implicit in the Constitution of these United States.

Here young citizens are again being made conversant with our unique traditions, our history, our ideals. Here they are imbued with the heritage of Freedom upon which their lives must always rest—taught in such a way that *they* discover how new and vital in the history of Man this thing called Freedom is, and what an adventure it can be.

Here they are being raised to think, and they are discovering the immutable principles which must forever govern all active life—whereas a "science" of today may become but the mythology of tomorrow.

Can we not also teach—and ourselves convince—that no mere clash of might, no technology, no materialism however scientific, can preserve the sovereign Freedom which is our human birthright?

Can we not raise our youth—and ourselves—to the utter, and sustained, conviction that the magnificent achievement of our American Way carries within it—and as far as wisdom yet can see, *only* within it—those divine principles which are embraced in the Constitutional Republic of these United States?

For here was brought to first effective maturity that for which—over countless centuries—men had so painfully strived:

The equality, and the dignity, of Man—as a sovereign individual on this earth.

Here, assuredly, was and forever is the essence of our unique system and wellbeing—our own self-government its base.

Individual, it is the antithesis of the collective; personal, it is the antithesis of The State; spiritual, it is the antithesis of the global mechanism now proposed.

Here is expressed the genius of our people, of our institutions and of our schools.

Millions of free men and women—known as Americans—were the first sovereign self-governing citizens on this earth. They faced their trials, their joys and hardships, their duties and their human responsibilities—even as they are facing them now. And always they have conquered, for that which is of the spirit will ever emerge supreme over that which is not.

From these principles, divinely inspired, sprang the *character* of our

---

* The two institutions will gladly supply details upon request.

[157]

people and Nation. And from that character have come, and are coming, American answers to the challenge posed by the guided movement in our schools.

Ten years hence, will your own son or daughter come to you—and express thanks for what you did today?

Sixty-seven thousand school districts

"The true source of all our suffering has been our timidity. ⁰ ⁰ ⁰ Let us dare to read, think, speak and write. Let every order and degree among the people arouse. * * * Let the pulpit resound. * * * Let the bar proclaim. ⁰ ⁰ ⁰ Let every sluice of knowledge be opened and set a-flowing."

John Adams, writing in the Boston *Gazette*, 1763.

One thing is clearly needed. It is indicated by the very nature of our school systems: Activity at community level.*

Each community, indeed, each State, has laws, customs and characteristics which are peculiar to itself. The laws should be examined. Where courses in State and American history are required by statute, the statutes must be enforced. Where such provisions do not exist, they should be written into law and the law forthwith enforced.

Where such ideologies as have been documented herein are found to be present in a school, no person or "authority" outside that school's community should be permitted the determination of whether they are to remain or not. It is a local matter, to be determined by yourselves.

Should this call for a change in the school board, the administration or in teacher personnel, the citizens of your community—and no one else—have the right to bring about that change, and it does not matter whether the officials are elected or appointed to their trust. This is equally true of the textbooks your sons and daughters use.

Community success can spread throughout your State, by will of the citizens, dynamically urged.

From that point it follows that the Nation itself can be brought to mirror the wishes of its citizens—according to substantive law.

Armed with original evidence, undeterred by all that has become intrenched since this movement started back in 1905, here is the answer for each community, and for each one of the 67,346 independent school districts in these United States.

The issue is clear:

What is *best* for our schools—what is *best* for the 40,000,000 young citizens who are attending them and who, so soon, will be governing this great Country of ours?

---

* Suggestions for locally-organized committees are to be found in the Appendix, page 172.

Of two alternatives, only one ultimately can prevail: Either the "Government" will provide the answer, or you and your neighbors will decide—as citizens of the community in which you live.

The same clear issue lies before us in the realm of government itself:

Is the Nation, as well, to be run from Washington—or, is *local* government to recapture those functions which the Constitution reserves to you and to your neighbors; is it to be brought back home, where we know each other and know, therefore, what is going on?

So similar are these two questions that it may well be that in determining the former, the latter will be resolved.

The initial steps have been taken. Here, assuredly, is the first light of a new, and happier, day—for ourselves, and for our children as they mature.

Let these matters be faced calmly, eagerly. As a great American once so truly—and so simply—said:

"Nothing is so much to be feared as fear."

Henry David Thoreau: *Journal*. (*Circa* 1860)

Thus, from quiet resolution, comes the turning of the tides.

APPENDIX

The material compiled in this Appendix is not found, to our knowledge, in any other single volume.   THE PUBLISHERS.

The Intercollegiate Socialist Society
and The League for Industrial Democracy

There were about one hundred persons at the 1905 meeting. Chapter organization began at once and during the ensuing years the following were some of the participants:

Amherst: Evans Clark, Leland Olds, Carl and H. S. Raushenbush, and Ordway Tead.

Amherst Agricultural College: John Spargo

Barnard: Freda Kirchwey.

Brown: Alexander Meiklejohn.

City College, New York: Jay Lovestone.

Clark: Isador Lubin.

Coe College: William Shirer.

Columbia: Paul H. Douglas, Benjamin Feigenbaum and Lewis Lorwin.

Cornell: Vladimir Karapetoff.

Harvard: Carroll Binder, Heywood Broun, Lewis Gannett, Walter Lippmann and Kenneth Macgowan.

Johns Hopkins: Broadus Mitchell.

Pittsburgh: Abraham Epstein.

Trinity: Alexander Trachtenberg.

Vassar: Mary R. Sanford and Edna St. Vincent Millay.

Wayne: Walter Reuther.

Wellesley: Vida D. Scudder.

Wesleyan: Harry W. Laidler.

Wisconsin: David J. Saposs was president in 1910. Attending meetings were William Leiserson and John L. Childs.

Others, members and/or cooperating with the movement, included:

Roger N. Baldwin, Andrew Biemiller, Eveline M. Burns, W. E. B. DuBois, Frederick V. Field, Felix Frankfurter, Lewis Gannett, Sidney Hook, Joseph P. Lash, Max Lerner, Charles Luckman, J. B. Matthews, Nathaniel Peffer, Victor Reuther, Will Rogers, Jr., Bertrand Russell, Anna Louise Strong, H. Jerry Voorhis, James A. Wechsler, Bouck White and Ellen Wilkinson.

Among the treasurers of the L.I.D. were Stuart Chase and Morris Hillquit. Algernon Lee was a secretary. Paul Porter and Paul Blanshard were active workers, as was George Edwards, an Oregon editor and contributing editor of *The New Republic.* Louis Budenz was on the board of directors in 1926.

Bishop Francis J. McConnell (former president of the Federal Council of Churches, president of the Methodist Federation for Social Service, president of the National Citizens PAC) was a vice-president during 1940-1.

Among the officers of the L.I.D. in 1950 were:

John Dewey, honorary president; Nathaniel M. Minkoff, president; and Francis J. McConnell, Alexander Meiklejohn and Vida D. Scudder, vice-presidents.

Among the 1950 Directors were:

John L. Childs, Louis Fischer, Broadus Mitchell, Carl Raushenbush, Victor L. Reuther and Boris Shishkin.

The following were listed as among the sponsors of the 45th anniversary luncheon held that year:

Roger Baldwin, Mary McLeod Bethune, Algernon Black, George S. Counts, Helen Gahagan Douglas, Sidney Hook, William H. Kilpatrick, Ernest O. Melby, Henry Morgenthau, Jr., Abraham J. Multer, Nathaniel Peffer, Franklin D. Roosevelt, Jr., Harold S. Rugg, Arthur Schlesinger, Jr., Rex Stout, Channing H. Tobias and Goodwin Watson.

Among the speakers were Senator Herbert H. Lehman; Oscar R. Ewing, of the Social Security Agency; George Meany, of the A.F. of L.; and (by proxy) Walter P. Reuther, of the U.A.W.-C.I.O.

Among the participants in the convention were Israel Feinberg, vice-president of the I.L.G.W.U., who spoke on "human rights"; and Dr. Eveline M. Burns. The latter was administrative assistant to the British Ministry of Labour between 1917 and 1921, and was an assistant lecturer at the London School of Economics. She traveled in the United States between 1926 and 1928 as a fellow of the Laura Spelman Rockefeller Foundation, subsequently becoming a citizen. (*Who's Who in America*, Vol. 27, 1952-3, gives further details of her career.)

Greetings were received from, among others, G.D.H. and Margaret Cole, on behalf of the Fabian Society of Britain; Morgan Phillips, Secretary of the British Labour Party; Mrs. Eleanor Roosevelt; Senator Hubert H. Humphrey; Congressman Jacob A. Javits, of New York; and Harry A. Overstreet, author of *The Mature Mind*.

On the National Council in 1953 were George S. Counts, Sidney Hook and Kenneth Macgowan.

Sources: The material for this Appendix and for Chapter I has been compiled from references listed in the Bibliography, pages 174-5.

The General Education Board

The General Education Board was established in 1902 by John D. Rockefeller, Sr., "for the promotion of education within the United States of America, without distinction of race, sex, or creed."[1]

In seven years' time, Rockefeller gave to it the following sums:

1902	$ 1,000,000	
1905	10,000,000	
1907	32,000,000	
1909	10,000,000	Total $53,000,000[2]

Those wishing to further inform themselves on this phase of the schools-program are directed to *The Ogden Movement*, by Edward Ingle (1908). This monograph was written

"In the hope of inducing such full publicity and frank discussion that enthusiastic adherents of the campaign of the General Education Board may be led to realize the danger in the fundamental error of that campaign, and that its promoters may be forever restrained from exercising the tremendous power which is theirs."

[1] General Education Board, *Annual Report*, 1947-8.

[2] Ayres: *Seven Great Foundations*. 1911.

Four years later the General Education Board published an address by Frederick T. Gates, the Board's chairman. A part of that address is reproduced below. For title reference, *cf.* the Bibliography, page 180.

6

A VISION OF THE REMEDY

Is there aught of remedy for this neglect of rural life? Let us, at least, yield ourselves to the gratifications of a beautiful dream that there is. In our dream, we have limitless resources, and the people yield themselves with perfect docility to our molding hand. The present educational conventions fade from our minds; and, unhampered by tradition, we work our own good will upon a grateful and responsive rural folk. We shall not try to make these people or any of their children into philosophers or men of learning or of science. We are not to raise up from among them authors, orators, poets, or men of letters. We shall not search for embryo great artists, painters, musicians. Nor will we cherish even the humbler ambition to raise up from among them lawyers, doctors, preachers, politicians, statesmen, of whom we now have ample supply. We are to follow the admonitions of the good apostle, who said, "Mind not high things, but condescend to men of low degree." And generally, with respect to these high things, all that we shall try to do is just to create presently about these country homes an atmosphere and conditions such, that, if by chance a child of genius should spring up from the soil, that genius will surely bud and not be blighted. Putting, therefore, all high things quite behind us, we turn with a sense of freedom and delight to the simple, lowly, needful things that promise well for rural life. For the task that we set before ourselves is a very simple as well as a very beautiful one : to train these people as we find them for a perfectly ideal life just where they are — yes, ideal, for we shall allow ourselves to be extravagant since we are only dreaming; call it idyllic, if you like — an idyllic life under the skies and within the horizon, however narrow, where they first open their eyes. We are to try to make that life, just where it is, healthful, intelligent, efficient, to fill it with thought and purpose, and with a gracious social culture not without its joys.

EVERY INDUSTRY IN A CURRICULUM

Let us take, for illustration, as the rural school unit, a territory or township perhaps six miles square, thirty-six square miles, containing some twenty-five thousand acres and at present one

The Wishing Well

Another type of questionnaire is illustrated by *The Wishing Well,* an "intercultural testing program" which originated in 1949 at Ohio State University, Bureau of Educational Research. At five cents per copy, its distribution increased each year through 1952. Specific directions were provided for "administering " the test.

There were 160 numbered items. For analysis, these were keyed to eight "basic needs". Each item begins with the words, "I wish". Students were asked to check the items "wished".

The "test" was for boys and girls of the 4th, 5th, 6th and 7th grades.

Thirty of the 160 items are here reproduced, without comment*:

5. I wish I did not feel so different from my parents.

8. I wish I knew how you can believe that God is always right and at the same time believe that you should think for yourself.

14. I wish I liked Negro children as well as white children.

15. I wish my vote really counted.

21. I wish I could talk over important things with my parents more often.

24. I wish I knew why factories sometimes shut down when people need the things factories make.

29. I wish I had good times with my parents more often.

35. I wish our family had a little money saved so we wouldn't have to worry about illness, or accidents, or unemployment.

36. I wish I were less afraid of being alone in the dark.

37. I wish I knew someone whom I liked very much.

39. I wish I did not have to agree with grown-ups so much of the time.

43. I wish our family could afford to give each other better presents at Christmas and on birthdays.

46. I wish I had never looked down on people who are poor and uneducated.

48. I wish I knew how you can make lots of money and still be a very good citizen.

56. I wish I knew what causes the trouble among Negroes and white people and Jews and foreigners.

61. I wish I felt like a real member of my family.

72. I wish I knew why people say that everyone is equal when some people have much more money than others.

77. I wish I liked to be around my parents more.

80. I wish I knew why we have so many rules made by grown-ups when everyone seems to believe in democracy.

85. I wish my parents liked me as much as they did when I was younger.

92. I wish I were more protected from the things of which I am afraid.

101. I wish my parents did things that would make me feel more love toward them.

110. I wish my parents never did things that made me ashamed of them.

120. I wish someone would help me to understand why people hate and fight each other.

129. I wish children in our neighborhood were friendlier toward me.

139. I wish that people would pay my father higher wages so that our family would not have to do without so many things.

146. I wish I were not thought of as a failure by other people.

153. I wish so many children did not dislike me.

[163]

156. I wish grown-ups did not try to frighten me.

158. I wish people would not tell me things that make me worry.

This "test" has been used in communities in Florida, Georgia, Indiana, Louisiana, Massachusetts, Michigan, New York, North Carolina, Ohio, Tennessee and Texas.

---

* The reader himself may like to group the above "wishes" under "the eight basic needs":

1) "The need for belonging"...................................... 129, 153.

2) "The need for achievement".. 146.

3) "The need for economic security"......................... 35, 43, 139.

4) "The need for freedom from fear and aggression".............. 36, 92, 156.

5) "The need for love and affection"........... 5, 21, 29, 37, 61, 77, 85, 101.

6) "The need for freedom from guilt"...................... 14, 46, 110, 158.

7) "The need for sharing and participation".......................... 15, 39.

8) "The need for a world outlook"............... 8, 24, 48, 56, 72, 80, 120.

The "needs" of the boys were tabulated separately from those of the girls.

The potential use to which such "tests" may be put is noted by some people, and denied by others. In Jugoslavia, for instance, education authorities are using questionnaires slanted so as to get schoolchildren to spy on "reactionary" parents. Ostensibly to gather data on the "social, economic and moral" surroundings of young people, this device is being employed in the secondary schools of Croatia.

In this case the slanting is religious. The "tests" ask if parents are urging their children to read religious books; whether the youngsters recognize that such books are opposed to "the Atheistic view of the world".

Questions such as these are listed: "Do your parents receive visits from ministers?" "How long do they last?" "What topics are discussed?" "Do your parents practice their religion?" "Do they regularly attend church services?"

The parallel, if any, between these questions and those in *The Wishing Well*, is left to the judgment of the reader.

Source: *Petrusblatt*, Berlin. From the *Tulsa* (Okla.) *Herald*, All-Church Press, April 6, 1956. (RNS despatch)

UNESCO Lullaby

While indoctrination proceeds behind the scenes, children are sewing UN flags, dancing folk-figures and presenting innocent pageants as part of their school activities. All is gentle and benign. The theme throughout is "Peace". This theme is being indoctrinated in the face of global war.

At higher levels discussion groups are formed, speakers are presented, and students participate in solemn conclaves on the great world brotherhood now about to dawn.

Symphony orchestras entertain with the world's most gorgeous music —with a themal overtone of "one united world".

These and similar "front" activities are what will be pointed out to you by those who prefer to waive the use of a detached intelligence, and to disregard such documentation as is made herein. From these activities, and from their sponsors in your own community, will come the resistance to those who are determined that the entire movement shall be stopped.

The "front" activities in your community are illustrated by the contents of a

Report of the Secretary-General of the United Nations and the Director-General of UNESCO

which was released to a limited number of recipients on May 2, 1952.

The full title of the release is

Teaching of the Purposes and Principles, the Structure and Activities of the United Nations and the Specialized Agencies in Schools and Educational Institutions of Member States.

United Nations. *Document E/2184/Add. 1.* May 2, 1952.

There are 136 pages, of which 72 are devoted to reports from all of UN's members but one. That one report takes up 64 pages. It is the report from these United States.

Concluding paragraphs of the UN-Unesco Report

"Looking back over the past two years, we have seen a steadily growing concern to expand and improve education for international understanding, and specifically teaching about the United Nations, at all levels from pre-kindergarten through college and university to the general adult population throughout the United States. * * *

"The widespread and spontaneous popular interest * * * has been given every possible encouragement by the Government of the United States and by the authorities of most of the individual states, and of the territories under its jurisdiction. State-wide programmes are often sponsored by the State Board of Education, usually with the close co-operation or under the leadership of a State University. Added stimulus is given by the official co-operation of all agencies of the United States Government with the major national civic, church, labour, business and educational organizations in promoting the annual observance of 24 October, through the efforts of the National Citizens' Committee for United Nations Day. Continuous encouragement and assistance is offered to teachers at all levels throughout the year by the Department of State through its publications and speakers, and by the United States Office of Education through its periodicals, pamphlets, bibliographies, and consultant service." (*P. 132*)

These paragraphs conclude the UN-Unesco Report.

These are the "front" operations observable in your community. The UN-Unesco Report itself states the result—in the form of a "typical kindergarten definition" which came from some child who might be your own:

" 'The United Nations is so people can live, so they'll be taken care of and won't be cold, and so we'll have peace.' " (*P. 81*)

Is this the truth?

Or does such indoctrination predestine that child to a disillusionment which can shatter his life beyond repair?

American Association for the United Nations.

American Association of University Women.

American Council on Education.

American Education Press.

American Legion (local Posts).

Boards of Education (many, State and local).

Carnegie Endowment for International Peace.

Center of International Studies, Princeton, N. J.

Church Peace Union.

Citizens' Committee for United Nations Day.

Civic Education Service.

Collegiate Council for the United Nations.

Committee on Foreign Relations.

Community Ambassador Program.

Council for Social Studies.

Federal Union.

Federation of Women's Clubs.

Foreign Policy Association.

Institute of World Affairs.

⁕ International Relations Clubs (in schools and colleges).

Junior League.

Kiwanis (local units).

League of Women Voters.

National Citizens Committee for United Nations Day.

National Commission for the Social Studies.

National Committee on Boys' and Girls' Club Work.

National Education Association.

—Committee on International Relations.

—Department of Classroom Teachers.

—National Association for Supervision and Curriculum Development.

—*UNIT (United Nations Information Service for Teachers).*

National Intercollegiate Christian Council.

National Student YMCA.

National Student YWCA.

Office of Education (Federal, and many State and local offices).

Operation Democracy.

Parent-Teachers Associations (local units).

Rockefeller Foundation.

Rotary (local units).

Scholastic Magazine.

Social Science Foundation, Denver, Colo.

Soroptomists (local units).

United States Government: all cooperating agencies.

—Department of Agriculture, Extension Service.

—Department of State.

—Department of State, Division of Public Liaison.

—Office of Education.

—Office of Information.

UNIT (See National Education Association).

United World Federalists.

Women's Civic League.

World Peace Foundation.

YMCA (*See* National Student YMCA).

YWCA (*See* National Student YWCA).

⁕ "⁕ ⁕ ⁕ organized under the auspices of the Carnegie Endowment for International Peace, in universities, colleges, and normal schools * * *"

International Relations Clubs Handbook: Amy Heminway Jones (Exec. Sec'ty.). Published by the C. E. I. P., Division of Intercourse and Education. November, 1929.

Excerpts from the American section of the UN report

"The United States Office of Education has been seriously concerned in trying to implement the obligations of the Government of the United States, as a Member Nation, to encourage teaching about the United Nations in our schools and institutions of higher learning." (*P. 70*)

"The Division of Public Liaison of the Department of State has published a number of useful pamphlets and charts concerning the United Nations, and given them wide distribution." (*P. 71*)

"For example, the Committee on International Relations of the National Education Association is inaugurating this year a unique United Nations Education Service for Schools, including a bi-weekly newsletter, UNIT (United Nations Information for Teachers); the distribution of selected Kits, pamphlets and audio-visual materials; preparation of spot studies, teaching units, and handbooks for school observances; direct assistance to subscribing school systems in planning conferences, visits to the United Nations, etc.; and the maintenance of a permanent representative of the teaching profession at United Nations headquarters." (*P. 71*)

"After World War I * * * The emphasis of political science teaching swung to the study of world organization", according to a 1930-1 analysis of courses in 465 colleges and universities by the World Peace Foundation. (*P. 97*)

In 1950-1 "Eight institutions—the Universities of Denver, Michigan, Pittsburgh; Columbia, Colgate and Yale Universities; Trenton [N.J.] State Teachers College and Vassar College—in co-operation with the Carnegie Endowment for International Peace and the American Council on Education, explored their own resources and practices bearing on international relations. The results have just been published in a report by Howard E. Wilson, *Universities and World Affairs* (N.Y., Carnegie Endowment, 1951.)" (*P. 98*)

"The obligation to educate for international understanding cannot be fulfilled adequately without preparing teachers to teach about the United Nations and to help their students develop concepts of international co-operation. * * * The education of new recruits to the profession * * * is but one phase of the problem; even more immediately effective is the in-service training of those already teaching in our schools and colleges." (*P. 109*)

Active in meeting this need are teachers, State and local boards of education, the NEA, American Association for the United Nations, and the United States Government through its Office of Information. (*P. 110*)

"* * * In many institutions organized groups of students—notably the International Relations Clubs, the World Federalists, the Collegiate Council for the United Nations—sponsor radio programmes, or send speakers to meet civic groups, distribute literature, or otherwise 'campaign' beyond the campus. * * *

"The Institute of International Studies at Yale, now the Center of International Studies at Princeton, exercised extraordinary off-campus influence by careful and focused distribution of the publications." (*P. 121*)

"The Collegiate Council for the United Nations is an intercollegiate organization set up by the American Association for the United Nations to arouse college students to an understanding of their position of responsibility in the United Nations and of what they can do to help make it work. * * * National CCUN services include: *News Notes on the United Nations* [monthly], * * * *UN on the Campus* [quarterly], speakers", etc. (*P. 128*)

Some of the activities reported, compiled by State

Arizona. In Phoenix, high schools "have for the past two years collaborated with speech and drama classes to stage a series of United Nations programmes for local radio and television presentation." (*P. 96*)

California. A monthly mimeo *UNESCO Bulletin* is circulated to all principals and directors and to the UNESCO chairman in each one of the Los Angeles city schools. Five "units" are entitled *World Citizenship*. Courses include study of such international organizations as the International Trade Organization and the Bretton Woods Bank and Fund. (*P. 90-1*)

"Each December the High School in Sacramento has sent two delegates, a girl and a boy to the state-wide high school UNESCO conference held at Stanford University. ⚹ ⚹ ⚹ Each year these delegates have presented a positive programme for student activity on a community basis * * * The United Nations flag was the theme used by the Girls' Drill Team of the High School at the 'big game' between Sacramento and McClatchy Senior High Schools, on Thanksgiving, 23 November 1950." United States History 7, required of all students, devotes at least one week to the United Nations. "In 1951, they stressed the success of the United Nations economic and social agencies in removing pressures that cause wars and what many of these agencies are doing to raise living standards. * * * A senior elective course, World Affairs 8, is largely based upon the United Nations, especially the work of the technical assistance programme and the accomplishments of the social agencies. Another selective course, Sociology 8, studies the 'Universal Declaration of Human Rights' ". "Many students use United Nations materials in senior English composition classes." Spanish courses include translation of UN pamphlets. "* * * pamphlets, maps and posters [are shown] in the United Nations display cases in the main hall and in the social studies corridor." (P. 94)

In the same high school, an " 'Education for Peace' faculty committee stresses teacher knowledge of and participation in the activities of the United Nations. * ⚹ ⚹ The main purpose of this committee is to further correlation of the United Nations activities throughout the school. Each year the committee is in charge of the school-wide display for United Nations week." (P. 113)

"At Claremont, California in 1950, Pomona, Scripps, and the Claremont Colleges sponsored a study programme in international affairs in both summer sessions ⚹ ⚹ ⚹ Courses and roundtables on international relations, international politics and organizations, and the United Nations were attended by teachers, research students, and others preparing to teach." (P. 116)

"Under the auspices of the Northern California American Association for the United Nations a study course on 'the dynamics of the United Nations' was held 6-30 August 1951 at San Francisco City College. This was primarily a training course in contents and methods of teaching for organization leaders interested in educating adult groups about the United Nations." (P. 116)

"The twenty-seventh session of the Institute of World Affairs sponsored by the University of Southern California was held at the Mission Inn in Riverside, California, 10-13 December 1950, on the theme 'World Leadership in mid-century' * * ⚹ Outstanding educators from the colleges and universities of the Pacific area addressed the plenary sessions and led round-table discussions." (P. 125)

Colorado. "The Social Science Foundation at the University of Denver climaxed its twenty-fifth anniversary year-long programme * * * with a five-week World Affairs Institute. The topic for the whole of the first week was 'The prospect of freedom through the United Nations', and for the last week 'Human Rights' ". (P. 119)

"Founded a quarter of a century ago and directed by the head of the University's department of political science, the Denver Social Science Foundation is devoted to high-level education of the community-at-large in the field of international relations. The Foundation, with the full cooperation of the University of Denver, aids in the conduct of surveys of public knowledge and opinion; it sponsors public forums in the University's downtown college; it serves as a distributing center for publications of the Department of State and of the United Nations; it sponsors a long-established radio programme called 'Journeys behind the news', which is an influential force on public opinion in the Rocky Mountain area." (P. 122)

"The University of Colorado sponsored a full Regional Conference, with twelve colleges participating, as well as a week-long spring Conference on World Affairs." (P. 130)

Activities are mentioned of the Senior High School International Relations Clubs, Colorado Springs. (Pp. 86-7)

Connecticut. "The Teachers College at Connecticut, at New Britain, Connecticut, has held a series of workshop conferences for teachers and students under the auspices of its UNESCO Council. On 22 April 1950, a workshop conference on International Understanding brought principles[als?] and teachers from 700 elementary schools in the State, as well as students from many New England colleges.

A week later a second workshop conference on Human Rights drew teachers and students from 168 high schools in the State. In April 1951 the Third Annual UNESCO High School Conference dealt with the work and current problems of the United Nations, drawing an attendance of over 650 students and teachers from more than 50 communities throughout Connecticut." (P. 117)

"The Connecticut Committee on the United Nations and World Understanding, appointed by Commissioner Engleman in December 1950, is composed of school and college teachers and administrators. It has developed an elaborate State-wide programme, including courses in teacher-training institutions, distribution of several issues of a mimeographed leaflet, the Connecticut UN News; preparation of inexpensive recordings of United Nations radio programmes for use in the schools; setting up of regional workshops and United Nations filmstrips, libraries, and model United Nations assemblies with High School youth playing the role of Member Nations." (P. 123)

"* * * the United World Federalists sponsored the Greenwich Student Institute on 8-18 August 1950, emphasizing peace through world government and world law, the need for educating the public on world government and some practical phases of federalism." (P. 131)

District of Columbia. Following a detailed preparatory program which involved the appearance of the word *Unesco* in gradually increasing tempo, "The instructor in charge commented: 'There is now not a child at Alice Deal [Junior High School] who does not know what UNESCO stands for' ". (Pp. 87, 89)

Beauvoir School is favorably mentioned. (P. 79)

Florida. Mock United Nations meetings were staged at Umatilla. A teacher is quoted: " 'The initial appearance of the United Nations official flag by a colour guard of CAP Air Cadets was of particular interest to our students.' " (P. 96)

"The General Extension Division of the University of Florida has for the past three years encouraged study of international understanding through a series of study outlines and a book of projects prepared by Hazel L. Bowman, a former member of the staff. The titles are *Practical Projects for UNESCO and World Citizenship; the E in UNESCO; Culture and World Understanding; the C in UNESCO.* * * * A special exhibit * * * on world citizenship was prepared for the annual convention of the Florida Congress of Parents and Teachers in Jacksonville in November 1951. * * * World understanding has been featured at the Parent-Teacher Leadership Short Course sponsored jointly by the General Extension Division and the Florida Congress of Parents and Teachers each June at Florida State University, Tallahassee." (P. 120)

Indiana. An examination to be taken by some 5,000 high school students enrolled in social science courses was prepared by Professor Frederick H. Stutz of Cornell, at the request of the Council for Social Studies and the Rockefeller Foundation. It contained fifty "carefully worded questions" on the United Nations and the Specialized Agencies. An "elaborate questionnaire concerning materials was sent to social science teachers throughout the State * * *" An "investigator, Colonel W. E. Burnham, exhibited UNESCO posters and publications for the State Association of School Board Members, for a state convention of city school superintendents, and for several teachers' association meetings * * *" (P. 92)

"Evansville College in Indiana is now, through its Library, offering five 'Songs of World Brotherhood and Creative Living' to discussion or service groups. * * * The first song, 'We Are United Nations' has been designated as 'The First International Anthem'. Its words were assembled from discussions of delegates and from comments of co-operating diplomats during the San Francisco Conference." (P. 126)*

"All CCUN chapters and International Relations Clubs in the Great Lakes and midwest region were invited to participate in a conference at Indiana University on 30 March-1 April 1951, on the theme, 'How can we bring world consciousness to the midwest?' " (P. 130)

Kansas. "Kansas State Teachers College, at Pittsburgh, Kansas, with the cooperation of the National Association for Supervision and Curriculum Development of the National Education Association, sponsored its second Workshop on Interna-

---

* Cf. page 127.

tional Understanding and Cooperation on 27 June-8 July 1950, open to college seniors and graduate students interested in a teaching career. Lectures [etc.] * * * were designed to give teachers a * * * desire for international cooperation through various subjects and activities from the elementary school through the Junior College." (P. 116)

"The University of Kansas sponsored in January 1950 its second annual United Nations Conference, designed to enable the people of the region to obtain first-hand information on the program of the United Nations." (P. 126)

Maryland. "McCoy College of the Johns Hopkins University offered in 1949-50 a special informal course for adults on 'The United Nations and world co-operation' * * * The weekly lectures were largely by members of the United Nations staff or delegations, or of agencies of the United States Government concerned with the United Nations. * * * Baltimore and Maryland branches of the American Association of University Women, Foreign Policy Association, League of Women Voters, Junior League, United Nations Association, United World Federalists, and the Women's Civic League co-operated in sponsoring the course." (P. 120)

Massachusetts. "American International College in Springfield, Massachusetts, offers a special evening session course in education, 'Teaching the United Nations'. A graduate course, open by special permission to seniors as well, it provides for teachers an introduction to the United Nations and UNESCO * * *" (P. 115)

"The Mount Holyoke Institute on the United Nations conducted four-week institutes for teachers and community leaders during the summer of 1948, 1949 and 1950. * * * Members of business and service clubs and civic organizations, leaders of community forums, radio and newspaper commentators, clergymen, librarians, and college professors as well as elementary and secondary school teachers participated." (P. 118)

"The United Nations Council of Harvard co-operated with NSA and the Harvard Graduate School of Arts and Sciences to stage a Conference on Under-Developed Areas in March 1951." (P. 131)

Minnesota. "A conference on Teaching About the United Nations was jointly sponsored by the Commission on International Understanding and World Peace of the Minneapolis schools and the Minnesota United Nations Association." (P. 117)

"Minnesota University is operating a World Affairs Center". (P. 123)

The Tuttle School in Minneapolis is favorably mentioned. (P. 85)

Missouri. The NEA Committee on International Relations and NEA Department of Classroom Teachers held a conference, attended by 400 teachers, at Lindenwood College, St. Charles, July 1950. "This conference was one of many activities of the National Education Association designed to encourage and improve teaching about the United Nations. * * * In 1950 the National Education Association compiled and distributed to teachers 1,000 United Nations Kits, with a handbook prepared by their Committee on International Relations. *A Teacher Handbook for United Nations Day and Week, 1951,* was distributed as the first of a series of special mailings to United Nations Education Service subscribers." (P. 111)

Maryville College, St. Louis, "also sponsors an annual Workshop on current United Nations developments for the pupils and private high schools of the St. Louis area." (Pp. 94, 100)

The "Grade School" at High Ridge is favorably mentioned. (P. 89)

Nebraska. "The State Department of Education and the University of Nebraska have co-operated in vigourous promotion of United Nations activities in that state." (P. 126)

The Bancroft School at Lincoln is favorably mentioned. (P. 84)

New Jersey. "The State Teachers College at Upper Montclair, N. J., with the co-operation of the New Jersey chapter of the American Association for the United Nations and the Cosmopolitan Club of Montclair presented a very successful United Nations Institute, 9-20 July 1951 * * * the Dean of the New York University School of Education spoke on 'The United Nations Challenges Education' ". (P. 118)

"Another World Government Institute was held at Miss Fine's School in Princeton, N. J." (P. 131)

[170]

New York. "In 1951 examinations set by the New York State Board of Regents in two compulsory high school courses, American history and world history, each contained a fifteen-point question devoted to the United Nations." (*P. 93*)

At the College of New Rochelle "department of education the United Nations is covered as background for a thorough study of UNESCO." (*P. 100*)

At New York University "One schedule of study leading to the M.A. and PH.D. degree specifically on the United Nations, includes a basic course in international organization." (*P. 105*)

"The library of Teachers College, Columbia University displays United Nations materials in the Social Science Reading Room where 10,000-12,000 teachers may see them." (*P. 111*)

"In 1951 the American Association for the United Nations completed its sixth annual in-service courses for teachers on United Nations affairs, planned in conjunction with the New York City Board of Education. Teachers taking this course get credit for it toward promotion or salary increment. During the past year with the co-operation of the University of Chicago, American Association for the United Nations also worked out two correspondence courses specially designed for teachers." (*P. 112*)

A Workshop in International Understanding was held on the Syracuse University campus July-August 1951. Invitations were sent to every school in the State, and with the strong endorsement of the State Commissioner of Education. "* * * one member of the group, a teacher of commercial subjects, decided to use selections concerning the United Nations for typewriting practice during the coming year!" (*P. 114*)

"Similarly, the annual Conference on American Foreign Policy at Colgate University usually attracts many social science teachers, as well as community leaders from New York State and the country at large. The Third Conference, held 21-26 July 1951 on the theme 'Nations of the Free World', assembled an extraordinary galaxy of national and international officials and experts to discuss major current issues. * * * Simultaneously, a round table on the 'Role of universities in world affairs', discussed for two afternoons the preliminary version of the Carnegie report with Howard Wilson himself participating.

"The 'Resources Fair and Exhibit' was a unique feature of the 1951 Colgate Conference. There was an elaborate display of materials from the Department of State, UNESCO, the United States Office of Education, and such private agencies as the Foreign Policy Association, American Association for the United Nations, National Education Association, Operation Democracy, the Committee on Foreign Relations, Federal Union, the Community Ambassador Program, and various churches and civic groups." (*P. 118*)

"Columbia University's radio station sponsors 'UN Revue' as a regular feature. Broadcast every Monday evening for fifteen minutes * * *" (*P. 130*)

"The National Intercollegiate Christian Council, and the national student YWCA and YMCA sponsored two United Nations seminars in New York City in 1950. * * * Designed to help students understand the United Nations, the relation of the United States to it, and the responsibility of Christian students for world citizenship. * * *" (*P. 131*)

North Carolina. "The Student Division of the United World Federalists of North Carolina held a student conference on the theme 'Peace through world government—is it possible now?' at Duke University on 21-22 April 1950. Problems confronting the United Nations and problems in strengthening the United Nations were among the leading topics." (*P. 131*)

Ohio. "The Teachers Association at Euclid, Ohio sponsored a United Nations Workshop on 21 October 1950, with an address by a United States UNESCO delegate, a panel analysis of UNESCO, and a roundtable discussion on presenting the United Nations at various levels in school and community. The workshop summary was broadcast over a neighbouring radio station that evening." (*P. 117*)

"With several other colleges participating, Ohio State University is sponsoring a spring conference on the United Nations, emphasizing the work of the specialized agencies." (*P. 126*)

The Boulevard School, Cleveland Heights, is favorably mentioned. (*P. 86*)

[171]

Oregon. "The University of Oregon, in co-operation with the Oregon Education Association, sponsors each year a study of the United Nations in the high schools of the state. It sends out a bulletin promoting the activities of the Oregon High School International Relations League * * *" (*P. 94*)

Pennsylvania. "At Pittsburgh an office of the Foreign Policy Association is set up within the University plant, with many faculty members involved, one as its secretary." (*P. 124*)

The Gillespie Junior High School, in Philadelphia, is favorably mentioned. (*P. 90*)

Washington. "A United Nations Workshop was conducted in the summer session at Central Western College of Education in 1950 and again in 1951. * * * It seemed therefore appropriate to offer a teachers' course in the United Nations as a direct and effective means of introducing the study of the United Nations into the public schools of the state." (*P. 115*)

West Virginia. "The third in an annual series of one-week institutes on world affairs was held at Shepherd College in June 1951. The 1949 sessions had been devoted entirely to the United Nations, with the United States Office of Education co-operating in sponsoring it as a pioneer project; this year the major emphasis was put on the role of the United States in the United Nations * * * to give some insight into the functions and achievements of the United Nations and the role of this country." (*P. 116*)

Wisconsin. The fifth annual student United Nations Meeting at the University of Wisconsin was held in February 1951, with delegates attending from Wisconsin colleges. A " 'Little United Nations' conference was held on 4, 5 and 6 May with noted speakers." (*P. 130*)

Virgin Islands. The Charlotte Amalie Junior-Senior High School, and Commandant Grade School, St. Thomas, are favorably mentioned. (*P. 87*)

The Committee in Each Community

In forming a committee in the community certain personality equations are, of course, to be considered. Among them may be listed these three:

1) That of the educator who appears to feel that he is the be-all and the know-all of the profession which he serves;

2) The teacher who forgets that he is a citizen, too;

3) The citizen who has been indifferent to what is being taught his child.

The solution appears to be a committee of citizens, locally-organized.

This committee, it seems, should commence its organization with no prejudice, with no bias preconceived—but with the view of first examining original evidence. It then may outline its agenda, strictly in accordance with the evidence admitted. Collaboration should be sought with present authorities—and when a clear division of opinion shall have disclosed the issues upon which the whole of the community must decide, the matter may be placed before the whole community for its decision.

The committee should avoid reaction—red or black. It should be *local,* and it should carefully determine whence comes the *finance* for any organization that is not exclusively a product of the community itself.

Rights have no dateline. In the course of his education, a child clearly has the right to information on both sides of controversial matters. He, in his own developing wisdom, should properly determine the course of his personal growth.

While respect for the rights and faiths of others is properly a part of education, its teaching should not fail to carry within it the conviction that similar respect, by others, is to be accorded to one's own. While the Commandments teach that we must love our neighbors as ourselves, this is subject to no interpretation that one should love one's neighbor better.

[172]

While understanding of other cultures is a part of proper schooling, so, too, is the development, in the finest sense, of one's appreciation of one's own. In America, this means a clear responsibility toward the Republic, and to the exquisite Constitution which is its base.

The rights of others are not to be purchased at the price of the hard-won Liberties of our own.

The local committee, then, must dispassionately assemble its documentation and its facts. And while it must work with citizens whose present views may widely diverge, this need not cause the sacrifice, on the part of anyone, of his own clear right of equally independent thought, openly expressed.

Let smear be avoided. Its use belies the depth of one's own position and convictions. Therefore, it is submitted, this shallow course is to be rigidly expunged.

A Junior Committee—composed of young people attending school—is suggested as an adjunct to the work. Prizes and awards might be offered to students—of all ages—who present to the Committee examples of attacks upon, or disparagements of, our American system which they may discover in textbooks now in use. Why couldn't local businessmen underwrite such awards?

It might be a good idea to consider not appearing as an entirely "new" body. A survey of existing groups will reveal, in many communities, that a strong, judicious agenda will attract their representation on a joint committee for the purpose.

It is suggested that the work be considered as no matter of several enthusiastic weeks; rather, that it be approached with a view to calm and patient work which may, indeed, endure for years. Perhaps the first item to become conversant with is the legal structure of your local schools—how they are financed; how they are administered; taught; how textbooks are selected; who is appointed, who is elected, and in general what is the structure of that system which is so essentially your own.

The present documentation is expanded in a Bibliography. There will be found a comprehensive guide which will show, beyond the peradventure of a doubt, that movement there is, and that its purposes have in no sense been exaggerated in this text. Rather than attempting to "combat" those of your friends and neighbors whose present views may differ from your own, let us freely grant that their views are come by as naturally as have been our own. And let us respect those views—so long as ours are treated with equal respect.

Let their interest but be aroused. Few minds are really "closed". Let us, then, ask that they impartially investigate this documentation, and such further sources as their first inquiries may suggest.

This, it seems, is the way to rational citizen-action. Once a majority conclusion is achieved, nothing can successfully thwart a citizenry aroused, determined to set free the minds of its youth.

This is self-government in dynamic action.

One last suggestion may be advanced, and it is this:

Let no "authority", organization or agency that springs from, or is financed by, those who are not of your own community, direct for you what is to be done in the schools which your son or daughter attends. Let schools, like government, be brought back home—where they can be citizen-controlled, and watched.

Their standards, like that of government, can properly be set only by ourselves.

BIBLIOGRAPHIES

Grouped under pertinent headings and according to year of publication, these references will materially assist independent inquiries.

1) The Intercollegiate Socialist Society and the League for Industrial Democracy. *Source references for Chapter I and for the Appendix to Chapter I.*

1883-1952   *Annual Reports* of the Fabian Society. London, England.

1908   *Constitution of the Intercollegiate Socialist Society.* The Society.

1910-1912   *Bulletin of the Intercollegiate Socialist Society.* (October 1910-May 1912)

1910-1913   *Annual Statements.* Intercollegiate Socialist Society.

1911   *Socialism and the Student.* Published by the I.S.S. (December)

1916   *International Government:* L. S. Woolf. Prepared for the Fabian Research Department, London. Introduction by George Bernard Shaw.

1913-1919   *The Intercollegiate Socialist.* Official organ of the I.S.S.

1919-1920   *The Socialist Review.* (Successor to *The Intercollegiate Socialist*)

1921   *Constitution of the L.I.D.* The League. (Mimeo)

1924   *A Year of Achievement. June, 1923-June, 1924.* The L.I.D.

1926   *New Tactics in Social Conflict:* H. W. Laidler. (A symposium)

1927   *The L.I.D., An Account of Its Activities, 1926.* The League. (8-page folio)

1931   *Poor Old Competition:* Stuart Chase. Published by the L.I.D.

1932-1941   Student magazines of the L.I.D. *Revolt,* Oct.-Nov. 1932; *The Student Outlook,* Feb. 1933-Oct. 1935; and *Student Advocate,* Feb. 1936-Dec. 1941. The first issue of *Student Advocate* listed the following staff: James A. Wechsler, editor; Joseph P. Lash, associate editor; Bruce Bliven, Jr., Robert L. Spivack, Budd W. Shulberg and Ben Shangold, contributing editors. It was published by the American Student Union, successor to the National Student League and the Student L.I.D.

1934   *Education and the Social Order:* John Dewey. Published by the L.I.D.

        Loose Leaves from a Busy Life: Hillquit. Macmillan.

1935   *Thirtieth Anniversary Report. 1905 . . . 1935.* The League. This *Report* states that the L.I.D. magazine, *The Student Outlook,* "published, during the past year ❋ ❋ ❋ significant contributions in Marxian interpretation by Professor Morris Raphael Cohen and Professor Sidney Hook." It also states that "The Student L.I.D., at its 1933 convention offered a pact for united action with the communist National Student League and has, throughout the year, cooperated with it in many ventures." It is at this point that is found the statement that "❋ ❋ ❋ the Student L.I.D. ❋ ❋ ❋ feels particularly proud that the last annual batch of Rhodes Scholars contained six members of the L.I.D." (*Pp. 14 and 16.*) (*Cf.* page 97)

1936   *The European Civil War:* Scott Nearing. Published by the L.I.D.

1938   *Dare We Look Ahead?:* Bertrand Russell, Vernon Bartlett, G. D. H. Cole, Herbert Morrison, Sir Stafford Cripps and Harold J. Laski. Based on the Fabian lectures of 1937.

        A SUMMARY OF EDUCATIONAL ACTIVITIES. The L.I.D. (An 8-page mimeo entitled *A Year of Achievement*)

1940   *Thirty-five Years of Educational Pioneering.* Published by the L.I.D.

1941   *Workers' Education Today.* The L.I.D.

1944	*Canadian Progressives on the March:* M. J. Coldwell, M.P. The L.I.D.

1944   *Canadian Progressives on the March:* M. J. Coldwell, M.P. The L.I.D.

British Labor's Rise to Power: Laidler. The League.

1945   *Forty Years of Education.* Published by the L.I.D.

1947   LABOUR BRITAIN AND AMERICAN PROGRESSIVES: David C. Williams. *Fabian Quarterly* No. 53, March; pp. 7-10. Fabian Publishers, Ltd., London. Williams was director of the London Bureau, Americans for Democratic Action (the A.D.A.); a former executive secretary of the Ohio Federation of Teachers and secretary of the Ohio Joint CIO-AFL Legislative Committee, and a candidate for the Ohio Legislature in 1944. He is a member of the Fabian Society and a former Rhodes Scholar.

Agreement between the United Nations and the International Labour Organization. United Nations.

1950   *Forty-five Years of Social Education:* Laidler. The League.

Freedom and the Welfare State. Published by the L.I.D.

1952   *Fabianism in the Political Life of Britain, 1919-1931:* Sister M. Margaret Patricia McCarran. Catholic University of America Press, Washington, D. C. The Heritage Foundation, Chicago, Ill.

The following works, all by Lewis (Louis) Levitzki Lorwin, illustrate how a graduate of the I.S.S. and the L.I.D. finds frequent publication by affiliates or beneficiaries of the great foundations:

1929   *Labor and Internationalism.* Macmillan. Copyright, Brookings Institution. The half-title states that the Institute of Economics was established by the Carnegie Corporation of New York.

1933   *The World Economic Conference and World Organization.* Brookings Institution. Lorwin is identified as a member of the Institute of Economics.

1941   *Youth Work Programs.* American Council on Education.

1943   *Postwar Plans of the United Nations.* Twentieth Century Fund. (Bruce Bliven is listed as a trustee of this Fund)

1945   *Time for Planning.* Harper & Brothers.

2) The movement in the schools of America. *Source references for the body of the text.*

1930   *Man and His Changing Society:* Rugg. A series which began in 1930.

1931   *The Soviet Challenge to America:* Counts.

1932   *Dare Progressive Education Be Progressive?:* Counts. (February)

Dare the School Build a New Social Order?: Counts. (April)

1932–1951   *Progressive Education.* Official journal of the Progressive Education Association, now the American Education Fellowship.

Proceedings, National Education Association.

1933   *A Call to the Teachers of the Nation.* Committee on Social and Economic Problems, Progressive Education Association.

The Great Technology: Rugg.

Bulletin of the American Association of University Professors. (November)

Rollins College Bulletin. Vol. XXIX, No. 11. (December)

1933–1951   *NEA Journal.*

1934   *Conclusions and Recommendations* of the Commission on Social Studies, American Historical Association.

NEA Proceedings. Report of the Committee on Education for the New America, Department of Superintendence, NEA.

1934–1939   *The Social Frontier.*

1935   *Liberalism and Social Action:* Dewey.

SOCIAL CHANGE AND EDUCATION. *Thirteenth Yearbook,* Department of Superintendence, NEA.

1935–1947   *Building America.* Monthly. October through May. Originally *W.P.A. Project No. 165-97-6046,* published with the assistance of the Lincoln School, Teachers College, Columbia University, and with the financial assistance of the General Education Board. Forewords of the first issues were by William H. Kilpatrick. This publication was recommended for use by students in the 7th and 8th grades. The Third Report of the California State Senate Investigating Committee on Education (1948) stated *(p. 19):* "The Committee finds the *Building America* Books to be unfit for use in our schools. . . ." The series was first copyrighted by the Society for Curriculum Study. Later, it was "published for" this Society. Beginning in December 1942 its masthead stated that it was "Published for the Department of Supervision and Curriculum Development, NEA", and in October 1947 *Building America* became "A publication of" this Department of the NEA. (*Cf.* page 180)

1936   A NEW EDUCATION FOR A NEW AMERICA: Laski. *The New Republic.* (July 29)

AMERICAN EDUCATION AND THE SOCIAL STRUGGLE: Brameld. *Science and Society—a Marxian Quarterly.* (Fall)

1936-1951   *Yearbook.* John Dewey Society.

1937   THE TEACHER AND SOCIETY. *First Yearbook.* John Dewey Society.

THE SCHOOLS AND THE PEOPLE'S FRONT: Frank. *The Communist.* (May)

Public Affairs Pamphlets, Supplement No. 2. Office of Education, Washington, D. C. *Bulletin.*

1938   *Dare We Look Ahead?:* Bertrand Russell, Vernon Bartlett, G. D. H. Cole, Herbert Morrison, Sir Stafford Cripps and Harold J. Laski.

1939–1944   *Frontiers of Democracy.* (Successor to *The Social Frontier*)

1942   SPECIAL REPORT ON SUBVERSIVE ACTIVITIES AIMED AT DESTROYING OUR REPRESENTATIVE FORM OF GOVERNMENT. House Committee on Un-American Activities. *Report No. 2277.* (June 25)

1943   *New Schools for a New Culture:* MacConnell, Melby and Arndt.

1944   *The American Way of Business; the Role of Government in a System of Free Enterprise:* Oscar Lange and Abba P. Lerner. National Association of Secondary-School Principals and National Council for the Social Studies, NEA. (*Cf.* page 180)

1945   *Design for America:* Brameld.

1946   LOOKING AT THE WORLD THROUGH TEXTBOOKS. Unesco. Paris. *Document C/9.*

THE STUDY OF TEACHING OF AMERICAN HISTORY. *Seventeenth Yearbook,* National Council for the Social Studies, NEA.

1947   *A Better World.* New York City Board of Education.

Raw Materials in War and Peace. U.S. Military Academy, Department of Social Sciences.

Making the American Mind; Social and Moral Ideas in the McGuffey Readers: Richard D. Mosier.

Report of the President's Commission on Higher Education. Vol. III. ORGANIZING HIGHER EDUCATION. (December)

1947, 1948   A NEW POLICY FOR THE AMERICAN EDUCATION FELLOWSHIP. *Progressive Education.* (November and February)

1947, 1951   *Yearbook.* American Association of School Administrators, NEA.

1947   *Draft Convention on the Crime of Genocide.* Unesco *Document E/447.* Mimeo. (June 26)

1948   *Report of the Committee and Draft Convention.* Unesco *Document E/794.* Mimeo. (May 24)

1949   *The Convention on Genocide.* United Nations.

1950   THE GENOCIDE CONVENTION. Senate Committee on Foreign Relations. *Hearings on Executive O.* (January-February)

1948   *Textbooks, Their Examination and Improvement.* Reference Department, European Affairs, Library of Congress.

Education for International Understanding in American Schools, Suggestions and Recommendations. National Education Association.

STRATEGIC AND CRITICAL MATERIALS AND METALS. House Subcommittee on Mines and Mining. *Hearings No. 38.* (February)

Investigation of Teachers Union, Local No. 555, UPWA-CIO. Committee on Education and Labor, House of Representatives.

1948-1951   *Towards World Understanding.* Unesco. Paris. Vols. I-VII, and Vol. X. Columbia University Press, New York City, is the official sales agency for the United States. The Unesco address is 19 Avenue Kléber, Paris 16.

1949   *A Handbook for the Improvement of Textbooks and Teaching Materials as Aids to International Understanding.* Unesco. Paris.

Unesco Leaders Speak. U.S. Department of State. *(G.P.O. No. 0-841574)*

Daily Worker. (March 28)

Review of the Scientific and Cultural Conference for World Peace. House Committee on Un-American Activities. (April 19)

COMMUNISM AND FASCISM IN THE SCHOOLS: DeBoer. *School and Society.* (October 29)

THE GOVERNMENT'S REACH FOR EDUCATION: Cowling-Davidson. A supplement to *American Affairs.* (Winter)

1949-1951   *Excerpts of Minutes.* Meetings of the Board of Regents of the University of California. Transcripts. (March 1949-October 1951)

1950   *American Education Under Fire:* Melby. Published by the Anti-Defamation League of B'nai B'rith. Sponsored by the National Commission for the Defense of Democracy Through Education, NEA; the Association for Supervision and Curriculum Development, NEA; American Education Fellowship, and the John Dewey Society.

Ends and Means in Education: Brameld. Harper & Brothers.

COMMUNISM AND AMERICAN EDUCATION: Brickman. *School and Society.* (March 25)

THE POLITICS OF SCHOLASTIC CRITICISM: Reinhardt. *School and Society.* (April 22)

QUACKERY IN THE PUBLIC SCHOOLS: Lynd-Case. *Atlantic Monthly.* (March, May)

Bulletin No. 35. National Commission for the Defense of Democracy Through Education, NEA. (July)

FEAR IS THE ENEMY. *School and Society.* (July 22)

WHAT IS THE ENEMY?: *School and Society.* (October 14)

1951   *This Happened in Pasadena:* Hulburd.

Teacher Handbook for United Nations Day and Week, 1951. Committee on International Relations, NEA.

Statement to State School Administrators. Michigan Commission on Educational Policies.

EDUCATION FOR A WORLD SOCIETY. *Eleventh Yearbook,* John Dewey Society.

THE DANGER OF AUTHORITARIAN ATTITUDES IN TEACHING TODAY: Hook. *School and Society.* (January 20)

POLICY AND LEADERSHIP OF THE AMERICAN EDUCATION FELLOWSHIP: Breed. *School and Society.* (February 10)

Eighth Report (L-1267), Senate Investigating Committee on Education. State of California. (March 3)

Guide to Subversive Organizations and Publications. House Committee on Un-American Activities. (March 3)

Hearings on the U.M.T. and Service Act of 1951 (*S. 1*), and U.M.T. No. 4 (*H.R 1752*), before the Committee on the Armed Services, Congress of the United States (*S. 1,* Jan.-Feb.; *H.R. 1752,* Jan.-March)

U.S. National Commission for Unesco—Summary Report of the Ninth Meeting. Unesco Relations Staff, Department of State, Washington, D. C. (May 9-11)

The Pasadena Story. National Commission for the Defense of Democracy Through Education, NEA. (June)

MR. BREED AND THE AEF: Benne, and THE SCAPEGOAT VALUE OF AMERICAN PUBLIC EDUCATION: Rugh. *School and Society.* (July 14)

WHY RAISE AN OATH UMBRELLA?: Woody. *School and Society.* (July 21)

WHO'S TRYING TO RUIN OUR SCHOOLS?: Morse. *McCall's.* (September)

WHO OWNS YOUR CHILD'S MIND?: Flynn. *Reader's Digest.* (October)

Daily Worker. (October 2)

IN DEFENSE OF THE CRITICS OF EDUCATION: Fraser, and ATTACK AND COUNTERATTACK IN EDUCATION: Brickman. *School and Society.* (October 27)

A JUNIOR HIGH SCHOOL LOOKS AT UNESCO. Procedure at Alice Deal Junior High School, Washington, D. C. Department of State, *Publication No. 4380.* (November)

1951–1952   INSTITUTE OF PACIFIC RELATIONS. Senate Committee on the Judiciary. *Report No. 2050.* (July-June)

INSTITUTE OF PACIFIC RELATIONS. Senate Committee on the Judiciary. *Hearings.* Parts 1-14 inclusive (July-June). A comprehensive Index is published as Vol. 15.

Communist Tactics in Controlling Youth Organizations. Senate Committee on the Judiciary. (April-March)

1952   *Teaching About the United Nations and the Specialized Agencies.* United Nations, Department of Public Information, New York. THE RIGHT TO EDUCATION. Unesco, Paris.

Universal Declaration of Human Rights. United Nations.

The NATO Treaty, *Executive T,* June 16. (In particular, Art. VII, the *Status of Forces Agreement.* This text can also be found in the *Congressional Record* of July 14, 1953, at page 9024. The Senate vote is at page 9088.)

THE SOCIAL ENGINEERS: Wythe. *Fortune.* (January)

ARE U.S. TEENAGERS REJECTING FREEDOM?: Houseman. *Look.* (February 26)

GROUPTHINK: Whyte. *Fortune.* (March)

YOUR CHILD IS THEIR TARGET: Irene Corbally Kuhn. *American Legion Magazine.* (June)

Teaching about the United Nations in the Schools and Colleges. Department of State, *Publication No. 4649.* (September)

SUBVERSIVE INFLUENCE IN THE EDUCATIONAL PROCESS. Senate Committee on the Judiciary. *Hearings.* (September-October)

The United Nations, Unesco, and American Schools. National Education Association, and American Association of School Administrators. (December)

3) Collateral references.

a) The Foundations.

1893   *Triumphant Democracy:* Andrew Carnegie. (Autobiography)
             THE REUNION OF BRITAIN AND AMERICA: Andrew Carnegie. *North American Review* (June). Published separately in Scotland.

1911   *Seven Great Foundations:* Leonard P. Ayres.

1923, 1927 *Direction des Relations et de l'Education, Enquête sur les Livres scolaires d'après Guerre.* Carnegie Endowment. Paris. Vol. I, 1923; Vol. II, 1927.

1934   *America Must Choose:* Henry A. Wallace. World Peace Foundation, and the Foreign Policy Association.

1936   EXAMINATIONS AND THEIR SUBSTITUTES IN THE UNITED STATES: I. L. Kandel. Carnegie Foundation for the Advancement of Teaching. *Bulletin No. 28.*

1937–1941 *Propaganda Analysis,* Vols. I-IV. Institute of Propaganda Analysis. Vol. I (*p. iv*) and Vol. II (*p. 13*) show this Institute as the recipient of monies from The Good Will Fund of Edward A. Filene. The Institute's Advisory Board included Hadley Cantril, Paul Douglas, William H. Kilpatrick, Ernest O. Melby and James T. Shotwell, among others.

1938   *Philanthropic Foundations and Higher Education:* Ernest Victor.

1940   *War Propaganda and the United States:* Lavine and Wechsler. Published for the Institute of Propaganda Analysis by the Yale University Press.

1944–1945 *American Oxonian.* (April-January)

1946   *The American Rhodes Scholarships:* Aydelotte.
             The Vision of Cecil Rhodes: Aydelotte. Oxford University Press. London.
             Treatment of Asia in American Textbooks. American Council on Education, and the American Council, Institute of Pacific Relations.

1949   *Intergroup Relations in Teaching Materials.* American Council on Education.

1950   *The United Nations, its Record and its Prospects.* Carnegie Endowment.

1951   *Universities and World Affairs.* Carnegie Endowment.
             Highlights Report. National Citizens Commission for the Public Schools. (Summer)

—   Rockefeller Foundation. *Annual Reports.* (Identified in the text)

b) The Council on Foreign Relations.

1933–1946 *Reports of the Executive Director.* (Directors included Isaiah Bowman, Stephen P. Duggan, Allen W. Dulles, Philip C. Jessup and Walter Lippmann)

1940–1949 *Annual Reports of the Executive Director.* (Philip C. Jessup is listed as a Director 1934-42 and Frederick V. Field as a Resident Member 1940-49)

1946   *The Council on Foreign Relations, 1921-1946.* The Council. (Its history)

1948–1949 *The United States in World Affairs, 1948/1949.* The Council (Allen W. Dulles, president. Introduction by General George C. Marshall)

1952   *The Challenge to Isolation, 1937-1940:* William L. Langer and S. Everett Gleason. Published for the Council by Harper & Brothers.

[179]

c) **The National Advisory Council on Radio in Education.**

1931-1932   *Economic Aspects of the Depression.* University of Chicago Press. A series of 30 economics lectures, broadcast under the auspices of the Council.

1931-1933   *Economics Series Lectures.* The Council. University of Chicago Press. The lecturers included, among others, Jane Addams, Stuart Chase, John Dewey, Edward A. Filene, Philip C. Jessup, Harry W. Laidler, Louis L. Lorwin, Isador Lubin, Felix Morley, Frances Perkins and Rexford Guy Tugwell. (October 1931-June 1933)

1931-1934   *Radio and Education.* (Annual proceedings of the National Council)

1932-1939   *Information Series,* No's. 1-19. (State that the Council was financed by John D. Rockefeller, Jr., and the Carnegie Corporation of New York)

1933   *Report of the Director.* (States that the Council, in addition to the above support, was financed, for specific purposes, by the American Political Science Association.) (May 1)

1934   *Radio and Education, 1934.* University of Chicago Press. (States that cooperation between the League for Industrial Democracy and the Brookings Institution began in the Fall of 1931 and continued with 28 broadcasts on economics, etc.) (*P. 160*)

Program of the Fourth American Assembly. (Includes addresses by Robert M. Hutchins, Robert Gordon Sproul, Harold L. Ickes, George F. Zook (director, American Council on Education), Bruce Bliven and Frederick P. Keppel (president, Carnegie Corporation of New York). (Chicago, October 8-9.)

America Must Choose. Originally a pamphlet by Secretary of Agriculture Henry A. Wallace. Debated in a series of radio talks presented in 1934 by the Foreign Policy Association and World Peace Foundation in cooperation with the National Council. (March 15-May 3)

1935   *Thirtieth Anniversary Report. 1905 . . . 1935.* League for Industrial Democracy. (States that the League cooperated with the National Council in a series of weekly broadcasts entitled "Economics in a Changing Social Order", Oct. 4-Dec. 20, 1934, over NBC's Blue Network.)

d) **The General Education Board.**

1908   *The Ogden Movement; An Educational Monopoly in the Making:* Edward Ingle. Manufacturers Record Publishing Co., Baltimore, Md.

1913   THE COUNTRY SCHOOL OF TO-MORROW. The Board. *Occasional Papers, No. 1.* (*Cf.* pages 161-2)

1914-1915   *Report of the Secretary.* (States that Andrew Carnegie was on the Board)

1915   *The General Education Board, An Account of Its Activities, 1902-1914.* The Board.

Report of the Secretary. (Lists securities of the Rockefeller Fund totaling $39,485,548.93.) (June 30)

1935-1936   *Building America.* The Board's *Annual Report* (p. 7, *e.s.*) notes its financial support of this series, and also for the Progressive Education Association. (*Cf.* page 176)

1944   THE AMERICAN WAY OF BUSINESS: Abba P. Lerner and Oscar Lange. *Problems in American Life: Unit No. 20.* Published by the National Council for the Social Studies and the National Association of Secondary-School Principals, NEA, from a grant by the General Education Board.

1947-1948   *Annual Report 1947-1948.* (States that the largest single gift by Mr. Rockefeller was of $50,000,000 in 1919. As of December 31, 1947, the total funds available to the Board are listed at $310,216,391.)

—   *Annual Reports.* Identified in the text.

[180]

e) Other references employed, directly or indirectly in the text.

1913   SOCIAL STUDIES IN SECONDARY SCHOOLS. Preliminary Recommendations by a committee of the NEA. First issued by the U.S. Office of Education as *Bulletin No. 41*, 1913. Reprinted in *The History Teacher's Magazine* of December 1913.

1916   THE SOCIAL STUDIES IN SECONDARY EDUCATION. Report of the Committee on Social Studies of the Commission on the Reorganization of Secondary Education, NEA. First issued by the U.S. Office of Education as *Bulletin No. 28*, 1916. Reprinted in *The History Teacher's Magazine* of January 1917.

1917   *Misinforming a Nation:* Willard Huntington Wright. (*Pseud.,* S. S. Van Dine)

1922   *Propaganda Through the Schools.* International Federation of League of Nations Societies.

1929   *Reports.* Committee on Propaganda in the Schools, NEA. (July)

1930   *Teachers Guide to Child Development in the Kindergarten and Primary Grades.* California State Printing Office.

1936   *Teachers Guide to Child Development in the Intermediate Grades.* California State Printing Office.

1937, 1942   *Education Manual. EM 763.* Published for the United States Armed Forces by Harper & Brothers. Two volumes. (Not available to the civilian market. Library of Congress File No. HB 171.5.G35.1944)

1938   SCHOOLS. *Report. House No. 2100* (pp. 229-274). Commonwealth of Massachusetts.

1940   THE BERTRAND RUSSELL CASE. *In the Matter of Jean Kay* vs. *The Board of Higher Education of the City of New York.* (*Cf.* page 89 for references)

1941   *The Fifth Column in Our Schools:* Gilbert. Zondervan Publishing House. Grand Rapids, Mich.

1941–1942   UN-AMERICANISM IN TEXTBOOKS: Gilbert. *National Republic.* (October-March)

1942   RAPP-COUDERT REPORT, New York State Legislature. *Legislative Document No. 49.*

1944   REVOLUTIONIZING OUR EDUCATION: Gilbert. *National Republic.* (July)

1945   *NEA History:* Mildred Sandison Fenner. Published by the NEA.

1946   COMMUNISM IN OUR SCHOOLS: Hon. George A. Dondero. *National Republic.* (August)

Canadian Royal Commission on Investigation of Espionage in Relation to Atomic Bomb Secret. *Report.* Controller of Stationery, Ottawa. (June 27)

1948   UNIVERSAL DECLARATION OF HUMAN RIGHTS. Department of State, publication No. 3381. *International Organization and Conference Series III, 20.*

NEW EVENTS ACCENTUATE ALIEN PROBLEM: Walter S. Steele. *National Republic.* (May)

1949   *Communism and Academic Freedom.* University of Washington Press. The record of the tenure cases at the University.

Report of the Committee on Subversive Activities to Governor Wm. Preston Lane and the Maryland General Assembly. (January)

A Bill of Grievances. National Society, Sons of the American Revolution, 1227 16th St., N.W., Washington, D. C. (April 19)

1950   TREATY LAW-MAKING: Hon. Frank E. Holman. American Bar Association *Journal.* Vol. 36, September; pp. 707-710.

Prejudice and the Press: F. L. Hughes. Devin-Adair.

1951–1952   *Neither Five Nor Three:* Helen MacInnes. A novel. (Harcourt, Brace, 1951; Popular Library Edition, 1952)

1952   *Report of the Committee on American Citizenship.* Bar Association of the State of New York. (January)

The Civil Rights of Conservative Men in Education. The case of Alpheus W. Ray, superintendent of schools at Roseville, Cal. Brief issued by the California Sons of the American Revolution, 926 DeYoung Bldg., San Francisco. (February)

The "Academic Freedom" Issue. Monthly newsletter of Harding College, Searcy, Ark. (May)

1954   *Elementary Schools, Chart of Comparative Educational Practices and Techniques.* THE LONG HOUSE, INC.

1955   METHOD AND CHANNEL FOR INDOCTRINATION (Group Dynamics). Chapter 6 in *Education or Indoctrination:* Mary L. Allen. The Caxton Printers, Ltd., Caldwell, Idaho.

Collectivism on the Campus: E. Merrill Root. Devin-Adair.

Economics and Action: Pierre Mendès-France and Gabriel Ardant. Unesco, Paris; Columbia University Press, New York.

1956   *The Vision and the Constant Star:* A. H. Hobbs. THE LONG HOUSE, INC.

1960   *The Report of the Working Party on the Draft Convention and Recommendation Against Discrimination in Education.* Unesco, Paris; *Document 11-C-PRG-36.* (Mimeo, with 3 Annexes)

1961   *A Federal Education Agency for the Future.* U.S. Department of Health, Education, and Welfare; Document *OE-10010.* Every citizen should obtain this official release and study it in the light of his understanding from *The Turning of the Tides.*

Freedom from War. Department of State, *Publication 7277.* This is "The United States program for general and complete disarmament in a peaceful world."

All other sources are specifically identified in the text.

The John and Abigail Adams quotations, and the excerpt from the *Suffol* *Resolves,* are taken, by permission, from *John Adams and the American Revolution* by Catherine Drinker Bowen. Boston. Little, Brown. 1950.

INDEX

Abbott, Leonard D., 57
Abraham, H. J., 99
Academic freedom, 13, 40, 74, 75, 181, 182
Adams, Abigail, 52
Adams, James Truslow, 68-9
Adams, John, 6, 60, 158
American Association for Adult Education, 56
———— for the United Nations, 75, 123, 167, 170, 171
———— of University Professors, 3, 24*fn*, 74-6, 86*fn*, 97*fn*, 101
———— of University Women, 170
American Council on Education, 64, 86*fn*, 87, 88*fn*, 100*fn*, 117*fn*, 123, 167, 175, 179
———— Education Fellowship, 3, 13, 16, 20, 23, 29, 41, 45, 52, 53-6, 58, 65, 68-70, 77, 86*fn*, 95, 104, 113, 114, 121, 123, 128, 130, 149, 150, 177, 180
———— Federation of Teachers, 42, 56, 91, 115*fn*
———— Geographical Society, 98*fn*
———— Historical Association, 16, 21, 22, 30, 39, 41, 76, 97*fn*, 101
———— Institute of International Relations, *and/or* of World Affairs, 98*fn*, 168
———— People's Fund, 100*fn*
———— Way, the, 68; alteration of, 153-7
Americans for Democratic Action, 56, 56*fn*, 175
Anderson, Archibald W., 53
Association of American Colleges, 113
———— for Childhood Education, 56
Associated Committee on International Relations, 107
Attlee, Clement, 3, 102*fn*
Aydelotte, Frank, 97*fn*, 179

Baldwin, Roger N., 160
Ball, Lester B., 69-70
Ballou, Frank W., 39*fn*
Beard, Charles Austin, 134
Beatty, Willard W., 20, 29, 45, 52, 86
Benedict, Ruth, 132 *e.s.*, 137-40, 149
Benjamin, Harold, 12, 14
Benne, Kenneth D., 41, 58, 63, 116
Benson, George, 156
Berger, Victor L., 2
Bethune, Mary McLeod, 160
Bible, The Holy, 45, 48, 111, 124, 132, 139
Biemiller, Andrew, 160

Bigelow, Karl W., 86, 86*fn*
Bill of Rights, American, 60, 115, 152
————, international, 86
Black, Algernon, 160
Blanshard, Paul, 2, 160
Bliven, Bruce, 2, 174, 175, 180
Bloor, Ella Reeves, 2
Bode, Boyd H., 37
Bowman, Isaiah, 21, 179
Brameld, Theodore, 18 *fn*, 25, 35, 42, 47, 50-1, 53 *e.s.*, 59, 65-6, 85, 106, 121, 129
Brotherhood of Man, 133*fn*
Broun, Heywood, 2, 42, 160
Budenz, Louis, 2, 160
Burns, Eveline M., 160-1
Businessmen, Leslie Gould on, 9

Call, for an Intercollegiate Socialist Society, 1
————, the first, *to the Teachers of the Nation*, 16, 20, 28, 34, 38, 40, 52, 68, 77, 86, 129, 149
————, the second, 52 *e.s.*
————, the third, 77 *e.s.*
Carmichael, A. Max, 47
Carnegie, Andrew, 97, 101, 149, 179, 180
————, Endowment for International Peace, etc., 75*fn*, 97, 98*fn*, 99, 100*fn*, 101, 117*fn*, 166, 166*fn*, 167, 171, 175, 179, 180
————, Foundation for the Advancement of Teaching, 97*fn*, 101, 179
Carter, Edward C., 98*fn*, 100*fn*
Chase, Stuart, 2, 25, 61, 160, 180
Chiang, Kai-shek, 75
Childs, John L., 25, 37, 42-3, 58-9, 141*fn*, 148, 160
Church Peace Union, 101, 166
Class-warfare, 9, 34-7, 40, 42-3, 92
Cohen, Morris Raphael, 174
Cole, G. D. H. *and/or* Margaret, 161, 174, 176
Collectivism, education for, 9, 14, 16-7, 19-22, 25, 29, 30, 35, 36, 47, 57, 63-5, 69, 72, 93, 114, 125, 139, 145, 150-1, 157
Collective security, 59, 148, 150
Collegiate Council for the United Nations, 167
Commager, Henry Steele, 117
Community, committee in the, 5, 63, 67-8, 71, 111, 140, 154, 155, 157-8, 172-3
Community Ambassador Program, 171
Congress of American Women, 133*fn*

[185]

[187]

Censoring with "does it serve our purpose?"

The strength of the ties
1) between NEA & UNESCO.
2) UNESCO's plan/agenda — ppl involved
3) Our current situation   ppl funding it

— list of "purpose" statements, for teachers
+ for certain classes

Steps in the indoctrination process
Globes, hule your community etc.

List of Books + publications
      Organizations
      Conferences
      Schools involved

Anti-Family quotes

great summation, 131, 133

CPSIA information can be obtained
at www.ICGtesting.com
Printed in the USA
BVOW06s1646280817
493305BV00021B/133/P